KL

ONE SIGNAL
PUBLISHERS
ATRIA

Kissing Girls on Shabbat

a memoir

SARA GLASS

ONE SIGNAL
PUBLISHERS

ATRIA

NEW YORK · LONDON · TORONTO · SYDNEY · NEW DELHI

ONE SIGNAL
PUBLISHERS

An Imprint of Simon & Schuster, LLC.
1230 Avenue of the Americas
New York, NY 10020

First Atria Books hardcover edition June 2024

ONE SIGNAL PUBLISHERS / ATRIA BOOKS and colophon are
trademarks of Simon & Schuster, LLC.

Simon & Schuster: Celebrating 100 Years of Publishing in 2024

For information about special discounts for bulk purchases,
please contact Simon & Schuster Special Sales at 1-866-506-1949 or
business@simonandschuster.com.

The Simon & Schuster Speakers Bureau can bring authors to your live event. For
more information or to book an event, contact the Simon & Schuster Speakers
Bureau at 1-866-248-3049 or visit our website at www.simonspeakers.com.

Interior design by Dana Sloan

Manufactured in the United States of America

1 3 5 7 9 10 8 6 4 2

Library of Congress Cataloging-in-Publication Data has been applied for.

ISBN 978-1-6680-3121-6
ISBN 978-1-6680-3123-0 (ebook)

For Victor and Jordan
It has always been for you, all of it.

Contents

Author's Note

This memoir represents my best recollection of events, along with my subjective feelings and thoughts. I have done my best to ensure that the experiences described within these pages are as accurate as possible, by cross-checking my words against a collection of past emails, journal entries, photographs, and conversations with relevant individuals who witnessed my story as it took place. Despite my best efforts, some of the people in my story may remember it differently. That is an inherent limitation of memoir writing—I lay no claim to the only version of these events.

I have changed the names and identifying information of many individuals. I hold a firsthand understanding of the intricate grapevine within Jewish communities and of the many possible implications of having one's name appear in a memoir like my own. Therefore, I have changed the names of all people who are currently connected with any branch of the Orthodox Jewish community. I have also changed the names of anyone whose actions appear as less than tasteful in this telling.

The goal of this narrative has never been to shame any single person or to seek revenge. Instead, the goal has always been to gradually address and reduce the larger systemic disparities, particularly concerning individuals diagnosed with mental illness or those who identify within the LGBTQIA+ spectrum.

Trigger Warning: This memoir contains content that includes themes of sexual assault, mental illness, suicide, and trauma. Reader discretion is advised, as it may be distressing or triggering for some individuals. Please take care and consider your emotional well-being before proceeding.

Please note that this manuscript was written prior to October 7th, 2023. There are references to Israel throughout this manuscript, and those references do not and cannot communicate the full context or complexity of that date. Nor do they communicate my feelings about what has taken place in the days, weeks, and months afterward. My heart breaks for the people of Gaza and the victims of October 7th.

For Clients: If I have ever had the privilege of serving as your psychotherapist, please flip to the end of this book to read my letter to you.

PART I

Watch Me Burn

First Night

They never showed me how to take it off, I realized, as I yanked yet another metal pin out of the hair that covered my own. The sink was already littered with dozens of bobby pins, mini tongs scattered over the white porcelain. Every time I swept my fingers along the thin net that separated me from the wig, I felt more pokes, more metal.

The white petticoat on the hook behind me had lost its fluff. It drooped toward the floor, random pieces of tulle pointing into the air. It was almost four a.m., and I wanted to wipe the rest of the thick wedding eyeliner off my lids and droop, too, into a deep sleep.

He was waiting though.

I found the last of the pins, felt for the clips over my ears, and bent them until I heard muffled clicks. Gone was the sleek haircut from the Manhattan salon, where a men's razor sliced the edges of my bob into a perfect line. I had only been wearing the wig for a few hours, but underneath it, my shiny strands had turned to static, like a halo of fuzz around my face.

Glitter and perfume slid down my body with the shower water. I ran a loofah over my skin, vigorous at the parts she last touched. I re-dressed, in the outfit I had chosen for this night: an ankle-length ivory silk night-

3

gown, covered by a mauve silk dressing gown. As I put my hand to the doorknob, my heart seemed to expand into my throat, until my breath felt stuck.

I was about to be alone. In a hotel room. With a man.

Alone, but not without a push from so many others. The women in my family had done everything possible to smooth the path for me, to lay out a silken carpet for my walk into a whole new life stage. My abba's credit card covered some of the cost of the bridal suite. My sisters lifted the train of my gown and, furtive nods of encouragement in place, helped me into the town car that would take me to Thirteenth Avenue that night. As I opened the bathroom door and stepped into the suite, though, the ground beneath me felt anything but smooth.

"You look nice," he said when I made it through the doorway, hiding my tremors in my slow, careful steps. He marked the place in his prayer book and placed it on a table, his eyes fixed on the soft pink carpet as he took his own cautious steps toward the tiled bathroom floor.

I slid under the sheets of the enormous bed, robe and all, and lay flat, waiting for him. I had trained for this night for so many years. I had sat in classrooms in New York, Toronto, and Jerusalem listening to pious women and men describe the holiness of matrimony. I filled notebooks with my own slanted writing, instructions for wifehood. I had reviewed my notes, discussed them with mentors and friends, committed my heart to the mission for which I'd been told it was created. But in that moment, as I felt my pulse race in my eardrums, thumping like a lunatic, I wasn't prepared at all. I had not gotten to review my notes from the last lesson, the one I needed the most, which had been received just seventy-two hours earlier in the back office of my wedding teacher's apartment.

From the look of Yossi's pale face in the dark, it seemed like he had not reviewed his final lesson either. He shuffled toward the other side of the bed, stood there for a moment, and then unbuttoned a plaid pajama top. He neatly folded it into a square and put it down. He removed his matching pants and settled under the sheet; his labored breaths audible across the inches of space between us. He lifted the white hotel blanket over his hand, providing cover as he tentatively moved to stroke . . . my wrist.

"Oh," he said, his voice more little boy than twenty-seven-year-old man. "I thought you were undressed." He grabbed the folded plaid off his side table, fumbled until he was dressed again, then lay back down. A cloud of Colgate and unfamiliar skin scent wafted in my direction.

"It is okay," I told him, as I turned my face toward his and put one hand over his side of the blanket. "My teacher said we don't have to do it the first night."

I heard his exhale, a long puff of air in the stillness of our space. "Maybe it is a little late," he said, a hint of relief in his voice. "You might be tired, right?"

"Yes, it is late." My voice stayed neutral. I did not want him to know I dreaded the act—consummation—we'd been placed here to complete.

He sat up, whispered the Shema prayer, put one hand over his eyes. I did the same, and then we both lay back down, flat shapes in the shadow of our evening, hat boxes and wig boxes and suitcases filled with expectation in the space around us.

Somehow the strangeness of it all was hilarious to me. It felt like a game of charades. I could not believe I'd wasted so much time fearing this night, wondering about this night. For nothing!

I turned to my side, away from him. I wished I could grab my Motorola Razr from my handbag and text Dassa.

You'll never believe what happened, I would start, just to mess with her. *He was even more freaked out than I was.* Then I felt it, the sadness that had been lingering underneath my nerves. It filled my chest, my limbs, slid down my cheek and onto the patterned cotton of the hotel pillowcase. I couldn't tell her. Not ever.

Unholy

At nineteen, I wished I could pretend, for my sake and for God's, that I had fallen into a trap. That my sins had been accidental. But I knew Dassa, with the auburn curls that fell over her shoulders, meant taking temptation by the hand and allowing it to tug me along.

As soon as she walked into my classroom, I knew she was not conventional. She looked nothing like the speakers they usually brought in to Torah Academy, matronly women who read from holy texts and smiled vaguely around the room. Dassa *strode* through the door. She dumped her purse down, sat right on top of my desk, and crossed one long leg over the other, metallic pumps dangling in the air. The tailored fabric of her dress framed her curves, the kind of curves one normally did not get to see under the garb of modest women.

She leaned forward and asked my students what their names were. I watched them stop doodling in the margins of their notebooks and sit up straight. They looked at each other, then at her, as they smoothed their collars and put their sneakered feet together and responded in careful, polite voices. She seemed unsurprised, as if she were used to feeling rooms become still when she walked in.

She smiled, turned her head slowly, caught the eye of each student. Then, she caught mine. She lingered in the gaze we shared, for just a few seconds. By the time she looked away, her careless grin turned to a businesslike nod. She pushed the sleeves of her blazer up, took a deep breath, and went on to talk about how she discovered God one night, when she felt alone in the world. She talked about the ways in which he helped her survive. She looked at me, every few sentences, until the lecture was over.

"I have never seen them so curious," I said to her after the bell rang and the chairs scraped against the linoleum tiles as the teens scattered.

"I don't usually do this," she confided. Her strong voice suddenly grew soft around the edges. "I am not sure if I am that good of a role model."

"Join the club," I joked. A chuckle, nervously but unsuccessfully squelched, hit the air instead as a short bark, and I worried that I sounded ridiculous. And I wondered why I cared about how I sounded at all, to a stranger I would probably never see again once she collected her things and left. I needed to see her, I realized; at least one more time, and as soon as possible.

By the time I said things about grabbing lunch one day, and punched her number into my cell phone, I knew. This was not the first time I had looked into someone's eyes and felt a thousand vibrations echo through my body.

Still, I lied, to myself and to her and to God, through our discussion about forgoing lunch and getting ice cream instead. I pretended, as we chose flavors and asked for sprinkles, that we were going to have a conversation about future teacher-lecturer collaborations. Perhaps she'd like to do a gratitude workshop for Thanksgiving next month, I suggested.

"If you do it with me," she said. Then she mentioned that she lived around the corner, just off Borough Park's Fifteenth Avenue, and we may as well head to her apartment where it'd be less noisy. Our pretenses melted quickly once we arrived, as quickly as the now liquid frozen yogurt we slurped from spoons as we sat on her bed.

She startled when she heard a door slam in the distance, and then answered the question on my face. "Just making sure it's not my mother coming into the apartment," she said, and her face turned bone white under her freckles, whiter than it had been. "The last time she found me alone in my room with a girl, it didn't end well."

She stared at the wall, then glanced over at me. I could have let it go right there. But the words "alone in my room with a girl" were a smoke signal, an encoded message released into the space between us, and I needed to respond.

"There was a while where I didn't trust myself to be alone with girls either."

She looked into my eyes, and for the first time she didn't look away. I saw myself in the coal of her irises, my own fear mirrored back from within her. When her lips moved again, more confessions spilling into the air, all I could think was *how much I want to kiss her.*

We texted each other later that night, and then again the next morning, and the next. We found reasons to meet and told ourselves, and each other, that we were building a friendship. We were cautious for a while, making sure that our meetings only happened in public cafés and kosher restaurants. I pretended not to notice the delicate swoop of her collarbone through her sweaters, the chiseled line of her jaw, the way her lashes hit her face extra fast when she caught me staring.

It started with a graze of her hand, the soft edge of her palm against mine as we left Mendelsohn's Pizza one evening.

"Let me walk you to your door," I said, with the chivalry of someone who was not just a friend. "It's late."

As soon as the elevator doors in her apartment building closed behind us, we merged. It began as a desperate, hungry embrace, and then my hands were in the thick waves of her hair, hers clasped around my waist, both of us inhaling each other's breath.

On the outside, we looked just like the other college-aged Orthodox Jewish young women in Borough Park. We wore skirts that ended well below our kneecaps. We covered our elbows and collarbones with loose sweaters and button-down shirts. We carried prayer books in our purses and paused to bow our knees to God after the sun rose each morning, and before it set each afternoon.

We participated in the *shidduch* process, the system within which we would meet our future husbands and prepare for our true purpose in life: bearing children. We helped each other apply modest hints of mascara from a tube we shared before we sent each other off to meetings with community matchmakers.

"How did it go?" we asked each other after the makeup was gone and the clothes were on the carpet at the side of my bed and our bare legs were entwined underneath the covers.

Dassa was almost twenty-one and I was nineteen. The only path forward was marriage, to a man, and lots of babies. We would follow the single mold created for adolescent Hasidic girls. *Our thing* was just a test to be overcome. We never said the words out loud.

Lesbian, gay, bisexual—those words described sinners, not us.

The love hit us when we expected it least. We were confused when our fights brought us to tears. When we wanted to be together all the time. When our hearts found ways to sneak into each other's home in the middle of the night.

She knew the code to my side door, and how to creep silently up the stairs, past my sleeping parents, and into my bedroom. We found ourselves wrapped in each other. So often. Too often. The springs of my twin mattress creaked in the dark, while we lived life deaf to the world.

My family lived in the Hasidic section of Brooklyn, New York. I'd had glimpses of the world outside, having spent two years in an Orthodox girls' high school in Toronto, and a year at a teacher's seminary in Jerusalem. I was aware that not all Jews lived their lives as we did, in the strict Orthodox fashion. Yet I also knew that to be a true servant of God *was* to be like us, and to belong to one of ultra-Orthodoxy's two main streams: the Hasidic and the Yeshivish.

My family was one of a minority: we belonged to the *Gur* Hasidic sect. Our sect was headquartered in Jerusalem, where our rebbe lived. We in Brooklyn made up only a tiny satellite group. Even with three Gur synagogues in the neighborhood, the Gur community was so small that all Gur girls in Borough Park could fit into one school building on Twentieth Avenue: preschool on the first floor, high school on the second, and elementary school on the third and fourth. A similar building existed that I was never allowed inside, and had been set up on Eighteenth Avenue for the boys.

Gur Hasidim take gender segregation to extremes even by Hasidic standards. Men avoid all contact with unrelated females—and sometimes even related ones too. The men frequently refer to their wives as their "*shtieb*"—their home—rather than by their given names. Many of the men avoid even speaking the words—*woman* or *girl*. Men do not walk beside their wives in public but several paces ahead of them. From a very young age, girls are taught to scurry aside in the presence of a man.

The gender segregation had become a part of my own identity. I had been made to understand that my body was powerful. That covering myself was a way to protect everyone *else* from its power. As long as I wore long skirts and long sleeves, I'd be safe from the scrutiny of men, and only then would the men around me be safe too—from the temptation my skin would cause them.

What Gur Hasidim lacked in numbers in our Brooklyn neighborhood, we made up for with the weight of our dread. Ours was a world of fear—the primary orientation of the Gur sect. Fear of God, fear of the Torah, fear of the rebbe, fear of our fellow community members. We also feared much that was unseen and not understood: the forces of evil that populated the universe. We were taught that Satan lived inside all of us, in the form of the yetzer hara, and that it was our job to fight the evil within ourselves.

Our history, as it was told to us, consisted of our people being burned at the stake, slaughtered in pogroms, executed over mass graves, gassed by the exhaust of diesel fuel and with the industrial efficiency of trains, camps, and crematoria—all of it because we sinned, and God, we were told, had been purifying us through our suffering.

"The sixth of God's thirteen traits," my seventh-grade teacher told us, "is *erech apayim*—slow to anger." Which was confusing, because everything else about God suggested a capacity for deep rage, rage that was meted out in calculated ways over time.

The teachings that governed my daily religious life illustrated grievous harm to body and soul of those who violated God's commands. Some sins were punished by disease and famine and brutal wars. Others were punished in a realm even more frightening, where the souls of sinners were cooked in boiling excrement; beaten by angels with fiery rods while still in their graves; or cast from a slingshot to hurl from one end of the universe to the other in an eternity of unrest.

There were also, of course, the ordinary fires of hell, which did not sound pleasant, though on the spectrum of available punishments, they were evoked for only the lightest infractions—a spell of gossip, missing an "amen" during prayer, or whispering to a friend during the Torah reading.

And yet, something about this reality was comforting. It was orderly. You sin, you must then accept a punishment. Don't sin, and you go straight to heaven. Theoretically, this should have made things easy.

Still, I had questions.

Hardest of all was to understand why I felt love that I was taught to hate. All love, except the love of God, was suspect, but one kind of love was singled out for extra damnation: loving someone of your own sex. I was taught that God found my desires repugnant, that they were unnatural, and wrong, and I spent my days in prayer trying to understand: Why would God create me this way?

The excitement my friends spoke of, about meeting a boy and living with him for a lifetime, was a strange and unfamiliar desire. The last thing

I wanted was to live with a boy for the rest of my life. Still, I was prepared to do just that. I knew that by giving my life to the service of my husband, I would reach closeness with God and receive His heavenly bounty, His love, His blessing. I would reach fulfillment.

"Your eyes, you know, they get lighter when you're happy."

Dassa's gaze held mine, and I felt my jaw clench. I looked down, away, anything to avoid whatever it was that she was feeling. Feelings were dangerous. Being seen, in the unfamiliar way she had seen me, was dangerous.

I saw the outline of her body through a thin layer of crimson lace. The contrast to her clear skin was striking. It made me feel things in my body that I'd worked to ignore. I felt my hands travel to places they shouldn't. Pure reflex.

She kissed my neck, did something with her tongue that made my breath catch. She bent her head, chestnut hair spilling over my chest as her lips burned a path of desire and shame down my body. My ribs, my stomach, they were hers. I arched my back and then clamped my legs together. "Stop . . . we can't." One of us always stopped before we went too far. Because we knew we did not want to burn with the others who had fallen out of God's favor.

But as much as we tried to place "do not cross" lines on our bodies, our hearts would not comply. And we fell. Harder and faster than we should. I denied it in my mind, the entire time. I told myself it didn't exist.

By Chanukah time, two months after we first met, I had a single rose delivered to her apartment on a day that I knew her father worked late. She burned a mixtape for me, our favorite songs all on one disc. By Presidents' Week, we booked our first vacation—a shared hotel room on North Miami beach. We told our unsuspecting families that we needed one last singles vacation before we found our respective husbands.

Before we left for Miami, Dassa placed an anonymous call to a rabbi and asked a question: Were two women allowed intimate physical touch?

The rabbi said that for men it would have been a very bad sin, but for women, it was merely disgusting. Still, he noted, that should we penetrate each other with an object, "like a cucumber or something," we would cross the line to actual sin. *A cucumber?* I wondered. A cucumber *where*?

We had received a *nisayon*, the rabbi said—a test from God. He offered Dassa a blessing for the strength to withstand it.

We were soon lying on a beach, fully clothed in skirts that covered our knees and shirts that reached up to our necks. The people around us formed a blur of tanned limbs, in the shorts and bathing suits one would expect from a Miami coastline.

We had traveled miles to be free, but I'd come to realize that the shackles were within. Even hundreds of miles away, I was still afraid to be caught. I knew that all it would take was one moment of impropriety, witnessed by one person familiar with our tight community, and my life, as I envisioned it, would be over. If I were caught holding hands with a girl, my prospects for a good match would dissolve like the thin wisps of cloud over Miami Beach.

We rented a boat for a couple of hours, and the tour guide let us have our privacy. Out in the clear blue ocean, we fused together, skin on skin. Our guide gave us a knowing glance when we stepped back onto the shore.

I wondered if the fear was just in my head. It consumed me, became indistinguishable from reality. More and more I wondered if this was worth it, the disintegration of my life.

When we'd returned home, Dassa handed me a stack of printed photos, the two of us leaning close, our eyes blurred in a bedroom haze, on a motorboat, in a tennis court, on sandy beaches. I found a Post-it Note within the stack, with words we never said out loud: *I love you.*

I tucked the note into a storage box of old schoolbooks, not wanting to see it, and not quite able to throw it out. I ignored her texts that day, played eight hours of *Roller Coaster Tycoon* down on the basement computer, hoping to freeze time. She should have known what was about to come next.

Her Body Is Bible

A few months before Dassa and I took our trip, my three older sisters—Hindy, Dina, and Goldy—decided it was time to find me a match.

I hesitate to say, but it was much like *Fiddler on the Roof.* Hindy arranged for me to meet with a matchmaker on a Friday afternoon. It was the eve of the Shabbat, the holy day of rest that we in Borough Park referred to in its Eastern European pronunciation: Shabbos. I stood in the matchmaker's kitchen as she prepared chicken soup for Shabbos and began what I thought would be an introduction to myself. It turned out, she already knew everything: the names of my siblings and their spouses, where each one lived and worked, and where their children attended school. It was a matchmaker's job to know these things, I realized, and that might be all she really cared to know. The meeting, I gathered, was an afterthought. If I failed to make conversation, the matchmaker would add "reserved" when she described me to future potential matches. If I were overweight or had acne, she would say I was "more focused on the spiritual than the materialistic." I was the product; she was in charge of packaging and marketing me.

I was nineteen and a half, and my friends were getting engaged one by one. I was falling behind—as if falling "out of step" had not been enough on its own. Weeks passed, and we did not hear from the matchmaker. I worried that our family was considered damaged, and that my chances of getting married were growing slimmer by the day. I had been on the market for nearly a year, and I was terrified of becoming one of those "older singles" I'd heard gossiped about throughout my youth.

Then the sister of an old school friend called. She knew of a nice boy from a good family, and my sisters set out to make phone calls and inquiries. They each returned with bits and pieces of information about this boy: twenty-six, studied at a prestigious yeshiva, parents of good stock. The father was in construction and the mother sold chandeliers.

Still, I worried. Unmarried at twenty-six? Something might be wrong with him. Dina, who worked to comfort me, would admit the word going around was that he could be a "little bit picky."

Hindy, always wise, had an addendum, "At his age, you know, he's probably motivated."

I could not disagree. Mission accomplished, I thought.

And with that, I was off to Miami. While we bent together over hookah pipes and shared bowls of French onion soup, Dassa had no idea that my sisters were sending me the results, in long voicemails, of their investigation of this boy's rabbis and friends and neighbors.

"They say he is very family oriented. He lives in the yeshiva dorm in Lakewood, but he drives home to his parents for Shabbos every week. He doesn't have a temper; no one's ever heard him raise his voice."

Soon, we knew that he wore dark socks, always, no patterns. That his father was very committed to his shul, but prone to sneaking a bite on some of the lesser fast days. That his sister had graduated from a Bais Yaakov religious girls' school just like mine, and that his brother's wife preferred wigs that were a tad on the longer side.

He sounded like a nice, devout boy. I, on the other hand, was sinning so frequently, so avidly, that I could no longer distinguish myself from Satan. I knew that lying in bed with another woman and tasting her on my tongue was forbidden. What I was unclear about was the fine print underneath that command: If I were in a forbidden relationship, and then I hurt my lover's feelings, was that part still a sin?

Was the sin made worse, in God's eyes, when I ignored Dassa for almost twenty-four hours after getting her love note, until she showed up at my bedroom door with puffy eyes and trembling hands? Or was it worse when I held her face in both my hands, told her that I loved her too, tasted the salt of her tears on my lips? Was it truly evil, the way her skin on mine made me forget everything else, including God? How wrong was it exactly, the way I whispered sweet lies all through the night, *you matter most* and *I'll never leave you*? Was God upset that in the morning, I could see the cloak of her pain lifted? Or by that point had he looked away in disgust, withdrawn his protection from us both?

I asked myself those questions repeatedly over the next few days as I prepared to meet with the vetted yeshiva boy. I played a game of hot and cold, fiery and freezing, with Dassa and God and myself, until I could barely function.

On a Sunday evening in February, Yossi Schwartz's green Mitsubishi Mirage arrived to pick me up and whisk me away for stilted conversation over Diet Sprite in the hotel lounge of the Marriott on West Street in Manhattan.

He's quiet, I thought, but I was not too bothered by it. I was capable of leading the conversation.

I asked about his family, and I told him about my students and myself. But then we ran out of things to say, and waited a little while in silence, until a little while grew into an hour. I'd been taught to be wary of a man who declined to tip, so I was relieved when he took care of the valet and the waiter.

"It was fine," I answered, when Goldy asked me afterward how it had gone. I told Hindy and Dina that he met my criteria, which was easy to do with a woman who had none to miss. I was afraid to admit it out loud, but I felt desperate, and I did not want to spoil my chances by being selective.

Yossi asked me out again, this time to an airport lounge, where we could watch planes take off, to fill the extended pauses in our conversation. For our third date, we went to a restaurant, and for our fourth, he took me to a planetarium. Our meetings were calm, quiet. He was a very safe driver. He wore a black hat to each date. I noticed him smile when he opened doors for me, which he always did, sometimes rushing awkwardly to grab the handle before I could reach it.

Later, in my room, I reviewed my notes from my post–high school year in Israel. I attended a "seminary" in order to get my teacher's certificate, although the time spent in courses on pedagogy were matched by that spent on how to set up a good Jewish home. I'd known from the moment I decided to apply to seminary that this was, in fact, something of a "wife school," which suited me just fine: I was keen on learning how to be a good Jewish wife.

My notes, scribbled in messy print, included directions on how to comport oneself when going out with a new prospect for the first time. Married teachers spoke of nightmare scenarios experienced by former students: dark drinks spilled on white shirts, and the like. It was wiser, we had learned, to order clear liquids, at least until after a couple was married. Hence, my order of Diet Sprite from the airport lounge. I was quite certain Yossi's teachers had suggested the Downtown Marriott as a good first date location. The lobby that night had been packed to the brim with men in black hats just like Yossi's, and women in long skirts like mine. It couldn't be a coincidence.

I continued on as the notes became more granular, less open to interpretation. They contained specific instructions about how to manage the emotions felt on a first date, the bodily urges one might confront when alone with a member of the opposite sex's attention for the first time. And they laid out a firm schedule for, and I quote verbatim, *dates one through ten*. Only in *rare* exceptions, it was made clear, was a couple to have more than ten dates. And in those rare cases, they were to seek rabbinic counsel. I was determined not to be one of those troubled few. Those people, I worried, were playing fast and loose with the whole concept of heaven. So, I sat on my bedroom floor and reviewed my instructions. "As long as you don't feel strongly one way or another," the lecturer had said, "you keep dating." At the fourth or fifth date, my notes read, "you should be able to imagine yourself liking them one day." By the sixth or seventh date, "you really shouldn't lead them on if you aren't ready to be engaged."

"The baby was up all night and Ezra got home late and I forgot it was Tuesday," my sister Dina whispered in one breath. It was another night in my Nutrition 101 class at Touro College, a building on Brooklyn's Avenue J where religious women attended classes, often in the evenings, after a day of teaching or working in offices. I was lucky Dina hadn't noticed the paper in front of me on my desk, now lined with practice runs of the new signature I'd imagine would be official soon: Mrs. Malka Schwartz.

Dina, sister and classmate, had arrived late, and slid into the desk beside mine. Her long wig flipped over the back of her chair, a pacifier fell out of her stuffed purse, and a wave of Lancôme Trésor settled in around her. I knew the scent; I had snuck spritzes from that peach bottle of perfume off her dresser for years.

Dina had been trying to complete a bachelor's in history for about ten years, initially studying at the college for Orthodox Jewish women back when she still fit in with the rest of the young single girls. The college joke was that people really attended just to bide their time until the matchmaker made them a wife. Dina, however, was determined to graduate for real, to be first in our post-Holocaust, first-generation-American family to have a college degree.

Dina scribbled rapid lines of slanted notes and jumped into the discussion, answering the professor's questions as if she'd been there the whole time. I couldn't be prouder. Despite her academic journey having been extended by marriage and childbirth, she was still a diligent student, and respected for it. She was also a showstopping beauty; her heart-shaped face and cashmere ensembles had appeared on the glossy pages of Touro brochures.

"Pssst. Read this!"

She passed me her notes, or rather, a list of questions that revealed itself upon closer inspection:

How do you feel when you're around him?

What do you think when you imagine a future with him?

Do you see him as someone who could take care of a house full of babies?

Have you disagreed on anything yet, and if so, how did he react?

Are you attracted to him?

The irritation erupted through me, down my arms and into my fingers clenched into fists. I looked at her and saw her waiting, beautiful hazel eyes wide and still. I felt like my brain was vibrating, like I had too much blood for my body, like everything that was supposed to be inside me was about to explode all over the room.

Did I seem blasé? I wondered. In reality I was anything but. Offended, now, but certainly not unaware of what I was about to commit to. My devotion to God and my deep, well-tended fear of his wrath didn't leave much room for choice. Feelings were irrelevant. Sexual attraction was irrelevant. Dassa was irrelevant. Aside from my role as God's servant, I was irrelevant too. I knew that. I had accepted that. I only wished Dina would do the same.

I visited Yossi at his home in Monsey for our fifth date. It was where I first met his parents. His father's eyes twinkled above a full, white beard, like a proud Jewish Santa Claus. His mother, in a well-coiffed blond wig and with a warm demeanor, offered me chocolate truffles and asked what

I loved most about teaching. On that night I showed them the virginal Malka, the version of me who wore cream bouclé blazers and blushed at their kind attention.

Afterward, Yossi and I went to a Chinese restaurant, and he smiled as he ate, pleased with how well the meeting had gone. I, too, was happy that I'd passed the night's inspection.

We talked about our futures, and I told him about my desire to obtain a PhD in psychology. It was something I was nervous about; an advanced degree would mean going outside the Orthodox-run, gender-segregated Touro College in Brooklyn. I would have to attend a proper university, and this was, to say the least, unconventional if not impossible. I could practically feel his alarm, all subtext and intuition, so I added quickly, "I asked Rabbi Levi, and he's given me permission."

He listened, then wiped his mouth with the cloth napkin, and silently nodded.

His economy of words was not unusual, but did present a problem. Later, I would learn from my sister Hindy, who had herself only learned from our matchmaker, that Yossi's parents approved of our relationship. I was "beautiful and sweet," in their relayed words. A match for Yossi, who was a handsome man himself. And to his credit, he was the product of a solid family and met the rigorous standards of my religion, while accepting the peculiar nature (for us) of my aspirations to a career of my own. No small thing. He was a "diamond in the haystack," we called it.

At our next meeting, Yossi told me he never expected to find someone like me. A woman who was adherent to God, yes, but also interesting and good at making conversation. It was an unceremonious buildup to the next question, shared no differently than if he were asking whether I'd prefer sushi or Chinese for dinner that night: Did I want to marry him?

I had no justifiable reason to say no. So my answer was yes, because that was what everyone expected of me. Yes, because I needed to get married to meet my mission on earth as a child of God. Yes, because no man was ever going to replace Dassa anyway, so why delay the inevitable? It would only become more painful over time. And yes, because he seemed gentle and had nice blue eyes and seemed to really want me to be his wife.

We walked back to his car in the same manner we had done everything up to that point: several feet apart, making sure that even the fabric of our garments did not accidentally come into contact. We had shared only several shy seconds of eye contact. The rest, I was given to understand, was to be saved for after we were married.

When we got back to Hindy's house, Yossi's parents were already in her living room with my abba, putting out loaves of babka and bottles of schnapps. Yossi's mother had brought with her three beautiful diamond-studded bracelets for me to choose from. I appreciated her generosity, but I knew that the large diamonds would be conspicuous in comparison to my simple gold studs and my thin necklace.

Somehow, in the hour between Yossi's proposal and our arrival at the house, three-foot-tall bride-and-groom helium balloons had been acquired and placed to wave in the air behind us as we posed with straight smiles and arms clamped to our sides for photos. Our families joined and were elated, the men clapping each other on the back and toasting each other with shot glasses—*L'chaim!*

To be engaged was to be relieved, spared the extended singlehood I had been dreading. I was lucky to have finally found someone willing to marry me, I reminded myself. Unlike Yossi's, my own background was filled with blemishes—both told and untold to this point in our relationship. There was very little I knew for certain at that time, except for one thing: no man would ever be *her*.

Dassa traveled around the city with me, helping me shop for all the outfits I would need in order to be a well-dressed religious wife. We took the Monsey bus to a dress shop that specialized in luxury clothing for women like me, garments that covered the elbow, collarbone, and knee. I purchased loose-fitting satin outfits for Sheva Brachot—the customary seven days of celebration following the marriage ceremony. I tried not to notice the tears in Dassa's beautiful brown eyes, tried to ignore the sharp pain in my heart. We soldiered on together, through the whole shopping trip, as we outfitted me in the wardrobe that would signal the end of us.

On the way back I took note of the curtain that ran the length of the bus back to Brooklyn, a barrier meant to separate the men from the women behind frosted plastic that barely hid the shapes of beards and long coats draped down to the floor. We ignored this as Dassa rested her head on my lap and then felt her way over and then underneath my skirt, finding a place inside me. My heart raced. How did she know? I pulled my skirt down and looked around. No one even glanced our way. And so, I returned the favor, pulling her close and feeling the heat between her legs, rebellious and evil and so right all at once.

The wedding planner stowed in my purse showed sixty-three days until we could never touch again. *Anything could happen in sixty-three days,* I thought, *he might even die.*

On a shopping trip to Manhattan, Dassa and I ran past a salesgirl and pulled a long, dark curtain shut. I could almost feel the salesgirl's mascara-coated doe eyes staring through the cloth. We were not inconspicuous, two girls in long skirts bearing armfuls of lace and spandex. I yanked the cloth as far as it would go, while Dassa leaned against the full-length mirror, laughing and rolling her eyes.

"It's Victoria's Secret. Trust me, they don't care!" She held up a miniscule piece of black string. "This would look great on you. Come on, try it!"

I felt my body freeze. I didn't want to try it. I was so modest that I slept in a long skirt every night. I needed a minute, so I flipped my phone open and checked phantom texts, not caring that I was being kind of rude.

Dassa laughed. I looked up and blinked. Blinked again. How did she do that? I saw her through what looked like a sheer black bathing suit, one that left so many miles of porcelain skin out in the open. I stared at her long legs as she came closer. She leaned down, hair brushing against my neck as she whispered in my ear, "You can do this. It'll be okay." I pulled her closer, as close as possible, until we felt each other's heartbeats, mine a herd of stampeding elephants, hers like the steady trot of a single Central Park Clydesdale. I inhaled her scent, Hugo Boss and pheromones. I felt the soft skin of her cheek. I looked into her eyes and saw the same dread that lived deep within my core. And then we were up against the wall, imprinting ourselves on each other. She spun me around and faced my bare, pale body toward the mirror.

"Look at you. You're beautiful."

I didn't believe her. But I knew that one thing was true. If I had any beauty, it belonged to her, not to the strange man with whom I had shared six awkward dates. In just a few weeks, Yossi would own me, acquired through the ancient ritual of purchasing a wife. My worth, according to the rabbis of the Talmud, was about four hundred gold coins. Except in modern times, all it took was a slip of parchment and a thin gold ring, and I, Sara Malka the daughter of Yehuda Hacohen, would become Yossi's. I barely knew him.

On that night, my bridal instructor told me, we would perform an act for which I should buy some lingerie. She would fill me in with more details when we got closer to the wedding.

The word sounded weird to me. *Lingerie.*

Dassa distracted me while I handed my father's credit card over the counter, and paid for a pile of wedding night lace and satin. She hated it as much as I did. But her love for me superseded all that. She knew what I was obligated to do. And so, she helped me prepare to do it.

The countdown chart in my notebook showed forty-one days left. I thought about backing out. How bad would a broken engagement look on my record?

"As a bride you have special mercy on your wedding day," Mrs. Levenstein, my bridal instructor, said as we sat at the folding table in her husband's study. "You can ask God for forgiveness, and he will wipe your slate clean, anything you have ever done wrong will disappear."

Mrs. Levenstein did not understand how much of God's mercy I would require. I sat before her with grave focus on my face, writing every word she said in a pink striped notebook. How could she know that very notebook had been purchased at an Old Navy in Herald Square, with the first girl who'd shared my bed, back in high school? The girl with whom I'd swapped long cargo skirts and shared headphones as we listened to forbidden Pink Floyd CDs and lay with our arms draped over each other's body. God knew how hard I cried into my prayer book, how often I fasted in repentance, and how many times I gave up and gave in and ended up face-to-face, tongue to skin, with her.

I am certain Mrs. Levenstein did not mean to say what I heard: I would get a free pass in thirty days. Anything I did prior to that, no matter how awful, would be forgiven. I was in a suspended moment in time, a liminal space between other spaces that secular people liked to blame on geography (Vegas, baby) or occasion (no bachelorette parties here), but I'd share with God: *whatever happens during an engagement period stays in an engagement period.*

I took her words and turned them into a signed permission slip. I could spend those last weeks with Dassa. All I needed to do was pray well, with some actual tears, on my wedding day.

Dassa was less calculating than I, though. I wanted to celebrate the bits of time we had left; she was already starting to mourn. We were stuck in the weeds somewhere to the left of where we began, tangled in the sodden mess, unable to free ourselves.

"We should run away to California," Dassa said one Shabbos afternoon as we sat on my lavender floral sheets and ate the crackers that my little sister Mimi slipped under the door. Mimi had become a good errand runner in the weeks before the wedding. I knew she was trying to get as many moments with me as possible before I left for good. I had done the same exact thing for weddings performed before, losing each sister to her new life.

"Stop it. Don't talk like that." I knew I sounded exactly like my school-teachers. I didn't care.

Sometimes I wondered how devout Dassa really was, deep down. She dressed like the rest of us and mouthed the prayers, but I knew her mind was not fully in sync with mine. There was a television set in her home, one of the greatest taboos in our world.

I had never watched a television show, not once. I had glimpses of the world outside from books I snuck home in unmarked bags from the Brooklyn Public Library on Sixtieth Street throughout high school. The Sweet Valley High series taught me what teenagers did when they were not bound by rules like ours. I knew that boys and girls flirted with each other, tossed their hair around and talked on the phone and rode surfboards on the ocean. I'd read pages and pages about people who laughed freely with others, who spent Saturday mornings at the mall instead of synagogue, and who were allowed to add cheese to their hamburgers.

I did not recall a single book about girls who loved other girls. Though it had been a few years since I'd cut the evil influences out of my life. Dassa must have had more updated information.

My mind traveled out west, and I imagined another version of myself, one with long curly hair flying free in the wind. She stood straight, this other me, wore flowing skirts and turquoise beads. She glided through cobblestone streets and cafés. She kissed Dassa out in broad daylight. Was there really a place in the world like that?

The real me shook my head, willing the image away. I felt the longing, the fear, the desires all coalesce until my body couldn't hold any of it. I was so mad that my fingers started to shake. I couldn't see past the foot of the bed. I gritted my teeth and the anger spilled from my voice. "Why do you keep bringing that up? You know I can't do that!"

"I'm worried, okay?" She sat up, tried to look me in the eye.

I looked out the window, at the blurred leaves and up to the blank sky.

I knew God was up there, somewhere, frowning down at me and writing notes in his ledger.

"I know him enough. That is not your problem." I hated the way she got into my head, under my skin. I didn't know why I was so furious. Why I even let her words affect me.

Perhaps because I wanted exactly what she suggested, but I knew it was impossible. Sure, I could probably have booked a flight on my father's credit card without him noticing, but then what? I was nineteen, without a college degree, and with little experience of the adult world. I knew how to follow my older sister to a bedding store and spend thousands of dollars on luxury sheets for my marital bed. But I didn't know how to do any of those things on my own, or how to earn the money to do so. I had the skills needed to decode Bible verses, but I didn't know how to drive a car or buy a movie ticket or pay bills.

"Hey," she said, bringing me back from my thoughts. "I love you." She put an arm around my bony shoulders, pulled me into her warm chest. I breathed against her bare skin until I stopped trembling, until my lungs filled with the scent of her cologne, until I sank back into the only arms that had ever made me feel whole.

It's okay, I told myself. *I'll end this next week.*

"We have to stop," I told her on the last Shabbos before the big day. I watched the mascara bleed from her lashes. I memorized the shape of her skin against the black satin she wore, just for me. My purity was so close, almost within reach. I was about to leave all temptation behind, to become the person I was created to be.

"Please," she whispered against my heart, as it broke and then froze over and went numb.

I walked up the concrete stairs to my bridal teacher's home, clutching my wedding notebook. There were eighty-seven boxes checked off on my countdown chart. Some of the boxes had roses on them, to mark the days of my menstrual cycle. There were only two left.

"Come in! Ready for the wedding?" Mrs. Levenstein guided me past a living room full of toys and into a study lined with leather-bound volumes. On the metal folding table between us, I saw what appeared to be an empty tube of toothpaste and a bendable pencil-shaped toy. I wondered why she had not cleaned up the mess. I opened my notebook and got ready to take notes.

"When a man and woman come together, it is the holiest act in the world."

I nodded, listening intently. I knew this. She picked up the tube of toothpaste and I noticed little stickers stuck on the white cap. They formed the shape of a face.

"This is the woman's body." She folded it and set it on the tabletop. She picked up the bendy toy. "This," she said, her intonation solemn, "is the man. His body enters the woman."

I felt my stomach lurch. I watched her take a little balloon out of a box. "This is a douche, but today it will be his *eyver*." She used the Hebrew word for *organ*, as if to sanctify the euphemism.

She demonstrated how the long stick at the end of the douche was the part on a man's body, between his legs. She pointed it down to the floor, and then up to the ceiling. "When he comes next to you it will get bigger and turn up, and that is how it will get into your private part." She pursed her lips to demonstrate what a vagina looked like, down there. I had been made aware of this, that the act would involve my vagina, because I had been told to visit a gynecologist a few days earlier, where I was deemed both fertile and a virgin.

She explained how my hymen would tear and there would be blood. The blood might be on the sheet after the act. She said that men could feel insecure if their *eyver* didn't become or stay erect, so it was my job to make him feel supported. I was to compliment him and act like it was no big deal if he didn't get it right on the first try.

That was what I would have to do with Yossi, the man I barely knew. I questioned this. Could no one have told me earlier? *It's too late to back out now*, I reminded myself as I popped another bubble of doubt in my head. The wedding was in two days. Hundreds of people were scheduled to attend. I had a gown, and an apartment, and dishes, and flowers. But I didn't want him anywhere near my body, never mind inside.

It all came together in my mind. The lingerie. The reason for immersion in the ritual bath. The way they kept telling me about the holy act of marriage.

I stumbled back out onto the Brooklyn streets, Mrs. Levenstein's voice calling behind me, "Call me the morning after if you have any questions!"

Maybe I'll Pray

I cleansed myself thoroughly the morning of my wedding, until I felt like my soul was scrubbed clear of its grime. Until it bore a hint of newborn pinkness on its surface, as if the inside of it were glowing white. I immersed myself in a purifying body of rainwater. I recited the entire book of Psalms. I cried to God and begged for the special grace of forgiveness he granted to worthy brides: absolution from all prior transgressions.

I was not sure if he saw my sincerity, when (or if) my record was indeed wiped clean. And to be honest, I was still unsure of my own sincerity. I had been sinning for so long that the line between moral and perverted, between holy and profane had blurred into nothing. Among the categories of sinners that exist in Jewish law, I was the worst sort. I had forbidden thoughts, committed forbidden acts, and brought others down into my depravity. My sins were premeditated and repetitious, even after I stood before God on Yom Kippur and swore I would stop.

I held the white leather book of Psalms that my groom had inscribed with my new married name: Sara Malka Schwartz. I held it all through the day, praying. Someone came to my house and twirled my thin hair up into a knot. I whispered words into the pages of ancient Hebrew text. Someone got me into a cab to the wedding hall. I did not look up.

"Try not to cry," said the woman who stood over me with makeup brushes. I watched my tears land on the book of Psalms now resting in my lap.

I heard it before I entered the room, the soundtrack I had chosen for this moment: "Bilvavi Mishkan Evneh."

I will build a tabernacle in my heart to glorify God's honor.
And I will place an altar in the tabernacle dedicated to God's divine
    rays of splendor.
And for the eternal, constant flame I will take upon myself the fire that
    fueled the Binding (of Isaac).
And as a sacrifice I will offer God my soul, my unique soul.

I walked down the aisle in a long white gown, flanked by my mother and mother-in-law, both bearing torches covered in elegantly shaped glass cones. I was there to offer God my body, my soul, all of me. If there was one reason I had chosen to marry a man I was not in love with and not excited about, it was for the tabernacle in my heart, as a sacrifice upon the altar inside it.

The crowd was full of devout men and women in black coats and dresses, watching and praying. I whispered words that only God would understand: *Please forgive all of it, please take my temptation away, please save me and rescue me and make me holy.* I promised to stay on the right path. I promised to stay pure. *Help me be your servant. Please.*

I heard the crack of a plate under Yossi's heel and the clamor of "mazel tov!" followed by jaunty musical notes.

"Let me help you," my mother-in-law said as she lifted my veil and wiped a delicate finger underneath my eyes. I saw the smudge of pigment like ash on her fingertip, the residue of my penance. I felt a clammy hand clasp around mine and saw the thin flash of Yossi's smile under the brim of his hat. We walked down the aisle as a couple, the tulle of my gown brushed against his pressed suit pants, and we accepted the exuberant congratulations of our wedding guests.

I had passed God's test. I made it away from Dassa and down the aisle and into a future of godliness.

Or so I believed, through the hours of dancing and accepting kisses on the cheek and leaving the wedding hall with my new husband. I even felt pure as I kept my body prone underneath the blanket of our hotel bed, as I prepared for the holy act of intimacy.

But when Yossi took his folded pajamas off the chair near our bed and put them back on, my body strayed so wildly, with so much audacity that I was taken by surprise. It ached. A comprehensive, organ-deep ache that made it hurt to breathe.

My soul wanted to be one with God, but my heart—it wanted Dassa.

Two mornings later, Yossi spoke into the receiver of our hotel room phone, and I listened to his Yiddish-inflected speech, the language of the yeshiva study hall. "It felt like maybe it happened but—but not for sure."

I stood in the space between the two full beds, several feet behind him. I wanted to lean forward, press my ear up against the phone, hear the rabbi's ruling for myself. I wasn't sure if I was permitted to do so that morning. We were in limbo. If it did happen, if we did successfully have marital intercourse, then I was in *niddah* status. That meant Yossi and I would observe "no-touch" rules until my bleeding stopped, I'd count seven days of purity, and then immerse in a ritual bath called a *mikvah*. We would repeat this cycle throughout our marriage, anytime I bled for any reason—random spotting, a menstrual period, childbirth, or contin-ued shredding of my hymen.

"How many fingers?" I heard him ask, as he held one hand in front of his face.

It felt strange, being on the outside of a conversation in which two men worked to determine if my vagina had been penetrated. I wished I could provide insight either way. But my instructions had been a touch too vague. Mrs. Levenstein had said I might feel a pinch, or a tearing sensation, or a blinding amount of pain. She said I might see a discharge of bright red blood on my sheets, or a light pink stain, or nothing at all. Apparently, every hymen was different, and that made for some confusing guidelines.

Yossi put the phone down on the bed and whispered to me, "The rav wants to speak with you." I turned sideways, took one step forward, gauged the distance between the phone and Yossi and me. I needed to get through the narrow tunnel between our beds without getting close to him. I had always been too long-boned, too pointy to have any sort of kinesthetic grace. In that moment, I was more awkward than ever. My hip crashed into the mattress and my legs jerked forward and I felt like a marionette on shaky strings. Something had shifted in the time since I re-purposed the limbs and organs that were my own and gave them to God. I was not sure how to move in this self that was no longer mine.

I tripped my way to the phone, said a soft hello.

"Mrs. Schwartz," the rabbi started. I felt my muscles spark in surprise, and then I remembered, that was my name. I was Mrs. Schwartz. Me, little me who did not even know what male private parts looked like until last night. Me, who did not know I had a hymen until last week. Me, who had never touched a boy before in my entire life. I was Mrs. Schwartz.

"I felt the *eyver*." I stated the proper Hebrew word for male genitals in my best married woman voice, clear and calm.

"Were you still able to fit more than four fingers in between you and your husband?" The rabbi sounded just as unsure as I felt, his questions coming in slow succession, euphemisms and similes and a discussion about centimeters of human flesh.

After a few more awkward phone passes, a call to Mrs. Levenstein, and another call from the rabbi, we arrived at our answer. We had not had marital intercourse last night. False alarm.

Yossi stopped his pacing and sat down on a corner of the bed and wiped a hand across his forehead. I felt hot too, under the layers of clothing and hose and wig, so much fabric and polyester fastened to my body. It was only noon, but I felt like it had been days since the sun came up and our phone calls began. We were scheduled to attend the second of seven post-wedding dinner parties later that day, where our family and friends would toast to our future. For seven days, the only item on our agenda was to get to know each other.

"Maybe we should rest a little," Yossi said, looking at me with a tenderness that had been absent all morning. "To tell you the truth, I am happy we have more time to be together." I tried to feel the joy that he did. But the biggest hurdle was still before me. The mysterious act that would hurt and break my skin and possibly make me bleed. The longer it took us to get it done, the more the fear grew. I just wanted it to be over. I did not need to spend any more time discovering the ways in which the hair on Yossi's chest extended down to the rest of his body. I did not need to feel the rough skin of his hands on the most delicate parts of my body. I just wanted to do the thing that would prove to God that I intended to keep the promises I had made in prayer and in our marriage contract.

But this was not about me. So I lifted a pair of baby-blue pajamas from my suitcase and headed to the bathroom to change. By the time I emerged, his suit pants and white button-down were folded over the desk chair, and he was sitting up in bed, waiting. I folded my legs underneath the blanket, sat upright and grasped at the static in my mind for an appropriate topic of conversation.

"Which of your family are coming tonight?" I nodded as he talked about his uncle Pinny, who would drive in from New Jersey; and his cousin Motti, who would make one of the seven blessings later; and his aunt Gittel, who was hard of hearing.

"You know what I meant to ask you—" He turned to me, and his brows crunched close together, a question on his face. "How come your sister Shani wasn't at the wedding?"

"The flight from Israel would be too much for her mental health," I explained. "She doesn't do well with missing sleep, it could trigger an episode."

He looked dumbfounded. "An episode?"

"Yes," I said, and tried to find words to describe what I had only seen flashes of. "She can get very depressed and end up in the hospital."

"Wow," he said, his eyes wide. "If I had known your sister was mentally unstable, I would never have married you."

How could he not know?

Didn't the matchmaker tell him all the facts about our family before he agreed to date me?

Didn't his mother vet me the way my sisters had vetted him—thoroughly and comprehensively, with pages of notes?

I thought he married me knowing all of these things, all the flaws. That he understood who I was and why I was pursuing a degree in psychology, and that he respected me for the challenges I had faced.

"I didn't mean . . ." He looked at me, his face red, his mouth starting to form words, his hands swiping back and forth against the blanket. "No, that isn't it."

Through the haze of my shame and my panic, I saw his brows curl closer together, tiny centipedes of regret, too small to make a difference.

I felt the old shame creep back through my veins, the familiar knowledge that my family was damaged, that I was broken, that none of it was reparable. It had lived inside me since I was seven years old, since my family splintered and then fell completely apart. Even worse than my damage was the fact that I had infected someone else with it, against his will and without his knowledge.

I was not just wounded, I had also become a perpetrator of wounds. I wanted to curl up in the corner of the hotel room closet and stay there with my hands over my ears until the world faded away and I was no longer in it.

Sound of Silence

The year I turned seven I huddled in corners, under the sloping stairs in our dining room, behind the coats in our front hall closet. There was comfort to the mustiness inside those spaces. The bits of dust that smelled like Abba's foot lotion, the occasional crumpled tissue that held Goldy's snot, hints of perfume that wafted off the wool jacket that Hindy left behind when she got married. In the darkness, I could feel the cracks between the wooden floorboards, the hard bumps underneath the paint, the scratchy fabrics against my face. Sounds that became distant, like they were echoes from faraway places, where the natives were losing their minds, but their madness could never reach me.

It started with the footsteps. They used to be light, the sound of my sisters Dina, Shani, and Goldy skipping up to their rooms on the second floor. Then, one day the steps slowed, grew heavier, like a tired elephant marking time as it grew near.

"Tell Shani she has to get dressed!" I remember hearing Dina shout down the stairs to my mother.

"Let her be!" my mother yelled back. "You're both late!"

We could all hear Dina bang on Shani's door one more time. Finally, she left, frizzy black hair and blue plaid skirt bouncing out the door.

It wasn't the first or last time Shani stirred up trouble. There was howling from the second floor another night, the sounds of Shani turning feral. It was like a shofar horn, the kind that was meant to pierce inside our souls every year on Rosh Hashanah.

Guttural, animalistic wails, then jumping, feet smashing into the ceiling above my head, thumps of wooden furniture thrown against the walls that sent the house shaking.

Finally Abba cut a path, heavy steps in clunky black shoes, up to the girls' floor that he never ever visited. "Shani!"

Through the walls of my closet. I could hear more screaming, more feet on the stairs, up, down, and then out the front door.

The house fell into terrifying silence in the hours after that door slammed shut. There were no sounds of sisters fighting over the phone, no mother calling us for suppertime, no walking around. Everyone stayed in their room with their door closed. And Shani was gone. I stayed at the edges of my room, where the floorboards met the walls, listening for quiet voices, trying to put the words together.

Hospital and *very sick* and *hold on, I will call you back from the bedroom* and *what are her chances.*

That Friday night for Shabbos, I brought my library book upstairs to read on the carpet, like we always did. No one left their room. There was no Goldy poking me with her toe and saying, "Don't block the light!" as we strained to read with the faint beams coming from the bathroom. Definitely no Shani, offering to read to me in funny voices. Just me and the gray upstairs carpet, both flattened by everything that had happened.

When Abba came home and called, "Kiddush!" the sisters slouched down the stairs, wearing their long velvet Shabbos robes, but with their faces pointing down. Abba went to knock on our mother's bedroom door. There were whispers, the sharp kind, and then he came back to the table and put the silverware and plates smack in the middle, no place settings, no napkins folded to look like wings. I wondered if our mother was just too tired to serve the gefilte fish this week. Too tired to remind us that we shouldn't play with our food, and then watch us form soft pieces of challah into squares anyway, and dip them into our soda.

Abba perched himself at the head of the table, acting like everything was normal. He read stories from the Torah, his black, glossy *bekishe* glinting under the light of our chandelier. He sang songs and asked me about school and told us that Bill Clinton would destroy this country if he won the election in November. He cut a cantaloupe into perfect slices for dessert, and he gave me an extra slice with a little smile through his wiry beard. He never said anything about the polished wood chairs that stayed tucked underneath the table all through the meal, the chairs where Shani and our mother belonged.

In the weeks after Shani vanished, we kept discovering more parts of us that had been misplaced and destroyed by our family's seismic implosion.

The first casualty was our mother. Sometimes she wandered around the house in her nightgown, holding half-full glasses of coffee, dark skin around her eyes. Other times she did not emerge from her room at all, not even when we ran out of groceries, when we started pouring water from the kitchen faucet into our morning bowls of corn flakes.

Then, another casualty became apparent, sparking in small flashes, like a flimsy electrical cord threatening to start a fire in the living room.

"Meshuggener!" *You crazy person,* I heard Abba tell my mother when he brushed past her, not looking at her face, not stopping to see who was around. When he finally went to work, our home left in sufficient upheaval, I heard my mother break—a thin wailing sound like the alley cats outside our window at night, coaxing its way into my bedroom. I wanted to hide, but then I thought of Mimi, my three-year-old sister, and how she'd need another memory to crowd out the first. I would teach her how to play the clubhouse game underneath our dining room table, I decided.

I padded the space between the legs of our chairs with blankets and pillows and teddy bears. I packed picnics, bottles of milk for her and baggies of Cheerios for me, and we read Little Golden children's books inside our hideout. I tried not to think about the old days, when Ma was the one who packed us picnics, bread-and-jam sandwiches that we ate on a blanket in the backyard. I wanted to peek out from under the tablecloth and call to her, *We are using our imaginations!* That used to mean she would come running, Nikon camera in hand, to snap a picture before sitting down on the floor and laughing with us, her face crinkling with deep dimples.

One day I worked up the courage to say the thing that no one was talking about. "What is Shani sick with?" I sat at the edge of my mother's bed, watching her, ready to slide off her sheets and walk away if she got upset.

"It's a very rare disease with like six or seven words that you would not understand." Her voice was tight and faraway. Her face fell. The conversation was over.

What disease could have six or seven words? I wondered. *Strep* was only one word, *strep throat*, two words. Even *ear infection* and *cold* were only four words altogether. When no one was looking, I took the dictionary off of the basement shelves and sat on Abba's brown recliner, using my pointer finger to trace the words. There were so many words near "sick," but none of them were six or seven words all in a row.

I wanted to ask the librarian at my school, to see if she had an encyclopedia with more words than we had in our home dictionary. I wondered if my science teacher might know about diseases that took sisters away from home for weeks. Both of those teachers had permanent seats at our shul. Both had husbands who sat in the men's section, just rows behind Hindy's husband, Meir. What if they said something to my mother, if their husbands said something to my brother-in-law, about the kinds of questions I was asking? They would wonder why a second grader wanted to study all the illnesses in the world. They might think there was something wrong with me. That there was an infection in our house, something that could make them all ill too.

I pretended I didn't hear the whispers dropped in the air in our house, parts of sentences like broken puzzle pieces that didn't seem to fit together. *Better doctors* and *there is a place in Israel*, Abba had said, to the walls around my mother, not waiting for an answer, not stopping to see her face start to crack.

When my mother told me that I had a doctor's appointment after school one day, I expected to have my height checked against a wall, get shots in my arm, and go home with a Mickey Mouse sticker. I did not expect a new office, strange, with a very still waiting room and magazines atop a small table instead of a VCR playing cartoons. I did not know what the word "psychologist," written in gold on the closed office doors, meant. My mother was in a weird mood, her voice frozen-polite as she signed us in at the front desk. Her closed lips curled up, her eyes moved back and forth. I knew that look. It had been with us many times since Shani left. The look meant that a scream could be inside her, ready to come out. It meant her hands might shake up and down until they dropped things on the floor.

My mother tucked her purse tight underneath her arm and walked me into a room where a fat man leaned back in a leather chair. I heard her tell him that she was worried about me. That I wasn't talking to anyone about my feelings. When she left, the doctor pointed across the carpet to a part of the office that looked like it was made for children.

"You may play with the dollhouse however you'd like," he said, looking at me like I was a real person, someone he saw and noticed. The experience was deeply unfamiliar.

I watched him out of the corner of my eye while he watched me move a girl doll around a wooden house. The doll was too big for the wooden rooms, like a blown-up person in a tiny world. "Tell me about her family," he said, scratching a pen on his notebook. I wanted to take the grown-up dolls and put them in opposite corners of the house. I wanted to make them whisper loudly—rock-like words that would take up the whole dim office. But my mother was right outside, in her weird mood, and I didn't want to make it worse.

"I had a dream about Shani," I said, casually setting the doll at the edge of the house, crossing her legs over each other.

I had figured it out, I thought to myself. This was what the doctor was for; because my sister disappeared, and I wasn't allowed to talk about it with anyone else.

"She was in Israel." I sounded the word out slowly, heard it echo in this room of shelves filled with books that had complicated words down their spines. "She was on a mountain being chased by soldiers with army guns. She was so scared."

I wanted to cry, but I forced the tears back down my throat, back inside me. It felt so real, the dream. It could have been real. Shani was the only one of us with olive skin and deep brown eyes, and I'd hoped that if she was in Israel, she would by now have become unidentifiable. That she would blend in wherever she needed to, a specter among the Jews and the Arabs.

"Mhmhm," the psychologist said, writing now as he stood and guided me to another room, one with flat chairs and no toys, where my mother sat stiffly with her brown pocketbook in her lap. "She had a nightmare," he said, as he dumped his large body down onto a chair.

I wanted to stand up and scream. Why would he tell her about the dream I had been keeping to myself? Had he never learned that mothers were not people you shared such personal things with?

They talked about me like I was not there. "She might be worried about Shani," he said as if it were a mystery that he had solved all by himself. My mother stared at him, said some words, all of it blending into a jumble of sounds that could no longer be understood. Her words, and his words, and mine.

After, when the streets were dark and we were walking home, she asked, "Do you want pizza? Ice cream?" She bought me a hot slice from Mendel's. I looked at her as she carried it all the way home, oil seeping into the brown paper bag. She looked almost like my *real* mother, the one from before Shani got sick, who would take us to Mendel's, but something was not the same. When she smiled at me, I saw too much gum over her teeth, noticed the bluish tint in the places where she had crowns. When she led me across the street, she did not look both ways. Instead, she looked straight ahead, as if she were seeing something past the traffic lights, past the tops of the houses, past our whole town.

That night I sat with my back against the door, the full weight of my seven years pressing on the hollow wood. *Remember*, I penciled to my future self, *do not trust her. Sometimes she is nice, but she is always weird again.* I twisted the thumb-sized tin key into the lock, turned it all the way.

"What do you want to be when you grow up?" Mrs. Abramowitz asked me, leaning back on one of Hindy's polished dining room chairs.

I tucked my white slip under the pile of my clothing on Hindy's radiator. Even outside the classroom, she was still my teacher, and I didn't need her seeing my underclothes.

"An author, a librarian," I started to say, and I watched her nod in approval. "Or a psychologist."

"What makes you say *that*?" Mrs. Abramowitz asked, her eyes narrowed to slits.

"Their job is so easy! All they do is sit in a chair and say, *Mm-hmm!*"

As soon as the words left my mouth, I knew it was a mistake. The room felt frozen in the moment and was also way too bright. Hindy looked at me, mortified, while baby Leibele kicked against her hip, making little creaking sounds.

Mrs. Abramowitz looked at Hindy, then back at me, and all of a sudden, she started talking about challah recipes.

I added *psychologist* to the list of things in my head that should never be spoken. It was now a long list. *Mommy and Abba fight. Mommy might be crazy. Mommy made Shani sick—or the other way around. Shani is sick, but I don't know with what. She lives in Israel, in a special hospital. I haven't seen her in a long time.*

I never spoke the thought out loud again, but I knew I wanted to be a psychologist, so I could help children in the way that they truly needed. The psychologists I knew told mothers what the children said. But sometimes, mothers were not safe. Sometimes, children needed a place to say the things they couldn't say at home.

By the time I started third grade, things had begun to settle around the space where Shani used to be. I found a pressed uniform skirt and freshly ironed shirt at the edge of my bed every morning. There were sandwiches in my knapsack each day, butter on rye bread in little bags. There was roast chicken for dinner most nights, like always, except for Thursday, when we had breaded flounder instead. It was almost normal—but I could see the cloud of darkness my mother wore surrounding her entire body, a murk that made her steps slow, her hands shake. My mother was there, but she didn't come back home after Shani left.

Abba went back to ranting about the state of the American government during our Shabbos meals. He couldn't wait for one of the Bushes to get rid of that Clinton before he and the rest of the Democrats ruined our society. Abba brought new Jewish novels home for us each week, gifts from the owners of Judaica stores who stocked their shelves with prayer shawls and yarmulkes from his factory. Unlike my mother, he was almost the same as before, except for the silver cup he kept filled with a clear liquid throughout dinner in the evenings, until he fell back in his chair and started to snore.

Shani wasn't there to see me get my ears pierced for the first time. She missed the time I broke my arm and spent two months of fifth grade in a neon-green cast. She wasn't there for my first period, when Hindy slipped a manual about growing up into my school notebook and I snuck maxi pads out of Goldy and Dina's stash in the bathroom cabinet. Shani did stay in touch however she could, with greeting cards and gifts for my birthday most years—stone bracelets she strung herself, tiny felt dolls, Israeli shekels. Sometimes there were glossy pictures, too, her hair long and curly, flowing in the wind atop her smiling face as she sat among a group of people I'd never met. The pictures more than anything made her seem even farther away. We didn't flow around in the breeze in our family. And Hindy's wig was straight as her long navy skirts, a style the rest of us sisters would follow, just as she'd followed that of our married aunts and teachers. We didn't do casual.

Shani wasn't there to see our mother crumble again when Dina got engaged, walking around the house in a stained nightgown, panic in her eyes. One day as the wedding date drew nearer, our mother grabbed on to Dina's arm until it bruised, begged her to stay home instead of getting married. There was a new set of sounds and whispers; the wailing of an ambulance siren, the silence afterward, the empty space where my mother used to be. Words like *straitjacket* and *the doctor already knows us and it's better if she stays until after the wedding*, murmured between Dina and Hindy and Abba as I eavesdropped on their phone calls. There were so many things I wanted to ask Shani in preparation for what I was sure was about to happen again: *Were they nice at Maimonides hospital? Did the doctors help people they took in? Would our mother be in a straitjacket the whole time? Did they have kosher food for her to eat?* I didn't have Shani's phone number, and by the time a letter about these goings on got to her, Dina would have already married, and our mother would be back home after a stint in the psychiatric ward. Besides, we didn't really talk about things like that in our family. Explosions were best ignored and then forgotten.

I was fifteen when I finally saw Shani again. I had lived without my sister for more than half my life. I was in therapy for real by then, with Dr. Genevieve, whose office was down the block from Bais Yaakov High School for Girls. I liked the independence of it, the ability to walk to therapy myself.

During our early sessions, Genevieve listened to my choppy narrative about my family's broken parts. She squinted as I told her that my mother had told us Shani was afflicted with a six-or-seven-word disease, and that no matter how many dictionaries and science books I consulted, I would never figure out what it was.

"Malka," Genevieve's voice took on an extra layer of tenderness, "have you ever considered that your sister *and* your mother suffer from mental illness?"

I struggled to push words past the panic in my throat, Genevieve waiting calmly as I put them together to form the most frightening question, "What if I go crazy too?"

Shani arrived two days before my sister Goldy's wedding, with suitcases bearing Hebrew tags and gifts of jewelry wrapped in soft patterned paper. The first act of hers I can remember back in the house was Shani, tanned golden like an exotic stranger play-acting at the role of Shani in a Hollywood production, trying on a plum velvet gown to twirl around Hindy's living room. She sparkled with laughter when I showed her the trendy black choker that I planned to wear with my matching plum gown, and said, "Good for you!" I smiled, a tight, forced motion of my jaw, wondering if her laughter was a sign that she was out of control, that she was about to go crazy again. Wondering if my own behavior—purchasing a choker at Claire's and hiding it from Hindy and planning to whip it out at the last minute—if that made me kind of crazy too.

No one stated, "Don't mention invitations or seating plans in front of Ma." We didn't have to. We had all seen what happened the last time our home was filled with lace and gowns and calligraphed envelopes. This time, we kept the wedding paraphernalia in Hindy's apartment, stashed underneath the table at which Goldy and her groom had met, and at which they had gotten engaged. No one officially said, "Hindy and her husband Meir are taking over," but I saw Abba slip his credit card to her and nod gratefully. No, we simply moved ourselves into position, took on our roles, donned our costumes like actors in a silent film.

Our mother did manage to get to the wedding hall without incident, to take her spot in the white wicker chair designated for the mother of the bride. Only the most astute guests noticed that our mother's lips did not curve upward for the pictures taken that day, that her eyes were fixed in a blank stare. When I told Genevieve about it later, she said, "She might have been heavily medicated," and that seemed to make sense.

Once Goldy was married and Shani was back in Israel, our house of sisters adopted a painful, achy sense of emptiness. My parents took to eating their Shabbos meals in separate rooms, at separate times, as Mimi and I made awkward choices about which of their tables we would join each week. I wanted to be there for my little sister, but I was disintegrating just as she began to wear the same distant expression that presaged our mother's own collapse. I stopped eating, in what even I was aware was a very cliché way to deal with circumstances outside my control. I felt invincible at first, in my skeletal body, in the way I could get through my days at school on only a single teaspoon of rice. It felt like a cool experiment, until Genevieve noticed and threatened to tell my abba if I didn't start eating again.

I gripped the edge and pulled myself back into the land of the sane, reluctantly shoving enough calories down my throat each day. Genevieve decided that my dances with insanity had grown too frequent, too intense, and that something needed to change. With the help of a sympathetic teacher at my school, I was accepted to the Canadian version of our Bais Yaakov girls' school, where I could stay with some cousins in Toronto to begin eleventh grade.

I made friends that year, girls who gently poked fun at my monotone

voice and then helped me relax enough to laugh out loud. It was easier to hold on to my mind miles away from my family, in a home where
the "mother" walked around in neat sweater sets, baked chocolate chip
cookies every Wednesday, and taught me how to set a table with multiple
forks at each setting.

My year of normalcy in Canada was strong enough to hold me through
a brief trip to Israel to celebrate Shani's marriage to a handsome military
veteran. By the time I entered twelfth grade, I was a candidate for some
excellent post–high school programs in Israel, an honor only the bright-
est girls in my grade were invited to attempt. My interests in research and
writing papers with well-developed insights that would please my teachers paid off as I gained entry to one of those schools, sorely needed proof
to myself that I'd defeated whatever genetic predisposition to insanity
might course within my veins. Who, after all, would want a wife whose
offspring were destined to lose their minds?

But by the time Yossi's family was approached about our wedding, I
was no longer just a girl from a complicated family. I was a graduate of
a reputable high school, an elite seminary, a student of psychology at a
religious women's college. Hindy and Dina handled the rest of the story
with practiced matter-of-fact delivery.

"His parents understand that our family is a little different," Hindy
told me. "Don't worry."

And so I didn't.

I didn't think I needed to ask if all our family's mental health history
had been disclosed to the matchmaker. It had seemed obvious to me—
that, I'd thought, was how the matchmaking process took place. Yossi
and I had also exchanged the results of genetic testing to ensure that we
weren't carriers of hereditary disorders that were common among Ash-
kenazi Jews, like Tay-Sachs or cystic fibrosis. Our rabbis had also been
clear; we were supposed to disclose any possible emotional conditions
that could affect our future children. I was confident, too confident it
turns out, that Yossi had consciously accepted the darkness hidden be-

hind my shiny straight hair, stylishly modest clothes, and poised Canadian posture.

I realized I had been wrong in our post-wedding bridal suite, as the afternoon sunlight filtered through our hotel room shades and onto my quivering body.

"I didn't— No— That's not," he stammered, as our stilted small talk about the families we'd readjust to post-marriage opened a crack in our façade. Yes, my mother was difficult. Yes, my sister had been hospitalized and fled to Israel to heal away from the people who'd pushed her to her mental limit. Yossi threw segments of words out between us, words I hardly heard above the ringing of alarm bells in my head, "I meant, I am happy I didn't know. I am happy we got married."

I dug the old armor out from inside, rebuilt my fortress, and found the will to stand up and face him. "It's okay," the shell of me said. "It was destined for us to be married, maybe it had to happen this way." I saw the relief in his eyes, and we readied ourselves for dinner, me in a floral skirt and softly curled wig, him in a navy suit and geometric tie. He looked at me shyly as we rode down to the hotel lobby in a mirrored elevator. "You look very beautiful," he said to the reflection of me staring back at him.

As we walked down Thirteenth Avenue to China Glatt, where a dinner had been arranged to host a select subset of wedding guests who wished for more private time to celebrate the bride and groom, I took notice of my image in the storefronts. My sharp chin unmoving against glass displays holding children's toys, then low-heeled shoes, followed by kosher salamis. I looked like I was holding it together, my face smooth and unbothered. I almost began to believe that I was fine. Then I saw the shape of her, inside the doorway of the ice cream store, standing still.

"Go ahead," I told Yossi, my voice as smooth as my expression. "I just want to check my makeup before I go inside."

I turned around, grabbed her by the hand, and walked her to the side

street away from the avenue. I was about to ask her what she was thinking, how she could think there was a happy ending to this night where
she'd show up uninvited to the celebration of my marriage to a man. But
as I felt the blood rush to my face, the anger form underneath my skin,
I stopped. There was anguish in her face. Her eyes were raw. I saw my
Dassa, trying not to be mine anymore.

"I just need to know," she said, in a voice so small that it was almost
dwarfed by the whooshing of tires and the honking of horns around us,
"are you happy?"

I stood on the concrete, feeling her hurt start to enter me. I wanted to
pull her close, to let my tears fall against her face, to cry with her until we
fused back together again. I wanted to wipe the past week out of both our
minds, to turn around and run until we were far away enough that none
of this would matter anymore. Until we were us again.

But I couldn't. I had made promises. To God. To Yossi. To myself.

"I am happy," I lied, through the iron tightness of my jaw. "I am fine."

I turned around before I could break apart, before she could see that
I was not me anymore. I moved my legs, one in front of the other, until I
was inside the restaurant and smiling at a room filled with my aunts and
sisters and cousins, saying "thank you!" as they kissed me on the cheek
with warm greetings. "Mazel tov, Mrs. Schwartz!"

I didn't know who this new Mrs. Schwartz was, but I did know Dassa
could no longer matter to her.

Watch Me Burn

Lakewood, New Jersey, is home to the largest and most prestigious Talmudic (Jewish law) academy outside Israel: Beth Medrash Govoha. And just like any secular college town, where the locale bends to the whims of the institution that drives its economy, Lakewood has grown to support the specific needs of its yeshiva. The local babysitters work from ten in the morning until two in the afternoon, because that is when the town's husbands are at the study hall; at two, the men pick up their children, while their wives often remain at their full-time jobs.

Seventy miles south of New York City, Lakewood is both a hub of Orthodox Judaism and one of the fastest-growing municipalities in the country. It is a secluded and self-contained world, its ultra-Orthodox residents maintaining cradle-to-grave amenities that allow them to limit their exposure to the broader American society outside its city limits.

Lakewood's clothing stores, for example, typically display the verse from Psalms: *All the glory of a princess is within*, a reminder for women to hide anything too conspicuously feminine. Shop attendants keep measuring tape handy, to ensure that all skirts fall four inches below the knee.

And Lakewood was where Yossi and I planned to settle down after our wedding. We rented a small basement apartment and labored to ad-

49

just to the strangeness of sharing a home with someone we barely knew. While Yossi busied himself with his studies at yeshiva, I filled my days with reading kosher cookbooks, followed by quiet walks down a dirt road to the nearest supermarket before I cooked what I'd just purchased. Thrice-weekly commutes to the classes I'd resumed at Touro College in Brooklyn were a relief, but this was never meant to last.

Yossi didn't hesitate when I tried (and failed, repeatedly) to get a driver's license. In fact, he turned out to be a patient and gentle guide, as he let me drive the Garden State Parkway on our way to his parents' in Monsey. "You might want to veer a little to the left," he said when I was about to hit another car, with not a trace of sarcasm in his voice.

But other things were more troubling. During my monthly cycle, the *niddah* period during which our faith told us I was impure and untouchable, Yossi insisted I sleep with my headscarf pulled tightly over my forehead, covering every stray hair. He avoided looking at my entire side of the room, just in case the kerchief slid backward in the night and a strand came poking out from underneath my blankets. "It happened a few times," he said, and his face turned dark, like the gloomy brown spines of the massive Talmud volumes that towered over us from our shelves.

His *niddah* went above and beyond. The law mandated that we did not touch, but in his reading, "only speak if necessary" and "minimize eye contact" were rules to live by for what worked out to be two weeks of every month. I gave in to his extremism, often mouthing the same prayer several times in the morning, until I was sure that I had pronounced every syllable with the right intention. I found reasons to leave conversations when I suspected that I might hear gossip. I dressed modestly as always, but as an added measure kept the volume of my voice down whenever there were men in earshot.

We were *machmir*, exceptionally devout even among the devout. It wasn't something we would label ourselves, for fear of coming across as arrogant. It was a compliment given by others: "Oh, you and your husband are so *machmir*." I would flush and pretend to wave the words away, while my heart swelled in pride. I didn't flag Yossi's extra restrictions as a concern. They were right on brand for people like us.

We were at his parents' home in Monsey when I started bleeding. It was on a Shabbos in early August, six weeks after our marriage. I was busying myself with inspection of the vomit-pink bathroom walls, the old porcelain bidet, the window screen; but in the corner of my eye I noticed the crimson drips dotting the floor. My belly was still flat under the lacy black belt, and less than a week had passed since the doctor's office called to tell me that I was, in fact, pregnant. Early days, but I could already feel my baby with every breath I took, with every bite of food I swallowed, with every step I walked. I loved the way the word *mother* sounded when I whispered it, *I am your mother*. I turned around, forced myself to look down. The water in the toilet had all turned to blood, like one of the Egyptian plagues. I felt it spilling onto my thighs. Thick, sticky, hot.

I stuffed a wad of tissue between my legs, sat down at the edge of the bed and waited for Yossi to come home from shul (synagogue). Moments passed. Years, maybe. Eons. Eventually, he swung the bedroom door open and put his black felt hat and prayer bag on the dresser. His accoutrements were brand-new just like mine, and the scent of leather and linen trailed into the air behind him.

"Good Shabbos." He nodded in my direction, square white chin over dark suit jacket.

I stumbled to find the words. "I am having some bleeding. I think we should call the doctor." I watched his transparent blue eyes stare out of the picture window at the wide Monsey lawn.

"I'm sure it is just a little bit, right?" he asked, in a tone more like statement than question. I wished he would look at me, see the panic in my eyes, understand that our baby needed to be saved.

He mumbled some words under his breath and walked out of the room. I expected he had gone to retrieve a cordless phone. It was Shabbos, but we all knew that saving a life superseded the restriction against using electricity. "My mother said a lot of people bleed when they're pregnant. It's normal," he said, returning with eyes trained on the moss-green carpet.

And so it was. We would not call the doctor on the holy Shabbos. No matter how furious or afraid I felt, I was not going to violate the most important rule of all: "*Isha Keshaira Asah Retzon Baalah.*" A kosher woman does the will of her husband.

Whatever happens, it is God's will, I told myself, but my words felt hollow, meaningless. I was so skilled at the movement, the turning off of my heart at its base, that my body betrayed nothing to the world at all.

"How are you feeling?" Mother-In-Law's falsetto wafted toward me, her smooth blond wig framing an empty oval face as we spoke in the kitchen.

"*Baruch Hashem.*" Blessed be our God. I picked up the crystal salad bowls and brought them to the grand antique-white table. Then the china plates, the silver knives and forks, the cloth napkins. *I am God-fearing just like you are,* my actions said, no room for the concerns of a woman, not-yet mother, in this house of rules and laws.

Later that night, when the sun set and it was permissible to use electricity again, we drove to the emergency room. I knew there was no good news to be found. I had been bleeding all day.

"How old are you?"

I couldn't even imagine what the doctor thought of me, with my neat brown wig and long black skirt bunched up around my waist.

"Nineteen." I was alone, watching the monitor blink, and decided this was a time to be matter-of-fact. There, on the screen, I saw the tiny triangle of my uterus.

"I'm sorry honey." The doctor's voice was soft as she put a hand on mine. "I can't find a heartbeat."

I blinked hard, willing the tears back through my eyes. They landed in the back of my throat and burned their way down inside me. My baby. How could my baby be gone? I thought, this whole time, God would see my sacrifice and give me his blessing. But my baby was dead. My first moments as a mother, and already I had failed. I clamped my jaw shut. Why cry if it was already over?

In the waiting room, I found Yossi sitting in a chair and clutching his cell phone, staring straight ahead, face blank.

"They told me," he mumbled. "I spoke with the rav."

I sat in the chair beside him, trying not to notice the way he whisked his arm into his lap.

"Fourteen days," he said, his words deliberate, slow. "We don't know if it was a male or a female, so we have to count the maximum." He said more things about how the sex of the fetus determined the amount of time we must count before I may purify myself in a ritual bath. He repeated the numbers, several times, as if speaking from a trance of sorts. "So, seven days plus fourteen days, okay?"

I turned the orange plastic bracelet on my wrist, noticing the stamped letters for the first time. PCN. I wondered what they stood for. Pregnant Child? Primary Care? What was the N? Suddenly it seemed imperative that I find out. A nurse came by, handed me a sheaf of printed papers, asked for the phone number of my pharmacy. "Excuse me?" I heard my own voice, urgent. "What does this mean?" She read the letters, "Oh dear, this is the allergy you reported. Penicillin."

Penicillin. I was ten years old, on the crinkled paper of another doctor's table, swinging my feet back and forth as she examined the bumps on my cheek. *No more penicillin*, she had told us, winking at me. *I recommend orange ices instead.* I wanted to curl up under my flower sheets and eat a popsicle while reading *Harriet the Spy* for the third time. I wanted to go back in time, back when doctor's visits did not involve invasive probes and the death of my child.

I looked down at the purse over my wrist, the diamond on my finger, glowing in the cast of red emergency lights. I was an adult now. There would be no turning back. Smoothing the strands of wig back from my face as we stood up, I followed my husband out the glass doors and back into the world.

We wandered around our basement apartment for a few days, passing dry words across the table as I prepared meals from ever deep recesses of the *Kosher by Design* cookbook. "It's hot for this time of year." One day he told me that he had a few weeks off before the next study semester, and maybe we should take some day trips. "My friend told me about a lounge in Long Branch," he said, and I nodded profusely, grateful for his effort.

We took the Garden State Parkway north the next afternoon, and it felt different being out of the apartment. As we passed strip malls of Michaels craft stores and RadioShacks, it felt like we were allowed to feel sunlight again, to expel our grief and allow the suffering to slowly dissipate behind us, a cloud of exhaust in the air.

Inside the oceanfront hotel lobby, Yossi did not seem to care that the bartender watched him like one would an exotic zoo animal. He did not even glance at the women around him, all shine and bare limbs and cleavage. He was one of the truly pious, happy with me and the long garments I wore to hide my body away. *I am lucky*, I reminded myself, *he is the real deal.*

I had not watched the news since the Gulf War in 1991, when my mother snuck us into our Italian neighbor's living room, and we watched bombshells explode over Israel in grainy black and white. I preferred to keep my mind on more purposeful things than TV screens. Then I heard the New Jersey governor Jim McGreevey's words cut through the tinkle of silverware and classical music: "I am a gay American." I nodded over at Yossi, who waited for our glasses of Sprite several feet away, as the small screens around the lobby played the same scenes all at once. The governor's wife looked so sad and stiff.

Kissing Girls on Shabbat

ssa's birthday, the CD she mixed for me, the roses we slipped into each
ier's hands, the oversized sweatshirts we swapped, the folded notes
ide pillowcases, the foil-wrapped containers of favorite foods sourced
·m restaurants across the city and eaten together cross-legged on my
d. Our gifts required effort, but never the forced kind.

Yossi's choice of gift on this *mikvah* night, moments before we were
ieduled to have marital intercourse, was another among many con-
ions. A wind-up music house? *He has never been with a girl before*, I
ninded myself. *How is he supposed to know?*

And *don't let her ruin this.*

I clenched my muscles, my teeth, my mind, until all I saw were the
·brew words from the silver-plated plaque near my Shabbos candles.
ang the words inside my head, keeping the melody on repeat, keeping
y thoughts in the holiest of places. It was my responsibility to reject the
ipure, unholy thoughts. I felt for the godly trail, where virtuous behav-
·r might be rewarded with a baby, like the one I'd lost before.

Vezakeini legadel bonim uvnei bonim
May I merit to raise learned children and grandchildren.

I heard the tune play as he turned the lights out, climbed into bed, felt
·r my body under the blankets.

Ohavei Hashem, yirei Elokim
Children who love God, fear God.

I saw the ancient letters before my eyelids as my eyes squeezed shut,
I felt the weight of his body on top of mine.

Anshei emes, zera kodesh
People who speak the truth, holy offspring.

I held my breath through the pain, the sensation of a serrated knife
rough my flesh. I felt him leave his mark inside my body. I heard his
gh, then felt the indentation of his weight on the mattress beside me.

How did they get her to stand there next to him in tw *and blow-dried hair and a plastic smile?* I knew what wo when they were being forced into shapes that were not th McGreevey looked so very squished.

"I have decided the right course of action is to resi McGreevey concluded, as his family stepped off the po screens all around the room. August 12, 2004, the day the g Jersey resigned because he was gay. My heart scrunched u rocking back and forth, thinking about Dassa. I didn't wan her breath on my skin, her whispers against my cheek, th cologne in my hair. I wanted to call her, just to hear her vo her how scary it was to lose my baby. Then I realized what (to tell me. This was a message. The bleeding and the sins w

I did bad things with my private parts. My baby bled th vate parts. God put the screen there, on that day, with that for a reason. *My child, you must scrub her from your mind,* hear his voice rumble inside my head.

We were parked outside the unmarked women's *mikvah* building at the end of our block, shrouded in greenery. I h: pleted the count of days since my miscarriage, and purified mersion in rainwater, following the directions as told in the hair beneath my wig drip, rivulets of water down my n

"For you," Yossi said, handing me a palm-sized house, wood, "it plays music."

I looked over at him, his knee bent underneath his | reaching over the console toward me. I had not seen his loose, his body this nonchalant, in weeks. I held the wood i smiled as he turned a knob and released simple notes into

"This is beautiful," I said, because it seemed like the co

I blinked fast, willing the images away: the locket I ha

Ume'irim es haolam
And light up the world.

I exhaled, the first full breath in what felt like hours. I heard his foot-steps along the tile floor. I had done it. I kept God in the bed with us during the entirety of our marital intercourse. I kept his spirit alive in every mo-ment of our actions, through every breath and every movement. I wiped the holy seed from my sheets, and said good night to Yossi, who was al-ready back in his own bed across the room. I whispered the Shema prayer, and I imagined golden rays of protection beaming down from above.

When I found out that I had conceived a few weeks later, I was elated. I sang the Shabbos prayer every Friday night after lighting flames atop engraved silver candlesticks from my grandmother. I prepared fine china plates of gefilte fish, garnished with carrots carved into the shape of flow-ers, and tiny cucumbers scooped out and filled with horseradish. I read Jewish magazines while I waited for him, the stories about rabbis and holiness would prove my worthiness this time, I thought.

The pregnancy held, past six weeks, past eight weeks, past the three-month mark at which we told our family members. For a brief period, my constant feeling of aloneness went away. My love for the life growing inside me was enough for now. Everything would be okay.

"I-I talked to the rabbi today."

Yossi looked down at the rosemary potatoes on his plate, moved them around with his fork. "He is a very smart man. His wife— His wife, she has a degree."

"The rabbi?" I kept my voice polite and interested. Did we have a ques-tion for the rabbi? I didn't recall us discussing any.

His next words were slow, mumbled. "He said that a social work de-gree is enough. You don't need a PhD." He leaned his head to the side.

The mumbled words turned to boulders midair and hit me one by one. I gripped the beveled edge of our glass kitchen table.

Was this his plan all along? Pretend to approve and then forbid it later, when it's too late?

There was nothing I could say without spitting in the face of God himself. I knew the hierarchy. My husband had authority over me, as the man in charge of spiritual matters in our home. His rabbis had authority over him. They had the final say. Game over.

It was already asked, answered, and decided. There would be no PhD. There would be no Dr. Schwartz from Lakewood, New Jersey.

He took my silence as acquiescence, exhaled, and picked up his fork. I went through the motions of being a person at a dinner table while he told me how it would happen.

"There are a few people from the town who go to social work school. He said it's better if you go with them in the same car. He said to look at the schools in New Jersey. You'll be very happy with a social work degree."

My presence was irrelevant as he decided how things would proceed from here on.

"I understand," I said, as I cast aside my lifelong personal goals, tossed into the reservoir of ambitious Orthodox girls' dreams with all the others. I had submitted myself to being second class in all other matters, but for reasons I now struggle to explain, I'd determined that accepting Yossi for all his faults had earned me this exception. I had given up my Dassa, my body, all of it. I just wanted one thing for me—with a PhD, I could figure out what was wrong with my sister. I would have been able to ensure those same illnesses did not befall me. This was a new level of surrender I'd need time to let pass through me, fully digested before my silent protest could transform to silent acceptance.

Hindy helped me find maternity clothes, skirts with elastic waists and tops that would grow with me through the trimesters. The sisters sent hand-me-downs, digging through piles in the backs of their closets. "This one got a lot of compliments," Dina said, handing me a black, empire-waist top. They called each other and then me every time I reported a new symptom. "Goldy said you had a cramp," Hindy said. "Try pointing your toes to the ceiling. Don't worry, she is the only one who had sciatica in our family, and we don't think it's that." They were amused by my avid reading.

Dina was pregnant with baby number four, also due in July, and she called to find out, "What's the fruit of the week?"

I didn't miss a beat.

"Cantaloupe." Our babies were the sizes of cantaloupes.

My dreams of becoming Dr. Schwartz shattered, I applied to master's degree programs at Monmouth University and Rutgers, and I was accepted to both. Rutgers was a state school and therefore more affordable. I asked Yossi to drive me to the campus so that I could look around and pick up brochures as I considered enrollment.

When we pulled up, got out, and walked toward the Admissions building, I noticed a sudden change in his demeanor. He stopped short and stood awkwardly at the edge of the lawn, leaving me to finish the trip on my own.

"You go ahead."

Afterward, when I suggested we tour the campus to see some of the buildings, he grew tense and shook his head silently. He refused to even step onto any of the walking paths carved out in stone. He appeared almost afraid of being infected by the air around us. My curiosity about the school I very well could be attending was no match for the burning anxiety pouring out from Yossi's every pore. We headed straight back to our car.

The performance at Rutgers did me the favor of removing any inkling there might be a difficult conversation ahead about how to handle my commencement ceremony from Touro College a few weeks later. My bachelor's diploma would be shipped through the mail after I graduated, in absentia, as they called it, in May of 2005. And besides, I was already the size of five cantaloupes.

On July Fourth, Yossi drove me down the highway through the crackles of fireworks overhead in the New Jersey sky. "My wife is in labor!" he said to the person manning the toll booth, his voice jumping up and down. We walked the hallways of the hospital all night together, pausing each hour so that I could lift my knees behind a curtain while a doctor measured my cervix.

"I'm going to break your water now," he said at some point after one of those check-ins, "baby's almost ready." Yossi's cue to leave the room.

I wished he were one of the husbands who believed it permissible to stand at the head of the hospital bed while their wives gave birth. They'd look anywhere but at her, but at least they were there to hear their baby's first cries. Yossi, though, did not want to risk seeing even a flash of my pale leg, never mind my vagina, in its moment as the centerpiece of the entire room. I gripped the plastic handlebars of my hospital bed as doctors and nurses fussed around me, telling me when to breathe, how hard to push.

"It's a boy!"

They handed him to me, little pointy limbs waving around. He fit right into my arm, and for once it didn't matter that my elbow was showing or that my messy ponytail had come loose from its covering. The only thing I cared about was my son, resting the most beautiful face against my chest, looking up at me, blinking. "Hi," I whispered against his tiny forehead as I felt him settle and relax, "it's okay. You made it."

I came home to an assembled crib and Yossi proudly showing me around the changes he had made to our apartment. My sisters had sent diapers and bottles and soft blankets in shades of blue. Our cousins sent baskets of onesies and teddy bears. We invited them all to a bris ceremony in a small basement shul with requisite platters of bagels and lox. I passed the baby to Abba on a brocade white pillow and watched the joy spill over his beard and out into the room. I heard my baby's cries from across the barrier that separated the men from the women, and I knew the *mohel*, the rabbi in charge of performing the circumcision, had completed his cut. A rabbi called out, "May his name be declared among the nation of Israel, Avigdor the son of Yossi HaCohen!" We named him after Abba's father, and I hoped Abba knew that in one small way, I was saying, "Thank you."

I rolled his porta crib right up to the side of my bed, and I watched him through the night to make sure he stayed alive. I scrutinized the chapters in *What to Expect the First Year* as much as I studied the rhythm of my baby's movements, the jellybean-sized indentations in his cheeks, the soft nails at the ends of his fingers and toes.

"Still bleeding?" Yossi asked one evening as we sat down to a quiet dinner, eight weeks after our baby was born.

So, it's this again.

As our baby grew, Yossi's gaze grew colder, more odd. Like his eyes could never focus on the mother and infant who'd come to inhabit his space. When he spoke, he looked at the chandelier, the floor tiles, anywhere but at me.

I had forgotten that in the first months of our marriage, he would only look at me in the weeks after I had been to the *mikvah*, when it was permissible for him to touch me. The *mikvah* cycle was suspended during my pregnancy, and I suppose I'd gotten too used to having face-to-face conversations with my husband. *Still*, I wondered: *We have a baby together. Shouldn't he at least smile at me once?*

I knew it wasn't meant to be personal, but it hurt. I felt like the handmaids in our Bible stories, there to bear children and to breastfeed. Wasn't I more than that? I'd been told not to trust myself in this time, that the hormones draining from my body could make me emotional in ways that should give me pause about perceived slights and failures of accommodation.

I couldn't seem to get over it though. With each passing day, my mind responded with a word that was new: *no*. No, I could not accept that this is how husbands and wives were meant to be. I wanted to fulfill God's command, but I could not believe that what Yossi had imposed was what God expected. Even for a holy wife, there was a breaking point.

I called Mrs. Levenstein, my bridal teacher, hoping for some words of encouragement.

"I know he wants to be extra careful not to touch me," I said. "It's just hard for me." My bleeding was almost done, and the fatigue of motherhood was setting in.

"Malka, how long has this been going on?" Mrs. Levenstein's voice brought me back into my body, curled up on the concrete stairs outside our basement apartment, out of earshot of my husband.

"Since the beginning," I said, beginning to suspect that even by the standards set by our laws and customs, this wasn't normal.

"Why didn't you tell me?"

I was silent. It was a good question, and now I felt ashamed, like it was my fault for not knowing it was a problem.

"So, he talks to you regular when you are clean, and then ignores you when you are a *niddah*?" I didn't want to cry. But my insides trembled like blades of grass on the front lawn swaying in the wind. "I am going to call his rabbi. This is unacceptable." She was firm, sure of herself, and I was ready to let her be sure for me, too.

She called me a few days later. "His rabbi said he'll talk to Yossi." She asked me to let her know if anything changed. "Don't fall off the map again like that. I'm here."

I heard her, thanked her, and then did exactly that. I fell off the radar, right into finding day care and getting ready to start graduate school.

Mad World

As I stepped onto the campus grounds to begin my first semester, I understood why Yossi and the rabbis spent so much time discouraging young women from the path I had chosen.

Under the trees on sprawling lawns, girls in mini tops and pants so short they looked like underwear leaned on broad-shouldered young men with swoops of hair over their smooth, tan faces. Were it not for the brick buildings, their titles in stone relief—"Alpha Gamma Delta," "Mille-doler Hall"—I would have thought I had fallen into a magazine.

Yossi's rabbi had recommended a college buddy system, to help ward off the spiritual dangers of the secular world. I stood with Zeldy, my fellow Lakewood wife and assigned college buddy. Zeldy was cool, unruffled, confident in her skin and her layers of clothing. I, on the other hand, did not wish to feel like an outsider in this space. I wanted a pair of jeans. I wanted to rip off my wig and tie my hair into a ponytail. I wanted to be twenty years old and ordinary.

But I couldn't change who I was, not with eyes watching over me. And so I stood tall in my black skirt and adjusted the diamond ring and wedding band on my swelling fingers. I tucked a strand of my wig behind my ear.

"Aren't we lucky *we* don't have to dress like that?" I said to Zeldy.

We sat through orientation with our new classmates. They had names like Melissa. Jack. Chad. Crystal. I was so glad that I had decided to use my second name, Sara, for college. Back home, my family and friends would still know me as Malka. But at least here, I wouldn't have to force a smile as I spelled and sounded it out to people who had never heard those sounds paired before.

Men and women sat at the same round tables, as if it were no big deal at all. They leaned back, silky blouses revealing hints of cleavage, colored button-down shirts and ties moving casually with their breaths. "Look around," the dean said, his bare, non-kippah-covered head leaning forward, "these will be your friends for the next two years, and your colleagues forever." The air might as well have been loaded with pieces of shrapnel. I sifted through the words in my mind, replaced them with others. *These will never be my friends, all I will be is courteous to them.*

The next words came, this time from a woman in a wraparound dress, one that looked like it could fall entirely off if the thin belt were to come loose, "Prepare to have your horizons expanded." I bit the inside of my lip, tried to eject her words before they could burrow into my consciousness. *I am preparing to learn how to help my own community, the holy children of God.* I felt the fatigue emerge from inside my body, the same body that lifted eight-week-old Avigdor to my breasts all through the night. This was going to be exhausting. I was already exhausted. And I hadn't even begun.

Rutgers University challenged my internalized censor more than I had anticipated. Some days, it felt impossible to wipe all the evil influences from my surroundings. It was easier to sit in the back of the classroom and keep my head down until class ended, physical distance as my shield against the secular world. Afterward, I would lift my Longchamp tote from the floor beside me and head to a bathroom stall, where I held a manual pump to my breasts while my classmates filed in and out, talking about weekend plans. I curled my shoulders inward when their profanities slinked through the crack in my stall door, blocking their impurity from reaching my baby's milk.

Some of my classes took place on the basement levels of undergraduate dorms, where the evidence of weekend plans lingered in empty bottles of beer that lined the windowsills. I struggled to understand how people around my age could still be single, more focused on drinking alcohol than finding a spouse.

In social policy class, I learned that not everyone was a Republican. They talked about President Bush as a person of nefarious intentions and who single-handedly botched FEMA's response to Hurricane Katrina. One of my classmates, who had just returned from New Orleans, spoke about passing out blankets in shelters and sitting with people who had just lost everything. I began to wonder about my preconceptions.

"Ugh, I can't stand his pig nose on the front page of every newspaper," Professor Adams said. I was shocked to hear an author of many academic papers use such language about a man of immense power. I was flabbergasted to hear these well-informed people disagreeing with my abba and everyone else I knew with such vehemence.

In my social work theory class, the content was more familiar. I had learned about Beck and Bowlby and Rousseau. But other references were entirely foreign. I was lost when everyone in the class referred to *The Simpsons* or *American Idol* or any other number of television shows I had never heard of.

I would have to stay vigilant between classes too, as I kept my eyes on the buffed wooden hallway floor and stepped rapidly from one classroom to the next. My mind's appetite had been piqued by the influx of stimulation, and once I started reading something, I never could seem to stop. So I was left holding questions pulled from student group flyers like, WHY ARE FEMALE ORGASMS UNDERVALUED? 8 P.M. WEDNESDAY, STUDENT LOUNGE. I was still trying to figure out what that word meant. It appeared in one of my textbooks as part of a case study. It wasn't in the glossary at the end of the book, though. I figured that *orgasm* must be one of those popular culture references to which I was always oblivious, like *Dancing with the Stars*. Probably for the best.

At night, I tiptoed out of bed in Lakewood to write papers, pausing only to put a sleepy Avigdor to my breast and to kiss the top of his soft blond head.

One day, I woke at the end of my Statistics in Social Sciences class over a puddle of my own drool on the lined paper beneath my cheek. Mortified, I began to apologize to my professor, until she stopped me. "I'm a mom too," she said with a knowing smile. "Glad you got in a nap."

In my actual life, miles down the Garden State Parkway and worlds away, I had worries unlike those of anyone at social work school. I had rabbinic permission to use a rubber diaphragm along with contraceptive foam for the first few months after Avigdor was born, but that time was almost up. It was supposed to have been enough time for me to heal, get used to being a mother, and be ready to conceive again.

I was not ready at all. I hadn't expected to care about school, to want to succeed. It was already hard enough with a baby that kept me awake most nights. I couldn't imagine having two.

I told Yossi, in very plain words, "I can't do this again right now." He seemed confused, as if he genuinely did not understand the problem. Finally, he let out a barely audible, "I see." He said he would make inquiries.

Yossi saw to it that we'd meet with the rabbi. I dressed carefully, in my longest skirt, my baggiest sweater. I spoke with great respect, referring to the rabbi in third person. "Is it possible that the rav may provide just a little bit more time?"

It didn't matter, in the end. The rabbi may as well have been light-years away, his bent shoulders behind a desk stacked with holy texts, his expression hidden by thick plastic glasses. He directed his questions to Yossi. "Is she suffering a physical malady?"

"No," Yossi said, just being truthful.

The rabbi's ruling was unequivocal. No more birth control.

Several weeks later, I dutifully hugged Yossi and told him the news. I was pregnant. As I stared out over his shoulder to the texture of the walls, I wanted to slide out of his heavy arms, away from him.

For the very first time since our marriage, I thought: *What about that love they said would come if I served my husband? Where is it?*

"Don't we have an appointment?" I said as Mrs. Levenstein stood in the doorway of her townhouse staring at me. She looked blank.

"Oh, Malka!" she exclaimed, as if a puzzle piece in her mind found its proper configuration. "Come in, come in!" She threw the door wide open and walked me past the toys and the book-lined shelves. "I didn't recognize you!"

She opened the door to her husband's study, and we sat down at the familiar old folding table. I looked around for the bendy toy and the toothpaste tube that were the sum of my sex education, over that very table, almost two years before.

She looked at me again, squinting through her glasses. "You look like a shell of Malka," she said. She was not one for tact, this woman. That was probably why she had been appointed as a bride teacher in the first place. She named the things that everyone else glossed over with euphemisms.

I am still me! I wanted to scream from deep down, from inside the body that had been following her instructions since the moment I left her. But I knew I was not the same person. Gone were my trendy chopped haircut, my carefree smiles, my poised posture.

She recounted the essence of her unsuccessful talks with Rabbi Turkel, the rabbi who prepared Yossi for marriage. She had been following up, determined not to let one of "her girls" suffer.

"You have to know the difference between the rules and the ones he adds onto them, Malka. He's adding his own rules. It's written nowhere that he shouldn't look at you for two weeks of each month. In fact, it is the exact opposite. That is the time he is supposed to connect with you emotionally!"

I heard her words, but I almost didn't care anymore. Something had just gone so wildly wrong, that a part of my brain had begun to think the unthinkable: *this marriage cannot be fixed.*

However, when she gave me the number for a reputable marriage therapist, I allowed myself a speck of hope. I owed it to baby Avigdor, and to the tiny new soul growing within me. Maybe, just maybe, my children would not grow up thinking it was normal for parents to communicate like strangers.

"I don't understand why they call it spring semester!" Zeldy stomped out of my green Chevy Impala and into a deep pile of snow. "*This is not spring.*"

I laughed. On campus, I was free to laugh and therefore I did not care how cold and snowy it was.

We walked past the dorms, past the co-eds in sweatpants that read PINK or FITCH down the legs. They had gone from wearing almost nothing to wearing pajamas, while Zeldy and I were in our long skirts, same as always.

In my classroom, a student named Andrea sat down near me, pulled a sandwich out of her bag, and brought it toward her mouth. I knew it was okay for non-Jews to eat cheese and meat together, but it just seemed wrong as I watched the deli meat overlap the American cheese between soft slices of white bread that passed between her lips. I had never seen anyone actually do this before. Certainly not from this close. My eyes lingered over this ungodly woman, and I looked away before she could catch me staring at the waistband of her jeans, the way it creased into a wide V when she leaned forward, revealing inches of smooth golden skin and a red elastic string where her underwear should be.

I was almost relieved when Professor Mary Ann stepped behind her desk. Her soft gray bob and round glasses reminded me of my grand-mother, but her ideas would shock anyone in my family. Her diversity class was one of my most perilous. Today she talked about female genital mutilation with a pained expression on her face.

"Little girls get their clitorises cut off to prevent them from feeling sexual pleasure."

I was twenty-one years old, and I did not know what sex had to do with pleasure. Or for that matter, what this *clitoris* she spoke of even was.

She went on to describe traditional places she had visited. "On one of my trips to the East, I found tribes that still endorsed marital rape."

I looked around, scanning quickly to see others' reactions. Didn't a woman belong to her husband? How could married people be raped?

They think that everything should "feel good," I scolded, internally, to no one but myself. *These people have different ideas about life.*

Tikva, the wife of an Orthodox rabbi in my neighborhood, joined our social work carpool.

"Hello, ladies." She threw herself sideways into the back seat of my car. "Muffin?" she asked, holding out a Tupperware container. "Sorry, sorry, sorry—I just wanted the kids to wake up with the house smelling like fresh baking."

Tikva had eight children at home, ranging from a toddler to a high school senior. We overheard conversations all the way up the parkway, "*Zeeskeit*, remember your spelling homework," and some singing, "Mommy loves you up to the sky." She had been counseling alongside her rabbi husband for so many years, she figured she may as well make it official and get a master's degree in social work. She was late to the carpool almost every morning, but we understood.

Tikva wore her religiosity to class like a badge of honor. She raised her hand in Social Welfare class and talked about how our community took care of our own, how we did not have a homeless problem, how no

Jew would ever go without food or clothing in our town. Unlike me, who had been slinking to the back of classrooms and trying to fit in, Tikva joked with professors and confidently asked about their vacations and prior publications.

We were often the only two people in any given class who were not in jeans or sweats. People mixed us up all the time, even though she was close to forty and I was twenty-two. "Tikva, want to join our group?" they asked me during group assignments, missing the way my straight brown wig differed from Tikva's blond wavy one. I knew that as much as they tried to be sensitive, they saw me by my long skirt, the only part of me that looked remotely like her.

Between classes, Tikva and I discussed the moral ambiguity of our attendance at college and found blank walls against which to pray. To her credit, Tikva acknowledged both sides of me, Malka the wife and Sara the student, and embraced them both equally.

One day, our professor wheeled a VCR into our classroom and pressed play on a film about gay rights. There had been no warning. Just a darkened classroom, me leaning against the wall, Tikva spilling chocolate chips into her palm across the aisle, and then a glowing screen.

I looked up to see women dancing across the screen, holding hands and then each other. The music slowed and the scene shifted to show men wearing eyeliner and feathered earrings, kissing each other on the lips. There were rainbows on flagpoles, waving against a still blue sky.

I can't watch this, I thought to myself, as I felt the memories of my sins snake out from the back of my mind. The lips on the screen were the lips on Dassa, and then my body was right back there, inches from hers. I tried not to stare at the shape of round hips in blue jeans pressed against bodies clad in leather, moving like we used to, like I wished I could, moving in the exact way that I would never move again, not with her, not with any woman, not ever. I held a hand like a visor over my eyes and turned my face down toward my desk when a tiny dark chip landed on the corner of my desk. It was Tikva, of course, who always noticed everything.

"Psst," she whispered. "Malka, you shouldn't be here. You're pregnant. This can go into your baby. Just tell her."

Oh, I was jolted by the thought. It wasn't just my own sins that those vile images evoked, but they threatened to contaminate my child.

Dr. Merritt leaned toward the screen, long locks swinging gently with the music. I motioned to her that I needed to speak, and we stepped outside the classroom. I found myself in the midst of an awkward conversation, mumbling words about pregnancy and religious observance and how it wasn't the film that was the problem, it was me.

"I'm so sorry," she said. "I had no idea this was against your beliefs. No worries. Just take the rest of the period. Do whatever feels right for you."

She waved her hand and smiled, no big deal. I thanked her. My evil inclinations had already cost me too much. I was still not used to Yossi touching my body, not even for a moment during our three years of marriage. The least I could do was stay far away from anything that would remind me of a world where people did the things that ruined me.

Rutgers, as the state university of New Jersey, had connections with internship placements across our state. Their field placement coordinator matched me with the internship closest to my zip code, an inpatient psychiatric unit in Toms River. She could not have known that the unit, though just minutes from my home, may as well have existed on a different planet.

During my first months, I interviewed a woman who shivered under four hospital blankets as she talked about selling her body for drugs on the streets of Camden. I stood in the corner of an isolation room and jotted notes while a large man strained against cuffs that kept his arms and legs tied to a vinyl recliner. I sourced a kosher meal kit from the kitchen and brought it to a young Lakewood mother who stared around the unit with wide, scared eyes. I shared a table with a tattooed man wearing a striped uniform with "Ocean County Jail" printed across his back.

On my breaks, I found quiet rooms to unlock, where I could unpack my kosher sandwiches and devour patient charts in silence. There were stories like, "Patient was found burning garbage cans outside and neighbor called the police. Patient tried to set self on fire at the scene." I was fascinated by it all. "Patient stabbed self in heart after a fight with her lover. Patient got staples in the ER prior to transfer." I memorized treatment methods and medication protocols, reading each chart for clues. I needed to know everything.

I knew Shani was back in the hospital again, in Israel this time. As per my sisters, she had gone off her meds, decided she was the Messiah, and announced it to all who would listen, right in the middle of the old city of Jerusalem. I had read enough patient charts and listened to enough stories to know what her symptoms meant. I was pretty sure she had bipolar disorder. I was determined to find a cure, or at least a treatment protocol that would finally give her relief.

By the time Yossi got home each night, the subtle layer of hospital disinfectant on my skin was masked by the aroma of home-cooked chicken liver or sautéed minute steak. The patient notes had faded from my mind and been replaced by the sensation of soft baby cheeks against my face, the sound of a sweet voice singing the Alef-Bais (the Hebrew alphabet), the sight of diaper after diaper rolled up and thrown into the nursery pail.

I selectively shared things each day like, "I had a Jewish patient today."

He would stroke his growing beard. "It's a good thing they aren't making you see, like, any unstable people."

It was easier not to mention the track marks, the four-letter words, the patient who tried to escape the unit by hiding inside a laundry bin. It didn't seem necessary to tell him that I found it simpler to just shake hands with men, instead of explaining that it was against my faith. I didn't want to burden him with the images now burned into my own consciousness, of distressed men displaying their penises in the middle of therapy group some days.

It's fine, I told myself. *I'm fine.*

Tikva began to come over to my place to do homework, and it was the first time Rutgers truly spilled out into my life. She arrived with a bag of textbooks, a giant box of Twizzlers, and gifts for my baby. She was as unabashed about being a college student in Lakewood as she was about being a Lakewood wife at college.

I watched her formulate term papers at my dining room table, feeling the muscles in my back tighten as she opened books and turned them upside down to hold the place, printed words directly on the mahogany table.

Yossi had asked me not to tell anyone about his aversion to cheap print. He refused to touch newspapers and would only read books if the paper met his delicate sensory needs. In our house, we mostly read magazines, such as the weekly *Mishpacha*. Only the parchment paper of holy texts was allowed on the table.

I didn't want to violate his privacy and I couldn't think of a good reason to tell Tikva to put the books away. And so, she sprawled. And then I sprawled. I sat cross-legged on the floor with a toddler on my lap while dictating paragraphs out loud to Tikva, who typed rapidly at the table.

"Are you coming . . . ? When are you coming upstairs?" Yossi stood sideways in the doorway of our dining room, fingers tapping against the wall.

"I have a very big assignment due tomorrow," I said, emboldened by the presence of Tikva, a real rabbi's wife, who sanctioned our past-midnight work session.

"Thank you, Rav Schwartz." Tikva nodded at him in deference, the fringes of her headscarf moving across her shoulders.

He looked at me, at her, and at the table strewn with open pages, with words he did not want to see. He lingered in the doorway for a few seconds, then seemed to remember where he was. He put one hand on the mezuzah, the scroll we kept on each of our doorposts with a square of parchment containing the Shema prayer. He brought his fingers to his lips, turned, and walked up the stairs.

Tikva looked away, down at the table, pretending she didn't notice the way I sat still, my fingers over my keyboard, until his footsteps faded into the distance. I knew my husband well enough to know that he was upset. I could see it, the way his eyes stared past me when he worried, the way his shoulders tensed under his crisp white shirts.

I could never have imagined how he would choose to cope with his feelings. Never. Not in a million years.

The next day, I came home from college to find Yossi on a stepladder, holding a package of Saran Wrap and a hammer. It was my turn to stand in the doorway of our dining room in confusion.

"It's better to double wrap the mezuzah," he said, adjusting his velvet yarmulke, then tapping a nail into our mezuzah case, newly encased in a plastic sheath.

In my twenty-two years of being an Orthodox Jew with very strict standards, I had never, ever seen a mezuzah scroll encased in both a decorative case *and* cling wrap. That was like wearing two pairs of sunglasses, one on top of the other, to keep the sun out of one's eyes. It was insane.

Yet, I knew that I was the one who had brought impurity into our home, in the form of secular textbooks that were quite unholy and threatened to contaminate the holy text. If he was anxious, it was at least partly my fault.

"It looks original," I said, offering a conciliatory note.

We both turned at the sound of Avigdor singing in the next room, "Red and orange, green and green!"

Yossi got off the stepladder, headed toward Avigdor and lifted him up. "I think we have a genius on our hands!" His voice was light again, the tension gone, the wonder creeping back in.

Yossi and I looked at each other over the wispy hair of our son, and our glance held a tacit promise. We would find compromises. We would find ways to keep our home holy. Even if it meant extra plastic wrap on our mezuzahs.

Girl on Fire

The compromises became more difficult to find as the walls between my universes sank through the ground.

"Marriage should be a contract that only lasts five years," Professor Deana said blithely, flipping layers of wild, streaked curls behind her shoulder. "And then every five years, we should be able to decide whether we want to renew."

Would I renew my marriage to Yossi?

I noticed the groove in my notepad before I realized how hard I was pressing my pen to paper; how hard I was fighting to keep her words from entering my mind. I was struggling to ignore the ways in which men in the outside world were different from my husband.

"I worry about long-term attachment wounds within the context of relationships," said Brian, my classmate, as he flipped his laptop open and cited a research study. I couldn't recall hearing Yossi cite anything other than biblical texts. Ever. *That's not fair*, I told myself. *Don't apply secular standards to him.*

I wished I could hold Yossi in my mind as the king of our household, the one to serve, the holy guidepost for our life together. I wanted to. But I couldn't help but begin to see things through newly opened eyes.

"She lays there, like . . . like a—" he whispered, paused, and looked down at the puffed arm of an overstuffed couch. "Like a board," he blurted.

We were in the office of the most highly regarded marital therapist in all of Borough Park. Mrs. H. had ornate cushioned chairs and tasseled rugs and gold frames everywhere. I had named this style of décor "Hungarian grandmother," coined at my in-law's house.

She lifted her glasses up by their beaded chain and placed them on her large soft nose so she could squint at the five-by-seven index card, the one that apparently held all she needed to know about our case. All on the one card. No thick chart, like the one in which I took notes about the patients I saw at my internship.

"I see here that you had a hard life, Malka." She looked over her lenses, across the paisley rug to me. I tried not to appear as stiff as he was making me sound. I unhooked my arm from around my rib cage and maneuvered it into a leaning position.

I was not sure why, but I felt compelled to give her comment a positive spin. "I am lucky to have a lot of support from my siblings. I went to some good therapy." I mentioned Genevieve, the religious woman who treated my sisters and me. She was another brand name around this twenty-block radius that comprised the epicenter of Hasidic life. Mrs. H. nodded; she knew the name. I could almost hear her wondering why I still wasn't normal, why I was lying like a board during intercourse.

They never told me that I had to move, I wanted to say. I would have moved!

No one had to instruct you to move with her.

I didn't want the moments to replay right then, the way my body found hers, the way my hands slipped underneath her long skirt as we sat in the back seat of city busses and car services and airplanes. I didn't want to wonder about the feeling inside me, the one that had made me press my lips to her skin, to the crescent beneath her breast, to the narrow crease at the top of her thigh. With her, I moved even though it meant risking an afterlife in a boiling cauldron of hell.

"How do you feel about what your husband shared?" Mrs. H. tilted her head, the short bob of her blond wig tilting in perfect synchronicity with her face.

I looked at Yossi, who tapped one pale finger on the crease of his navy pants, his gaze aimed squarely at the ground. I wondered how long he had been holding that inside, how long he had been wishing for a caress, a loving touch. The throbbing started, right where my wig was clipped to my temples.

I couldn't tell her the truth about how defective I was.

"I'm happy we are here to work on our marriage," I said. I knew I answered the feelings question correctly when I saw Yossi look up at me and then nod in acknowledgment. Mrs. H. moved her heft to the back of her armchair, settling in.

It hurt. It hurt so much that I felt it through the layers and layers of numb I wore underneath my skin.

"I'm just going to take your vitals for a quick minute." Her name tag read Maura and her scrubs had teddy bears on them.

I tried to keep my pain inside, but it slid between my teeth and out into the hospital room. "Oohh." I bent over, holding my swollen belly and squeezing my eyes shut. And then I felt it. The softest fingers on my arm, stroking. My eyelids lifted so fast at first, all I saw was a blur. "Sweetheart," Maura was next to me, watching me, "it is all going to be okay." I choked on the feelings coming up through my throat. Sorrow that I had been swallowing for days and weeks and years. This was the first gentle touch I had felt on my skin since before. Before him.

I couldn't tolerate the pain any more than the comfort. When Maura asked if I wanted an epidural, I said yes. I wanted all of the feelings to stop.

I was strapped to monitors and wires when Yossi came in to see me.

He brought a plastic bag with a prayer book and a cheese Danish, my favorite.

"I can't move this time." I explained that the epidural meant I could not walk the hallways like I did during my last labor. I was stuck to the bed. "Can you pray here?" I asked him to stay.

He looked down at his shoelaces. "I think it is better if I wait outside. I will pray for you." He left the Danish on a side table, nervously touched his untamed short beard, his worn leather belt, and then his beard again. Then he was gone.

Maura came back, the scent of vanilla wafting in the air around her. "You're four centimeters dilated, still," she said with one gloved hand up my birth canal. "We should start a Pitocin drip to speed things along."

I remembered hearing about Pitocin during the childbirth class I had taken. Mrs. Kessler, plump and comfortable in her plumpness, was a registered nurse who wore a long, puffy black wig. She was the portal to all things baby-related. I had sat in a circle with the other young mothers, all of us with smooth unlined faces, growing bellies, wedding rings, and no husbands in sight. They did not need to learn these things. Personal things about women's bodies and labor. We, however, learned to get extra calcium into our diets, to recognize the stages of labor, and what our own uteruses looked like. We learned that epidurals could slow labor, and sometimes labor would completely stall without intervention. Mrs. Kessler, bless her soft Lakewood soul, also told us to have a voice. To advocate for ourselves. "You need to know that you have rights, and you are allowed to say what you need in the hospital."

"I need to ask my husband first," I told Maura. I was exercising my voice! I was proud of myself. I would not allow protocol to get in the way of the real rules. Decisions needed to be made by the man.

"You got it, honey, I'll go grab him for you." She removed the latex and walked toward the door. I started to say, "He's the one who is about five foot seven, blue eyes, dark hair, white shirt, and . . ." She lifted an eyebrow, her warm eyes twinkling, and smiled.

I looked down at myself. Oh. I was at a county hospital in a New Jersey beach town. I had a kerchief tied over my hair. I wore a long skirt underneath my hospital gown. My chart said I just turned twenty-two and this was my third pregnancy. Yes, Maura could probably figure out which man in the waiting room matched with me. Of course.

I heard Yossi mumble from the corner of the room, his back facing me. "They said they want to add a medicine. I have to call Rabbi Hanover and get permission for that." I had not realized even this needed a rabbinic stamp.

"Please call him then." I spoke up. Again!

Yossi fumbled for his flip phone and dialed. A few murmured words and then he asked me, "The baby is fine, right?" It wasn't a real question. As usual, he stated his preferred response and put a question mark at the end for politeness. I checked the monitor. Baby's heart rate looked perfect. I had been checking every five minutes. Baby's heart rate. My heart rate. The paper with lines going up and down measuring my contractions. That was the only company I had. "The baby is fine." I was annoyed, but I was not about to lie.

"The rabbi said we should wait." I heard receding footsteps.

It was just me again. The epidural dulled the pain, but I still felt an electric shock to my uterus every few minutes, radiating through my nerves. I was scared, so scared. Midnight turned to one a.m., and the exhaustion weighed my limbs down. They kept telling me to rest but my heart was clenched, and I felt my baby moving, miniature limbs poking through my skin. I put both hands on my belly. "You will be okay. I know it's scary to come out into the world, but I will be right here. I will always be right here." It was a prayer and a hope and a vow.

"How are we doing in here?" Maura was back, looking at me and then her simple plastic watch.

"Four centimeters." Her hand in my vagina was the most natural part of the entire process. "Let's get your husband back in here about that Pitocin before my shift ends." She was leaving. Fuck. The bad word slipped into my mind, and I shoved it back out. That was what they meant when they talked about the influences of college. I was thinking in curse words.

Dragging footsteps. He was back. "I don't want to wake up the rabbi. It is so late. This could wait until the morning, right?" Another statement phrased like a question. I pleaded. I wasn't sure if it was the bad influence of Professor Jozef, who had analyzed the social constructs of gender in my Practice II class. His floral Hawaiian shirts and his tenderness had been as confounding as his ideas. Maybe he put doubt in my mind somehow. Or maybe it was Madison, my colleague at the inpatient psych unit. She wore fitted T-shirts over her growing baby bump and talked about her detailed birth plan involving a swimming pool and CD player. Either way, I had broken the seal around my protected world. I could not seem to stop myself from talking back to the husband I was supposed to obey.

The nurses came in and out of my room silently. They checked my vitals with mouths held in straight lines and piteous eyes.

An hour after the sun came up, after morning prayer time was over, the rabbinic permission came through. Pitocin. There was a flurry of movement. Two nurses, an IV pole, and another needle stab. Finally. Relief for a moment, and then the real agony kicked in. The epidural had worn off. I was strapped to the bed, gripping the handlebars, tears sliding down my face. This was like nothing I had ever felt. This couldn't be right. My organs felt like they were shredding, tearing. I couldn't breathe. My toes curled up inside my thin knee socks.

I looked around for someone. Anyone. I looked outside the large double window, at the rays of sun bouncing into blue sky. *God. Please. I promise I will be good. I will raise this baby to do your will. Please. Help me.* My belly was on fire. "Mommy is right here. I love you. I promise." I asked the baby for forgiveness. Hoping he or she would never know the circumstances of their creation.

"She's nine centimeters, get the doctor in here stat!" I tried to hold my body together. People. White coats. Someone yelled, "Push! Push, Sara!" More people, but my eyes were on the one holding a tiny blanket and running to the other side of the room. And then I heard it. A thin cry and someone saying, "It's a baby girl!" They brought her to me, and I reached with both arms. I studied her tiny straight nose and clear closed eyelids and little fuzzy black hair. I held her, cradled her, rubbed my face against her little sweet cheeks. She had arrived. I had a daughter.

"Someone go tell the husband!" More moving and doors and a doctor between my legs stitching things up and blood everywhere. The beauty of it all was that nothing mattered anymore. I had her. And she was everything.

She burrowed into me, five pounds and eleven ounces of brand-new. I gave her my promises and in return, she thawed my heart.

At my six-week postpartum doctor's appointment, I lay on the table and stared at the uterus diagrams I had stared at almost every month for the last two years.

"There's a bit more tearing than last time," I heard him say from between my legs. "Just remind me when you're in your ninth month next time, I can sew it up right after you deliver."

I watched his silver-streaked hair rise above my vagina-level as he snapped the glove off his hand, revealing the gold wedding band that had been up inside my body so many times before. I wondered about his wife. She was probably a blonde with perfect hair, and I bet if her vagina ripped apart in childbirth, he would have been much less casual about it. I walked out of the office, through the waiting room of women with baby bumps, women in long skirts praying out of little books, with nary a man in sight. He was right, the doctor. We would all keep having babies, as was God's will, so we may as well fix my torn birth canal next time.

I was helping little Avigdor brush his teeth, cartoon toothbrush in one little fist and strawberry toothpaste in the other, when the nurse called with the results of my bloodwork.

"How are you feeling?" she asked, knowing full well at this point that I was both severely anemic and in a state of hypothyroidism.

"I'm fine," I said, the spikes of irritation coming through my voice. I had decided to be fine. I did not have time for my body to disagree with me. Not when I was way too tired and too busy to load both children into their car seats and go to the pharmacy and get the pills she droned on about.

"Would you like me to add a script for birth control?" Her voice sliced through my haze and suddenly, I realized what this meant. I had a real, diagnosed, physical illness! According to our rabbi, that was sufficient justification for a pause in the baby-making process.

"Yes!" I almost sang. "Yes please."

I moved through my days, feeling the sluggishness in my steps around the kitchen each evening. I clenched my fists to warm the bluish tips of my iron-deficient fingers. I saw the paleness of my face in the mirror, the darkness under my eyes that concealer couldn't hide.

Each symptom painted a small smirk onto my face.

I had cheated the system! I had earned myself a break.

I finally stopped bleeding when baby Shira was twelve weeks old. I swiped a white cloth around the folds of my vagina every morning and evening for seven days, and then I dunked in the ritual bath. I tried to muster the same devotion to God. I begged him, from underneath the rainwater of the *mikvah, Please help me make this holy. Please be with me tonight.*

Later, lying flat beneath Yossi, I was not thinking about God at all. Instead, I kept thinking about Brian from class. Brian with the peace stickers on his laptop and delicate stubble along his chin, and jeans that were tight over the shape of his thighs. Brian, who flew overseas and volunteered in an orphanage with his girlfriend. I couldn't stop wondering about Brian, and how he acted when he was naked with the blonde I'd imagined for him. Did they talk? About their feelings? Did he look at her and stroke her body and hold her in his arms? I was still wondering when I felt the weight come off my body and Yossi's seed begin to leak out.

Another fucking thing leaking, I thought before I could control myself. *I'm sorry,* I whispered to God as I pulled the nightgown back over my head and down the torso that felt like it belonged to someone else entirely. *I will do better next time.*

I rolled baby Shira's bassinet right near my bed and fell asleep with one hand on her stomach, breathing in sync with the tiny puffs of her breath. I woke up and felt the dampness under my arms, the wet fabric on my chest, the slippery feeling between my legs. I was drenched in sweat. I sat up, gasping for air in the darkness of the room, and the nightmares flashed back into my mind.

I had dreamed about a baby in a mauve blanket snatched from my arms by a Nazi soldier with a swastika on his army hat. I dreamed about a little girl in an embroidered dress locked in a cellar, standing in the corner, smart enough to stay silent. Then there was a teenager, run over by a truck, her legs exposed on the sidewalk, tire tracks on her face.

I had been in social work school long enough to know that dreams were meaningful. I wanted to believe that mine simply meant that I had read too many case studies. But the theme emerged, the thing Freud would point out: There was a girl in danger. I didn't know if the girl was me, or baby Shira, or both of us. These were not nightmares drawn from fiction—that would have been too easy to dismiss. These scenes had been implanted by the ancestors, the community of and descended from survivors. My mother and father had both been born into the wreckage of war, and those stories were shared and passed down with purpose, with care. Something deep within me was awakening now, raising the worst from our memories to prepare me and my babies through traumas past for traumas still to come.

I just knew that it was up to me to save her.

Every few months, the tension we kept pushing under the rug rose, and the sharpness of our differences hit us in the face. Yossi wanted me to wear looser sweaters. I wanted him to ask me how I felt instead of monitoring what I wore. He said he couldn't ask me things like that when I barely even paid attention to him these days, when I was always busy outside the house.

I'd accepted a position at the local religious community center, where I treated women and children. Yossi called Rabbi Turkel, who called me, and recommended that we see another marital therapist, this time a rabbi. We visited a basement office in Brooklyn together, bought the recommended books, watched Therapist Rabbi stroke his beard and shake his head. He recommended a more experienced expert. We tried that for a few months, until the new therapist suggested that perhaps Yossi might want to do some of his own work, with an anxiety specialist. At some point this led Yossi to stop attending altogether. One day, marital counseling now all on my own, I stared at the therapist from my side of the empty sofa as he raised the query we'd avoided all along:

"How did you two end up married to each other?"

I stayed, caring for my babies and avoiding Yossi. He followed my childcare instructions without argument. "Take the broccoli patty out of the plastic wrap and microwave for thirty seconds. Feel it to make sure it's not too hot," I told him over the phone, as Tikva and I studied for our licensing exams.

"Was that your husband?" She looked at me, the incredulousness creeping out through her voice. "It sounded like you were talking to a developmentally delayed babysitter."

I explained that he was a really good father, but my voice broke. I sighed and told her the truth. How my marriage had turned into a business arrangement. How I had begun to feel weak and nauseous all the time. She hugged me. Told me that the rabbis were doing their job, trying to get me to stay, but that this was not normal.

I had another nightmare that night. I saw a young bride taken from her own wedding, men in black masks shoving her into the trunk of a car, the white fabric of her gown billowing in the wind as they drove away, far, far away. I sat up in my bed, my chest heaving, my legs trembling. I was safe, technically. There were three brass locks on our front door. Outside that door were rows of homes identical to ours, in which the mothers tied headscarves at the nape of their necks, in which fathers sang ancient songs around the Shabbos table. Still, I couldn't stop feeling like something terrible was going to happen, like the danger was on the inside.

I continued to immerse in the *mikvah* each month on the prescribed day. I mumbled the blessing on my way out of the building, *Bless me, dear God, in body and in spirit… Bind me and my beloved husband in a long, peaceful, harmonious marriage. Give my children easy lives without strain or struggle.*

When I got home from the *mikvah* one spring evening, I was so sick to my stomach that I couldn't find a single shred of strength for the sacred act of intimacy. "I am really not well," I told Yossi, sinking to the floor of our bedroom. I paused to lift the pink plastic hand-washing bowl closer to my face. My guts started to rise through my throat. I forced myself to breathe in.

"You have to ask! It is *mikvah* night." He dialed a phone number. I dug my bare fingernails into the gray pile carpet and breathed through my teeth. I focused hard on staying still. If I did not move, maybe he would just walk away.

Then there was a phone at my ear. "Hello? Mrs. Schwartz?"

It was Rabbi Turkel. I wondered why he was taking the time out of his evening, stepping away from his wife and children, to busy himself with my bedroom matters.

"Hello. I have a question." I straightened myself out enough to pace along the side of my bed. "The rav is aware that our marriage is not doing well. I just wanted to know if it is okay to use birth control for a little bit longer." My heart beat fast. Hard. My children, they lived in my heart. They were carved into my being, and I felt them in every moment of every day.

Their sweet faces, their little voices, their soft arms tight around my neck. It was a miracle, the amount of love I created from scratch, that I poured into them. I did not have any more in me for another child. Not with a man who sucked the air right out of me each time he tossed an awkward glance my way. No.

"How old is your baby?" The rabbi was matter-of-fact. Emotionless.

"Fifteen months." I scrambled through the dense fog in my brain. That wouldn't do. We were maxed out on birth control permission! Six months was a stretch. Twelve was allowed only because I had anemia and the doctor said I had to wait to get pregnant again. Another three months because we had just started working with a new marital counselor. "I think we will be getting divorced." There. I said it. The words that I needed to get permission. He could not possibly want me to get pregnant under those circumstances.

Except he did. "Mrs. Schwartz, I cannot give you a pass. Your baby is fifteen months. It should be with blessing."

I placed the phone on the gold-patterned sheets and hurled, all of everything from my entire being, right into the plastic bowl.

Yossi waited until I stopped vomiting. He cleaned the bowl in the master bathroom right near me as I continued to disintegrate, silent. And then he shut the light and took from me what was not his. The disgust turned to pain and then to sadness. I felt teardrops fall backward over my ears, one by one, until the gold-patterned sheets were soaked with all that was unholy.

When I lost my next pregnancy, I felt nothing. I was done. I was done. I was done.

I was done being a vessel. I was done being owned. I was done with men telling me what to do with my own body. I was done fighting to stay alive just enough to shield my babies, but not enough to truly live. I was done.

PART II

Darker

Crossroads

A woman in Orthodox Judaism cannot simply decide to get divorced. The rules mandate that a woman remains married to her husband for as long as he wishes, with divorce only coming at the time of his choosing. Until then, she may not marry anyone else. She may not date anyone else. She must remain celibate and alone.

My decision to get divorced, in a practical sense, lacked meaning or power. It was equivalent to announcing to myself, "I am the next president of the United States!" A delusion, at worst. A dream, if I was willing to work for it.

The first thing I needed was rabbinic permission to begin the process of divorce. Only brazen women would dare to tell their husbands their wishes to separate without a rabbi's approval. I would be dismissed.

I knew what happened to those who did not follow the rules as proscribed. They left blank spaces behind, shadows cast over their families. I remembered the darkness within Rachel, from my seminary dorm, whose mother was said to have walked out one day and never returned. I had seen a dark cloud over Chaya from high school, whose brother wore ripped denim and hung out with girls on Ocean Parkway before he was sent to rehab. Each absence was marked by whispers: *she lost her mind* or *he became a drug addict.*

As a fully licensed social worker, I sat in rooms where the words were not whispered but spoken out loud. "Poor kid," my supervisor said, as she handed me a file and smoothed a dark skirt over her knees. "The father went crazy and married a non-Jew."

I did not know what happened first, leaving religion or losing one's mind, but it was always both of those things. We kept careful notes in those cases. There were times when crazy nonreligious parents called our offices, that we sat around the conference table and discussed whether their children were in danger.

I knew that as a woman choosing to get divorced, I had to walk a thin tightrope. I had seen the signs on lampposts in our town, those that said, "Please contribute whatever you can. A Jewish father needs expensive lawyers to fight an evil woman who seeks to rip his children away from the path of Torah and good deeds. Help save their innocent souls!" I had probably even donated to such causes, to keep children with their devout parent, to ensure they were not poisoned by the one who'd defected.

At home, I handed baby Shira pouches of applesauce and helped Avigdor break the crust off his challah bread, and I strategized. I let the children play in the pile of tissues they freed from boxes and scattered over the guest room carpet, and I strategized. I rolled them through the kosher supermarket in a shopping cart, stopping to pick up pomegranates for Rosh Hashana dinner, and I strategized.

My first-choice rabbi had a divorced daughter of his own. I figured he might not be aghast by the idea of a marriage breaking up. When I walked into his office, he was sitting on a metal folding chair, eyes closed, swaying over a book of Jewish law. His wife bustled past the open door in a floral housedress, and little boys in velvet yarmulkes raced around behind her.

"We tried everything," I said after laying out, in careful detail, the failure of my marriage.

The rabbi opened his eyes, glanced at his Talmud and flipped the page, then murmured for me to continue.

I told him about the years of counseling with multiple therapists, and I shared with him the conclusion of the very last one. "Dr. K. said this will not get better. He said that my husband cannot change."

He thought in silence, then asked, "So the problem is you are not attracted to him?"

I nodded, not because the simple distillation of our marriage was how I saw it, but because my words were stuck in hot lumps inside my throat, and I needed to stop myself from leaking tears. If I cried, he could use that against me, label me emotional, or capricious, or weak, or needing only a gentle caress to make things right. I needed to be clearheaded and determined and strong.

"But you have two children with him, so it can't be that bad, *nu?*" It was not a harsh tone, the one he used to strip me of myself. But I could not argue with his logic—that birthing my husband's children meant that I consented to and reasonably enjoyed the acts required to get pregnant.

Instead, I tried to frame it as a health issue, which it was, and which I know rabbis took more seriously than a woman's mere pleading. "I am feeling so physically weakened by this marriage. I am not able to be a good mother to my children under these conditions." I held my breath.

For this he had a quick answer. "Maybe you can take a little medicine. I heard there are pills that help. Prozac."

The nascent flame of self that got me to go see the rabbi was dying. I wanted to ask him why he mentioned that particular medication. I wanted to tell him I had pages of notes about every psychotropic medication on the market, and that none of them treated marriage problems. But I couldn't get the words past the panic rising through my body, making my hands quiver as I held them modestly on my lap.

I realized that he was neither refusing nor granting my request, and I wondered how one played this game, when the subject kept changing. The rabbi stood up, marking the end of our meeting. The air between us bubbled with the scent of warm paprika and garlic. It was time for him to eat dinner with his family.

"May it be with a blessing and success," he said. "May you be guided on the right path."

I stood and took small steps backward, facing him all the while, as I had been taught to do. I looked at the ground, my black ballet flats soundless on the gray linoleum.

What just happened?

I assembled a list of rabbis who dealt with "emotional questions," such as obsessive disorders, porn addictions, and family strife. I presented my case to each, over the phone and in person, and sometimes, to wives who screened their calls.

Each time, I was left holding comments that seemed oddly unrelated to my question:

"Here is the number for a man who has saved many couples." I asked what his credentials were, religious or professional. There were none.

"What is the rush? You have young babies. I am sure you are tired."

"Please ask your husband to call me."

I felt the rage snake through my veins, through my fingertips, until my hands clenched around the base of my phone. I knew their hesitations and misdirection meant I would never break free. I knew the longer I stayed, the more they would use that as evidence that it wasn't that bad after all, that maybe it was time for me to conceive yet another child.

For my twenty-fourth birthday, Yossi bought me a toaster oven and a bread machine. It was confirmation of all that I had already known. To him, I was not a woman. I was a vagina who could cook.

Despite the inscrutable maze of rabbis and busy signals, I refused to be powerless any longer. That very night, I searched the phone book for a local hotel. As I turned the thin yellow pages, I gathered the words I had found in psych charts, in Rutgers classrooms, and in case study textbooks.

"I don't feel safe with you here," I said to Yossi, while keeping my eyes on the listings for Marriott Hotel and Ramada Inn.

For once, I felt Yossi looking directly at me.

"I will just sleep in the other room. No one has to know." His breaking voice floated over the plastic Lego blocks on the playroom floor and past my wooden heart. I didn't have any care left inside me.

As I dialed the hotel phone number, Yossi's tone became urgent, deeper, almost desperate: "Maybe we could talk to someone about this."

I had already tried talking. I had tried therapists and rabbis, I had listened and followed, agreed again and again to try one more time, and now I was no longer willing.

On the phone, the hotel operator took my credit card number as I booked Yossi a room. I tried to act like I was not shaking as I watched him shuffle upstairs, then back down holding a small suitcase. He stopped at the foot of the stairs, waited. I kept my head pointed down at the desk, my body still. My body was acting as if he were a predator, assessing me, looking for weakness. Full freeze response. I couldn't have turned toward him if I tried. I was stuck in place. Finally, he left.

As I heard the front door swing shut, I suddenly felt terrified. My toddlers were asleep, oblivious to their lives being shredded apart in the night. How was I going to get divorced and keep them safe?

Most of all, I was afraid that Yossi would simply return, and an army of rabbis would destroy my resolve. They would tell me that I had gone insane, that I had crossed a line, that my insistence on determining my own fate was of no consequence to them.

I needed backup, someone who knew I was not crazy, who knew I was able to care for my children, who knew I, too, was devout. With Yossi gone, there were no barriers to calling my own rabbi, from my year of post–high school study in Israel.

"Malkaleh," Rabbi Levi said with so much tenderness, with no hint of the years that had passed since we last spoke. "Why didn't you tell me?"

I didn't know how to tell him that my husband did not think he was pious enough, or stringent enough, and that his rabbinic rulings would've meant little within the walls of my marriage.

"I lost myself," I said, and he understood that in the way that mattered.

I told him as much as I could, though my brain felt like a dish left on a Shabbos hot plate, turned into a pile of mush. I knew my words told only a fraction of the story. I got my main fears across, that my own voice felt so small, and that I didn't know if it would hold against the weight of all the forces so much stronger than me.

"Don't worry." His voice was a salve of warmth and kindness across the oceans that separated us. "I'll call Yossi and make sure he doesn't try to come back. I will explain everything to your father. You are going to need him. Just rest."

I swallowed hard and dragged myself to bed. The sharp pain in my throat felt like it could turn into an endless stream of tears, but it wasn't time to cry. Not yet. I had too much planning to do, and I was so, so tired.

"He is a good man, Malka. You need to stop this immediately. You are going to destroy your children."

My sister Dina was lecturing me, just as I'd finally started to believe there was hope Yossi would not finagle his way back into our home again. She went on to tell me how unreasonable I was. I had only one thought as she went on for what felt like hours:

Thank God, he told someone.

I imagined the phone tree, a sorrowful reversal of the sparkling wires that got us engaged and married. Yossi must have told his parents, who called my sisters, who called each other, and then appointed Dina to call me.

My sister Hindy called. "How are Avigdor's teeth?" she asked, as if picking up from a prior conversation we never had.

"They're fine," I said. I grabbed a chicken nugget from Avigdor's little fist before he could smash it onto his sister's head. "I'm a little busy."

"Oh, okay, go take care. Yossi was just wondering if Avigdor had a cavity. We'll talk later. Bye." I heard the phone click before I realized, she had been talking to Yossi. She wasn't even trying to hide it.

I called her later that night, after the kids were tucked into their gingham sheets, and asked her why she was talking to the man I was about to divorce.

"Well, he called Meir," she said. "He is just very brokenhearted, Malka. He looks destroyed."

I was mystified. "How do you know he looks destroyed?"

"Oh. Well. Goldy invited him for Shabbos and then he dropped by." Hindy shifted the focus to other people so swiftly that I could barely keep up. "We're all just not sure you know what you're doing, Malka."

This was how they spoke, my sisters—in phrases dropped like little grenades, and then quickly walked away from. I was left standing when their words exploded, when I processed their meaning. They were all commiserating with and helping Yossi.

Hindy and Dina, the lead sisters, made their position clear. If I wanted to get divorced, it meant I was losing my mind. I must have inherited my mother's neurosis or Shani's bipolar disorder. They theorized that I had been poisoned by the liberal ideas of college. They took turns calling me and begging me to get serious therapy. Whatever it would take to stay married. Not once did they ask, "Are you okay?"

Abba sounded resigned. "Malk-ah, I talked with Rabbi Levi. I am mailing you a check." He did not ask questions, did not want answers.

After a while, I stopped calling them. It was just too painful, the way their lack of understanding turned my chest hollow when I hung up the phone. The place in my heart where my sisters had been was suddenly empty. I felt their support vanish as they ganged up against me in support of Yossi.

I learned to choose the size of my chicken thighs without Dina's input.

I learned to talk to the hair stylist about the frizz in my wig without Hindy's advice. I learned how to make teriyaki salmon skewers sort of like Goldy's, but from a cookbook instead of from her.

After a few weeks of living on my own, I discovered I was a fantastic mother—way better than I had ever been. I had kisses and hugs and bath time and bedtime all figured out, without any help. I allowed the children to snuggle on the couch with me even when their fingers were sticky. I fed them chicken tenders and homemade soup with no rush at all, once I did not have to cook a formal dinner for my husband every night. I kept my heart open and light, instead of locking it away as soon as I heard the front doorknob turn. Contrary to what my sisters thought, Avigdor and Shira were fine. They were better than fine. They looked me in the eye now, and when they caught me smiling back at them, they full-on giggled out loud until I laughed right along with them, sometimes for no reason at all.

I kept Rabbi Levi updated every week.

"There's a Sandcastles book," he said, "about helping children cope with divorce."

I drove to Barnes and Noble and bought it that same day, studied it like it was the Bible. The book had some good tips about how to help three-year-old Avigdor and sixteen-month-old Shira feel secure during this time of transition. I composed a little song, which we sang together before and after each visitation session with their father, until they learned to expect that I would always be there at the end. I talked with them in simple language about what was happening. I nodded politely at Yossi when he picked up the children, so they wouldn't feel the tension between us.

"Well-wishers," we called them at the counseling clinic. People who were not directly involved in our clients' lives, but who had definite opinions about what our clients should do. Aunts and neighbors and former high school teachers who would call the clinic and try to bypass our HIPAA requirements by leaving long messages about people they suspected we were treating.

I had not anticipated getting my own "well-wishers," but sure enough they descended upon my two-family townhouse in stages. Each time, I set the Italian wood dining table with crystal and pastries and listened as I was trained to do. I really heard them though, and that was where it went wrong for them.

An older aunt said, "Sometimes you have to sacrifice for your kids. My husband, he can be very unkind. When we are intimate, if I don't have the reaction he wants, he gets mean. I have learned to use imagery. Soft waterfalls. That helps. And look at my beautiful family! It is a sacrifice for them." She had ten children. Ten. I wondered when she started sacrificing. She left puzzles and stuffed bears for my babies and blessed me with the wisdom to make the right choice.

A high school friend came by, someone I had not seen in years. She asked me what happened. "Did he hit you?"

"Oh! I'm so happy you weren't hit," she trilled with visible joy, and then proclaimed that my unhappiness was not bad enough to warrant a divorce. "I was so worried about you when I heard you were separated. So, there's hope!"

She knew me well enough to catch the slight twitch in my eye as I stared blankly at her over the sliced babka.

"Malka. You cannot ruin your kids like this. They will never get into school if they come from a broken home!"

None of them realized that I knew better than the myth that staying married for the children was for their benefit. That myth had set my childhood on fire. I could still see the embers, the images. Plates of food crashing past my abba's beard and shattering against the wall. Mother's shaky hands waving at him. Words that sucked the air out of the whole damn house. Holes the shape of big shoes marking the wooden bedroom door.

Me, hiding at the top of the stairs, covering my ears with hands that were too small to block any of it out. Hiding myself behind stacks of sweaters and boots and long black coats in the back of the closet, waiting for it to end. And then silence for days and weeks and months. Icebergs slashing through our Shabbos table. Her hissing insults over pots of potato stew. Him reaching for the tall clear bottle of Finlandia, pouring it into his silver cup and downing it like water. That was what staying married for the children looked like.

My children deserved better.

The rabbis began to call me, an ironic reversal of the many months during which I sought them out. They each started with concern: "I heard things are not going well." They let some time pass while I spoke, and then they ended with the inevitable, "He says he will not grant you a divorce." They sounded helpless, even as I knew, and they knew, that with a single firm command they could get him to set me free.

My in-laws came to visit and sat down, somber. My father-in-law ignored the neat rows of chocolate rugelach as he focused on frowning at me with sufficient intensity across the table.

My mother-in-law said, "We had never seen our son so happy before he met you. He dated for so many years and couldn't find anyone before you."

She confirmed what I had begun to suspect. I had been told that he'd gone out on dates with about a hundred girls who were not good enough for him. I was beginning to infer that those one hundred girls were just a lot more intuitive than me.

My father-in-law said, slowly, "He will never give you a divorce." It was a threat. Clear and simple. I heard him.

I felt the steel forming in my core, anger heating up, growing sharp enough to cut. I looked at my mother-in-law. She seemed old and wizened, the bangs on her blond wig like straw over her wrinkles. The next words were for her. "Yossi was abusive. He abused me in the bedroom."

Her face folded inward, fine lines coming through the makeup. I wanted to take the words back. She was a delicate woman, one who worried about things like food being cold when the men came home from their prayer services. She had endless patience for pulling the same tinfoil trays in and out of the oven until the men arrived, so she could serve slow-cooked ribs and chicken soup and homemade potato kugel at just the right temperature until they all patted their stomachs, satiated. She lived her life to serve. She did not deserve this stab to the gut.

Besides, I was lying. I knew all about marital rape from college, and I knew that its essence was the lack of consent. But I never said "no" with Yossi, not once. The rules were the rules and we both followed them, even when it hurt me, even when I cried, even when I felt sick. I would never have said "no." That was not Yossi's fault, as I understood things then.

Did I wish the rabbis had allowed me to at least use birth control? Yes. It was an unholy wish, but I did wish I had been allowed that much autonomy. I had not dared to wish for a world in which the decision to have sex in the first place would be mine to make. I had not gone that far in risking my chance at heaven.

Yossi and I had many, many other problems, but those were not enough to make anyone listen. So, I stuck to the story about his abuse in the bedroom, hoping God would forgive me for flattening the truth to fit my agenda. With hindsight I see the choice of words is less straightforward than I felt as I spoke them back then. "Abuse," unspecified, in modern terms might include what I experienced in my marriage to Yossi. I had not processed enough to know the language best fit for what I experienced in Lakewood, but I knew what I felt would end the conversation when I needed it to end.

It would be more than a decade later before I learned that my body was truly my own, before I began to believe in a God that would never want me to subject myself to any sexual acts that felt violating. In that moment, back in my pre-fab beige house, in my small town, I gathered the gumption from inside my twenty-four-year-old self, hoping God would forgive me. I believed I was sinning by choosing divorce. Then there was the little added sin of my untruth.

But I hoped God would understand I was only doing those things so I could serve him better in the long run. I hoped that my Machiavellian logic would hold up, at the end of my days, when I showed up old and wrinkled in the heavenly court of law.

My mother-in-law tried to speak, but her mouth quickly opened and then closed without words. My father-in-law glared at me, his eyes in little narrow slits over the snow-white beard. He said nothing. I knew, then, that was my way out. *Abuse* was a strong word, one that they would not want floated around the social circle of their shul.

"I don't want to tell anyone that he hurt me. I don't want to say bad things about the father of my children. But if he refuses to give me a divorce, I'll have to." I sat up, held my resolve together. I could make threats too. They were parents, and I knew what that meant. They needed to protect their son. If they couldn't save him from divorce, they could at least save him from disparagement.

Two days later I got the message. He was ready to negotiate.

Far Away from Here

I met with Rabbi Shemaya three months after Yossi moved out. He was the director of the niche segment of rabbis in charge of organizing religious Jewish divorces. It was almost like they saved the kindest rabbi for last—one would need to wrangle through thorned bushes, scoot past rows of angry lions, slide in the mud between the thick legs of heavy elephants, and only then did they earn a rest in the meadow. Rabbi Shemaya was the meadow. He handed me a glass of water, leaned forward, and asked me how I was doing. He listened, really listened, and sat at his big Dell computer screen typing everything I said, stopping occasionally to stroke his brown beard or to give me a chance to catch my breath. Rabbi Shemaya treated me with warmth, with respect. It had been so long since that happened, that I just wanted to cry.

This rabbi, he saw my eyes dampen. He handed me a box of tissues. "I will call your husband and we will get you a divorce, Mrs. Schwartz."

He passed me a brochure for Sister to Sister, an organization that helped divorced Jewish women, and I looked at the pictures of campgrounds and glossy descriptions of retreats.

"You might want to call them; they can help you through this."

I swallowed, picturing myself in a grassy field, in a circle of other bewigged women without wedding rings. That's where I would soon belong, I realized. On the outskirts.

As snowflakes drifted over our beige town, turning the streets white and then dark, slushy gray, I realized that I had a new problem. Yossi was living in the attic of a local shul, I learned through the stricken voices of my sisters. Those voices were fading into the background, becoming less present, and I heard a shift in them. They were no longer trying to convince me to get help. They had given up on the mission to get me to regain my sanity and stay married. Instead, they called me to fish for information. "So did you get a lawyer?" they asked, their tones coiled tight enough that they threatened to snap the tenuous connections between us.

They suspected my religious devotion, I realized. They were trying to find out whether college had ruined me so much that I had become a threat to my children's spiritual well-being. According to the rules of our religious world, my divorce would be granted before a tribunal of rabbis, called a *beis din*. At the *beis din*, there would be no attorneys to present arguments in my favor.

As I stood in my kitchen, my thoughts scrambled, quickly losing coherence. *What if I lose my children? What if I lose my children?* The thought spun in a loop, faster and faster, until I was hyperventilating. I sat down at our glass-topped kitchen table and attempted the deep, diaphragmatic breathing from the treatment manual on my shelf.

Why was I so worried? I asked myself, parsing the components of my panic. *Yossi does not want the children.* He had called me to come home early during his scheduled visitation hours. "Shira is crying; she might be getting sick," he said, and I rushed home to find him with a helpless look on his face, holding her sideways. I did not believe there was a universe in which he was capable of or willing to be responsible for the day-to-day raising of the children. He would only seek custody if he believed I was not going to raise them in accordance with our religious laws and customs.

All I need to do is stay calm. The calmer I am, the less power they have, I coached myself.

It took so much effort to crush my panic. I scheduled a session with Genevieve, the therapist who treated me way back when I was fourteen, when I wanted to starve myself out of existence. In her familiar star-carpeted office, I allowed myself a measured amount of vulnerability. I made sure she took note of my rational decision-making and my consistent parenting just in case she was questioned by the rabbis. I wanted to sign that release of information form when the time came, with full confidence that waiving my confidentiality rights would work in my favor, and ultimately in my children's favor.

A few days later, Yossi joined me at a meeting with Rabbi Shemaya so we could mediate the necessary details of our divorce. He looked at the empty folding chair near mine, looked back at the rabbi across the softly dented desk, and deliberately moved his chair until it was in the corner of the room, as far away from me as possible. He looked like something dragged out of an attic, creased and frayed at the edges.

His mumbled responses to the mediation questions left the rabbi very puzzled.

"I maybe don't want to really commit to anything," he said, when asked about a visitation schedule. "I want to just maybe see the kids when it works out. Like maybe something like one time every week, but only maybe sometimes."

His speech patterns had devolved from circuitous to unintelligible. I was shocked. Had it always been this bad, or had I been the one holding him together until now? I had books at home with lists of labels for the inability to commit to even the words in a sentence, never mind to an entire schedule of custody. But in that moment, pressed against the back of the metal folding chair, watching the rabbi's eyebrows shoot up toward the top of his dusty black hat, for the first time, I felt like I was not the crazy one.

"If she ever writes a book, I don't want it to be about me." The clarity in Yossi's words betrayed the amount of thought behind his request. I was grateful for the layered strands of my wig over my nose and chin, over the curve of my lips as they held back a laugh. He did know something about me, after all. Maybe he did see the things that made up the real me, but just never knew quite what to do with them.

The rabbi said there was no preset language for a request like that.

"Let's move on," the rabbi said, scrolling down to the next section of our divorce agreement.

Yossi spoke. "I want the kids to be everything *frum*, like regular."

The rabbi leaned forward and offered Yossi some phrases. This religious part, they both spoke fluently. At the end of their discourse, the rabbi asked me if I was okay agreeing to the following paragraph, which mandated that I raise my children in accordance with the most stringent of Jewish law:

> *It is agreed by both parties that the children will be raised according to Halacha as stated in the Shulchan Oruch and the Mishna Berura. If it is determined by Rabbi Turkel of Lakewood, NJ, and Rabbi Levi of Jerusalem, Israel, that one party is not raising the children according to Halacha, custody will be transferred to the other biological parent.*

Even as I agreed, I knew it was a trap. I was as certain of this as I was that the sky was blue and the grass was green. I did not want to think of how the clause would affect our future lives, what I would be allowed to do, and how I would provide for the children.

I knew that if I mis-stepped I could fall into the shadows with the other rebellious parents who lost their children. Hesitation would show that I was unsure of my willingness to sign the document, and they would question my religious commitment and my faith. I could not give them a reason to deny me the precious document that would set me free, nor could I risk gaining that freedom without being able to care for my children.

Instead, I scoffed at the words on the thick computer screen. "Of course! I don't know why he'd have to put that in. Obviously, I want the same thing."

I acted indignant. It didn't matter anyway. I would have to want that, the faith and the commitment to religious observance and all it entailed. Because there was no way I would allow any man to take my babies.

When I left the rabbi's study there were stars in the distant sky, over all the neat rows of identical lawns. *I'm sorry,* I offered the words up to God, hoping he could still hear me, even as I abandoned my holy mission of marriage, *I really tried.*

I slid into the front seat of my secondhand Chevy and hit play on a CD I'd purchased at a Barnes and Noble off the Garden State Parkway. Secular music.

The music filled me, from the inside of my rib cage and expanding outward on all sides. She got me. Sarah McLachlan. Her voice, soft and strong, somehow reached inside my ice walls, words about holding on to oneself through the pain. I didn't know I was crying until the tears hit my hands on the steering wheel and I bent over it, folded in half, face dripping. I heard the guttural sound of my insides as they hit the glass all around me. Hoarse, choking gulps against my eardrums, along with gentle tones of a piano. All the sounds I had swallowed as my flesh tore apart and my dreams broke into pieces for so many days and years, all the sounds spilled out at once.

The lyrics were a promise. Not to God, not to him. It was the first promise I made that was just to myself: *I will be strong tomorrow.*

"He called me."

That was why I trusted Genevieve. She always told me, right at the start of the therapy hour, when one of my family had called.

"Do I even want to know?"

The room was dim, but I saw pain in the marble green of her eyes. I heard the pauses in her breath just as well as she read the tightness in my voice.

"He asked if you would sleep with him one more time because he does not know when he will be with a woman again." She looked as sick as I felt.

So, Yossi called my therapist to ask her to make me give him one last piece of myself. I grabbed the little metal garbage can off the carpet as bile fought its way up my throat.

"Malka, it's over." Genevieve passed me a fresh bottle of water. She sat back. She invited me, all of me, to speak.

I watched the minute hand trace its way over waves of colored stone on the side table. I wanted to put a finger right at the edge of it and stop time. Whatever tricks Yossi was trying to use to get at me on the outside, they had no power inside my session hour.

"Thank you for being honest with me."

In the space between the two of us, I was not a robot wife. I was a woman. A woman so close to freedom I could almost taste it. A woman days away from that final divorce. A woman who would finally, finally be allowed to say no, even by the most stringent of rules.

The night before *beis din*, I sat on the carpet of my children's playroom, reviewing the document Rabbi Shemaya printed for me. The document that would be signed and stamped in front of a rabbinic court.

I called Tikva. "It's happening tomorrow," I said. "Why am I suddenly freaking out?"

"It's intimidating facing the rabbis," she offered, her voice gentle but sure. "Do you want me to be there?"

My eyes filled with tears. Tikva was offering me the support my own family denied me.

"I can handle it," I said, but my voice faltered, and I knew she heard it.

"I'll be there," Tikva said. "I will be there."

I thanked her and hung up and then curled up, knees against my forehead, body shaking. I was getting divorced. I was twenty-four, and already I had ruined my own life. *Forgive me*, I begged of God.

I thought about the religiosity clause in my divorce agreement, the words that would keep me tethered to God's will. I wished, for a quick moment, that I could shuck God's rules along with the rules of my marital contract. That I could throw the wig out the window of my car and drive away into the sunset with the wind whipping through my hair. I wished I could move to California and wander the streets until I found women like me, lesbians, and then make friends with them over mugs of coffee. I wished I could wake up late on a Saturday morning and then drive to a bookstore and read for hours, instead of staying home and serving stew.

But I had children, and they deserved to be raised with a mother in their lives.

I stood up, placed the stapled pages on the corner of my kitchen counter, and got ready for my last night of sleep as a married woman according to Jewish law.

I would be free of Yossi. Not of God, not of my responsibilities, but I would be free of a husband I could no longer tolerate, and that was good enough.

As soon as the divorce papers were signed and sealed, I ran so fast and so hard and as far away as I could. I left the stapled sheaf of documents in my old bedroom. I drove Avigdor and Shira to Dina's house, where they were embraced by their little cousins and given fresh hot potato kugel right out of the oven. I raced down Dina's driveway, waving back at her scarved head. And then I was on the plane. Flying far, far away.

The first thing I did in Aruba, after leaving my wig in the glass-walled hotel room along with my kosher tuna packets and small travel bag, was pray. I headed to the rocks outside, right along the shimmering waves. I looked out to God, to the space between clouds and sea and my small bent body.

I am ashamed to admit it, but I am going to need some leeway, Hashem. I felt like I was letting him down, but I wanted to be honest. *I can't be perfect* anymore. *Not that I ever was perfect. But you know what I mean. I can't be like I was before. I couldn't keep it up. I tried. But I failed you.*

I bargained, holding my prayer book to my face, whispering into the thin papyrus-like pages. *God, I will find my way back to you. I promise. Please keep my babies safe. Please.*

And then, I sinned.

I dug tiny red pieces of spandex out of my suitcase. I opened my phone's internet browser, connected to the Sheraton network, and found the Victoria's Secret model who made the spandex seem like the key to a whole new life. I tied the fabric onto my body just like hers, strings above my hips and double knots around my back. Not bad. My skin was whiter. I had purple stretch marks on my thighs and silver ones along my stomach. Instead of golden cleavage, I had small pale lumps underneath the triangles tied to my chest. But all in all, I was passable as a person who may or may not have birthed two babies.

Down on the beach, I blinked in the intense brightness. I scanned the palm trees, the bare glistening limbs on beach chairs, the children running into the sea. Good. No women in wigs, no plastic kosher supermarket bags at the foot of chairs, no telltale side-curls framing the faces of little boys. If there were Orthodox Jews here, they too were defecting, and therefore I was safe. They would not dial their relatives in New Jersey and whisper about the therapist who got almost naked in Aruba, not if they were here doing the same.

Young men in polo shirts carried silver pails of ice back and forth, wiped sweat from their thick brows with cloth napkins. Women in big sunglasses snapped fingers at the young men and handed them folded bills.

It had been so long since I acknowledged the feelings in my body that I barely knew who I was anymore. Was it the gentle teasing of a man's attention that I craved? Or the delicate touch of a woman on my skin? I had not the slightest idea. Either way, I was sure that once I revealed myself on the wide-open beach, I would have more than one person try to get my attention. I could always decide then.

I slid my body down onto a towel and removed my knee-length denim skirt, slowly. I expected the wafting music tones to stop or crescendo, or something. But all of it continued right on. I pulled my long-sleeved black T-shirt over my head.

I wanted to yell and twirl and run around until the warm ocean wind whipped through my hair. But I was just stuck in a haze of wonder. I lay flat on the striped beach towel while my heart raced. I felt the sun on my skin, warming the parts of me that had been cold for so many years. For once, I sank into the body I had been trying to uninhabit. Yes.

I knew it was bad, the light on my body and people all around me who could see so much more of me than what God allowed. I wanted to close my eyes and rest, the sort of lazy basking I had read about. But there were men here and this was not a novel, I reminded myself. This was not safe!

A tinny voice from my old seminary classroom in Jerusalem rang in my mind, the voice of Rabbi Ostreicher. "Ladies, retain your feeling of shame. It is an important one. The world outside wants us to believe that anything goes. Do not let them influence you. We feel shame for a reason."

He also said, in his lilting British accent that seemed, at the time, to contain all the wisdom of the world, that it was our duty as women to protect our men. If they were to see the bodies we hid under long sleeves and skirts, they might get aroused. It would be inconsiderate to tempt them in those ways.

I felt liable for the sins of every man on the whole entire beach. I saw the crease in some tan shorts right near my head. A male, muscled calf. Every nerve ending in my body felt tightly attuned. If I had not shaved every bit of hair off my pale legs, I bet each would have stood straight up. The bit of fabric felt way too thin, the one between my vagina and the rest of the world. I flicked at the edge of the towel with my toe, sending granules of scorching hot sand over myself.

"Ma'am, may I bring you something from our menu?" He looked at my squinting face and waited for my order.

I looked at his smooth tan ankles and prepared to be assaulted, and then be sent directly to hell for it.

"Ma'am?" He looked away, at a couple of bouncy buttocks in a hot-pink string on the next beach towel, tapped his pen against a leather-bound pad. It appeared that all of my skin, right there, out in the open, was not going to make him sin.

"No, thank you." I got the words out into the warm air, and exhaled as he moved away in the sand, relieved but so very confused.

On the whole vast beach, not one person looked at my near-naked body. None of it made any sense.

Later, Google and the nice hotel concierge led me to something called Nightlife. Google was all over the place about what to wear for the experience, so I did my best. I knew to bring lip gloss and a box of condoms. I had seen too many diseases with scary names like chlamydia on the inpatient charts of women who did Nightlife. I had seen scars on their bodies from babies they never wanted, and from the substances they injected to forget. I did not know what happened in the outside world after dark, but I did know that I needed to stay alive and safe for my babies.

I tossed the pink leather Coach purse over my very bare shoulder, checked my eyeliner in the mirror, and plunged myself into the mystery of the island after dark. I found somewhere dim but not too dark, with polished wood and smiling people and English phrases in the air along with soft notes of a piano. I sat up on a tall chair, near the flashing white teeth of a bartender who checked my ID and then gave me glasses holding clear drinks with names I could not identify. I felt the sharp edges of pain in my gut start to fade. It was nothing like the small sips of wine at Shabbos dinner. Those just left me feeling slightly tired. With the clear drink, I was present. I noticed that the lights darkened and the music sped up and the space filled with the scent of flowers and the glint of jewels. I was there, but nothing on the inside hurt. I wasn't worrying about the rules or the sins, and most of all, the constant fear I wore on my chest—it was gone.

A small group formed around me. Sasha slung a long brown arm over the back of my tall chair, revealing tan skin between a miniscule T-shirt and pants so low they almost fell off her hips. Zafar handed me the next glass of sweet cocktail and leaned a smooth dark chin toward me. Amelie sent the fluted notes of her laugh around all of us until we laughed too. I was in Nightlife!

"You have beauty in that smile." Zafar whispered something behind a girl's long wavy hair, and then offered me a small packet. "For your sunburn. May I?" I looked down and saw my arms, red and starting to peel. It did not matter at all. He was already taking care of me, smooth and sure and making the hot feel cool as he rubbed aloe over my skin.

I paused, glass in hand, when the giant screen behind the group came alive. The voice behind the music was there, a woman who waved her body around like it was the thing all songs were about. Her lips coiled around the words, her eyes dared me to look away. I couldn't. The men in the video, open shirts over carved chests, they looked at her too, as she told them to read the signs of her body. The words filled every bit of air around me as I watched her move, the liquid gold shape of her finding a space beneath my core and making it come alive. If this was dancing, it was not like any dancing I had ever seen. It was nothing like the shuffle of women at Jewish weddings, in navy or black garb and stockinged feet in sensible heels as they formed a circle around young brides. Shakira believed that hips did not lie. My mind, wonderfully intoxicated, could not agree more.

When the song faded out and I came back to my very still body on the bar stool, I saw my new friends moving their bodies on the dance floor. A responsible-looking couple had sat down near me, a woman with graying hair and a cardigan who leaned into a gentleman in an ironed button-down and wire-rimmed glasses. They were from Boston, they said. I thought of brick college buildings and scholars and autumn. I told them things, those safe, solid people who did not seem fazed by any parts of Nightlife. They nodded when I talked about being Jewish and Orthodox. They looked at each other knowingly when I said I left an arranged marriage.

"When did this happen?" The woman had a voice like warm knit blankets, and so I was truthful.

"I got my divorce three days ago."

They murmured and walked me out of the bar, surrounded me with a cloud of their protection. The woman guided me into the back of a cab, told the driver the name of my hotel. When I looked up, I saw the man handing the driver some bills and telling him to get me back safely.

I didn't know what made them do that. But as I leaned against the vinyl seat and saw the lights fade into the sight of brick and glass and shapes outside, I was relieved. I would not have to figure out any more things. My box of condoms was still sealed in my bag. I had done alcohol and music and met real people in a real world and not gotten hurt.

After conquering the wearing of a bathing suit in full view of people and doing Nightlife, I relaxed into my own skin. I felt the sun warm every inch of me as I lounged at the clear blue pool and then down at the endless sea. I felt the sand on my feet and the waves as they lapped against my thighs, smoothing the thin silver scars left over from childbirth. I had drinks, clear and leafy and cool, and they glided down my throat with more ease than I had ever imagined.

At the end of the weekend, I boarded the plane back home, allowed the sun blisters on my shoulders to cool against the glass windows. I watched Aruba, and my brief freedom, fade away below me.

I may have made it to the end of the first tightrope, but just barely, and there were many others ahead. All it would take was one pious acquaintance at Newark Airport, catching sight of my naked hair in a ponytail, and it would be over. I had promised to hand my children to their father the moment I stopped following God's law. "Custody will be transferred," I agreed in the presence of three rabbis, one of whom pulled a stamp out of his drawer and affixed a legal notary seal near the shaky Hebrew letters of my signature.

As the pilot announced, "We are about to begin our final descent," I took my bag into the small bathroom. I emerged devout once again, hair pinned back beneath a shoulder-length brown bob of someone else's shorn hair, and my body cloaked in long layers. I ignored the scratching of cloth against my burning skin. *I will be righteous*, I vowed. I pulled a small photo out of my leather wallet, Avigdor in his velvet yarmulke and tiny dimpled smile standing on a red scooter, little Shira standing up right beside him, soft brown curls falling over round toddler cheeks. They were all that mattered.

Sweet Madness

After my Aruba trip, I felt the first tendrils of my freedom waver. I couldn't let the sunlight touch upon my hair anymore, not within miles of Lakewood. I needed to find other ways to figure out who I was, who I would become outside my marriage. My entire life plan had been demolished. Everything I knew about how to be a person no longer applied. I needed information. The only problem was that information in Lakewood was scarce.

We were under a town-wide internet ban. As the internet became a standard feature of modern life, the rabbis decided that it was for the secular world, not for us. In special cases, such as for work purposes, one was permitted to use the Yeshiva Net provider, which allowed access to "whitelisted" websites. I had a dial-up DSL connection monitored by Yeshiva Net, which meant that when I first wanted to access the Rutgers University Library website, the Gap, or Children's Place, I had to call the Yeshiva Net office to ask them to allow those sites. When I called to ask if I could add Google to my list, the sleepy male voice at the other end said, "Mrs. Schwartz, many people find that to be a strong temptation. We don't allow search engines." How could I admit that I wanted to explore more temptations? He would ask to speak to my husband.

I called the secular phone company and talked to them about getting a cable connection installed. I knew that I was walking the tightrope again. The shadow world was close, so close, and I was inches from falling. My children were still in day care, but in two years it would be time to apply to local schools, and I would have to sign a contract stating that our home had no unfiltered internet connection. *I will get rid of it by then,* I promised myself, *it's just for now.*

The AT&T technician arrived, and I watched him through the window of my townhouse as he took tools out of his belt. *He could just be here to fix my phone,* I rationalized, as I scanned the windows across the street, and hoped none of the neighbors were looking too closely.

He came to the door a few minutes later.

"Ma'am," he said to me, his face lined with confusion, "there is no cable in this zone."

He pointed at all the matching beige semi-attached townhouses, twenty on our block, each housing two or more Orthodox families. He gestured beyond, to the streets on either side of mine, and explained that none of the people in any of those houses had cable internet or TV services. If they had, he would have found a wired connection somewhere outside.

"I can do it for you, but it will take a few hours." I ignored the static in my nerves, the worry crackling through my body, and nodded.

I needed this.

After the technician left, I sat in the one corner of the kitchen floor that was close enough to the magical white cable wire that ran all the way around the house, down the back porch, and somewhere below the concrete. That wire and my nine-inch, metallic pink Dell Inspiron laptop were portals to a new universe.

I googled how to install antivirus software and felt invincible. I googled everything. How to watch TV. What to watch on TV. And then I was in a cloud above and outside our beige town. Every night, after the children were safely tucked in, I got comfortable on the tiled kitchen floor, back propped against the wall, and I lived inside *Grey's Anatomy* for hours and hours. I couldn't stop watching. I already knew some secular people from college, but on my screen the women were all so beautiful that it made my eyes tear. I watched their smooth faces and long wavy hair, their silhouettes that moved casually around, filling spaces with confidence. Television people seemed to just meet each other and then have sex within moments. They did it in the light and standing up and they laughed and smiled about it. They were having so much fun. I had no idea.

I viewed my colleagues at the hospital in a whole new way. Suddenly I was thinking about what was underneath their scrubs. I looked men in the eye instead of scurrying to the side when they passed. Were they all thinking about skin and laughter and the many rooms that locked on our inpatient unit?

I googled hair salons and found one in a town miles away. I felt the edges of guilt rise through my fingers when I took my stiff wig off in my parked car and threw it under the seat. When I sat down in the fancy chair and a skinny, bronze-skinned girl named Chloe came up behind me, I realized I still needed to explain. The wig was in the car, but its evidence remained in the bald spots above my ears, the mousy mess around my face.

I was always explaining something to someone. My life was upside down. At the hospital I explained why I ate plastic-wrapped sandwiches from home while everyone else at the table enjoyed non-kosher cafeteria food. In Lakewood, I explained why my mother never came to visit when all the other young women had mothers who brought homemade challah and watched their children. At home, I gently told Avigdor and baby Shira why Totty was not at the Shabbos table anymore.

I sighed. "I cover my hair, usually, and I haven't had a real haircut in a few years. That's why it looks like this." I gestured to the uneven brown tufts poking out around my ears. "Please just make it look normal. I think I might stop covering it all the time. Just do whatever you can." I used way too many words, awkward words.

Chloe put a hand on my shoulder and smiled. "I got you. No problem at all! How about a couple of highlights to bring out the pretty hazel in your eyes?"

Highlights! She was talking about highlights! I was so relieved. That sounded like the type of thing you told a normal person.

"Sure!" I chirped. I never chirped. But I didn't feel like a monotone anymore.

I began to notice the little shopping mall strips along the long Jersey highways, even the ones that did not contain kosher shops. There was a whole world out there for me to discover. On my drive home from work one day, I spotted a sign that I was sure I had passed hundreds of times before without seeing it at all. In big bold blue letters it read, $399 divorce. I swung into the parking lot in front of the sign, strode inside without pause.

"I am already divorced," I told the confused woman who looked up at me from behind tortoiseshell frames. "I just need the legal paperwork." I explained that I had already completed my divorce proceedings in Jewish court. According to Jewish law, that was the divorce that mattered in the eyes of God and everyone I knew. The legal divorce was a technicality, something I needed to check off my list before I renewed my children's health insurance so I could get better rates. I knew that Yossi wouldn't even read the paperwork. To rule followers, the stack of legal papers was much like trashy magazines in the checkout lines at our local Stop & Shop. We walked by those without reading the headlines, an inconvenience to get through so we could complete our purchases. We would sign the divorce papers as fast as possible, and then once a judge stamped them, we would never look at them again.

I walked out carrying the promise of a divorce for a flat fee of $399, no add-ons, no questions.

"You're here!"

My sister Shani ran down the city block toward me, curls blowing in the wind, a big white grin across her face.

Then she hugged me, so fast and tight that my stiff arms didn't even have time to consider hugging her back. She thrust a cellophane-wrapped package at me. "Happy Divorce!"

I laughed. Shani was the only sister who would see the happiness in this.

When I called to tell her about the divorce, her response was, "Welcome back to the world!" She didn't need any reasons. She was unfazed by the sisters. She was used to living in defiance of labels or categories. "You always seemed so much more interesting than he did," she added. That was Shani: direct, colorful, exuberant, and fiercely protective of those she loved.

"To be honest," she said, "when I saw your house, and that town, and all the people in black all over the place, I thought it felt like death."

In fact, she'd made that very remark when she and Felix visited Lakewood for the first time, right after moving back from Israel a year earlier: "It looks like a funeral out there," she'd said as she walked up the stairs to our taupe townhouse. "Who died?"

She had come wrapped in a paisley scarf and tie-dyed skirt, and her husband Felix was in dusty sandals. I remembered holding the door open and trying not to scan the street too hard, but I knew there'd be questions later: *So, you had a visitor today, huh?*

Outside the AMC theater in Midtown Manhattan, we laughed at the irony of our meeting spot. "Can you imagine what Abba would say if he saw us now? His daughters going to a movie!"

Shani decided to ease me into the real world, and she chose a PG-13 title for us to watch, *Did You Hear About the Morgans?* We debated getting popcorn, despite its lack of kosher certification, then decided it was best not to break too many rules at the same time.

As we sat in the movie theater, we dissected every move on the big screen, in true sisters' style. We were an analytical species, us sisters. As Shani and I whispered our observations to each other, I felt a familiar sense of home wash over the red plastic movie seats surrounding us. We watched Sarah Jessica Parker and Hugh Grant enter witness protection and start new lives with new identities. We compared that experience to ourselves, our attempts to re-create our own identities.

When the movie ended, I thanked her for the basket of vanilla-scented candles and lotions. "I have to run; I'm so sorry."

"I feel like I got my sister back!" Shani kissed me on the cheek.

"Me too." I muted my tone appropriately, back to permissible levels, but my heart sang. At least one sister still loved me.

I blew a kiss over my shoulder as I checked the small ticket in my hand and tried to remember where I parked. I was always breathless and running. I wanted to grab the entire world in my hands and devour all its wonders at once. I wanted to run and feel and taste and see all the things that had been forbidden. But I needed to pick up my babies from day care at five o'clock.

The exploration was fun, but only because I had it under control. I looked but didn't let my gaze linger on things that would make me want to wander. I felt, but not too much. I tasted new things, but only at shops that also had kosher items, so that no one would see me walk in and think I had fallen. Most important, I was making sure there was always plausible deniability of my defiance.

In the following weeks and months, I learned more about the years Shani and I had spent apart. There were big chunks of Shani's life that I knew nothing about. The sisters had banded together to shield me from months and years of her existence, and then eventually from Shani herself. There were whispers on the sidelines of our holiday dinners. "She's in the hospital again," and "It's really bad this time." When they saw me eavesdropping, they shushed one another and moved on to taking care of whatever cluster of children was running around nearby. "You don't need to worry about it," they would say. "Abba is paying for the best doctors. You focus on your marriage."

There was a hint of hesitation during her early confessions, as Shani tried to shield me from the worst she had endured. She was still my big sister and protective of me, but it felt more like love and less like a cloak of secrecy. After a while, she trusted me with the darkness underneath her gushing charm. She appreciated the expertise I had gained on the inpatient unit, expertise that finally felt useful in the way I had always hoped.

I was relieved to hear that she saw an expert psychiatrist who specialized in bipolar disorder. "Now that I'm not pregnant anymore, he put me back on lithium. It's working for me. I'm actually better than ever."

I ran a quick calculation. We celebrated the bris of her baby three months earlier, in a large wood-paneled shul filled with our relatives. Abba was among the men in black down on the first floor. I had leaned over the railing of the women's section as he held Shani's newborn on a white silk pillow and the rabbi called out his name, "Adam ben Felix." Abba's face had flushed above his beard, the pride in his eyes glistening, his joy filling the entire sacred space.

I remembered Shani being sort of frantic at the bris, greeting me with run-on sentences all piled on top of each other, and I remembered thinking, *She must be off her meds.*

Shani had been writing about her experience with bipolar disorder. She'd sent me pieces of her work and had asked how the family would feel if it were published.

I was so sick of the family secrets. So tired of everything being taboo. If Shani was our family's black sheep, I was the sheep veering very close by—dark charcoal, perhaps. It was selfish of me, but I'd hoped she could dispel some of the stigma around us both. Through the base of my Palm Pilot, I said, "You should tell your story. The sisters will have to handle it."

She hesitated. "I don't want to hurt them." She talked about Hindy, whose son was beginning the search for his destined marriage partner. Shani knew that if matchmakers read her article and connected Hindy's son to a family history of mental illness, his chances of finding a good match would be significantly harmed.

"Shani," I interrupted her. It was the only way to get a word in through the breathless rush of her worry. "People should feel honored to marry into a family with you in it." And, by extension, me. People should be honored to marry into a family with me in it, I wildly, recklessly wished.

When I, at age seven, wondered where Shani had gone, she was in and out of psychiatric facilities, both in the U.S. and in Israel.

She shared a diary entry with me, nearly two decades old:

I have not stepped out of this small room for 120 hours, excluding the minute it took me to get my lens case. Now I know why so much fuss is made about solitary confinement—it's a painful ordeal. I got in here Friday afternoon and tomorrow is Friday again. I don't even know whether or not I hate it anymore. I'm apathetic. Do I have any higher aspirations than a one-bedroom in a mental hospital? Here I'm safe. I've proven to myself that I can't handle the swirling, rushing whirlwind outside.

She'd attempted suicide, and as a result was placed in a straitjacket, with her arms and legs locked and fastened to a bed. Somehow, her mind cleared after a while. Still, she remembered it not as a time of healing but of torture. She was locked into that room, with nothing but a bed, and treated like a nonperson. When doctors and hospital staff discussed her case, they spoke as if she weren't there.

At the time of her first inpatient hospitalization, she was only seventeen. Seventeen and strapped to a table, helpless, among total strangers. I had been desperate to figure out what happened to her for most of my life, and once I knew, I felt it in my own body, as if it were happening to me. As if my arms were held down, my legs bound together, my own breath catching in my throat.

She recounted the way she came to see being locked up not as treatment but as punishment for her sins, and became obsessed with religious minutiae, praying for hours, and taking on all sorts of religious strictures of her own devising. She would experience hallucinations, at times looking at people and seeing something in them, an angelic aura—or, in some cases, a demonic one—and would begin to shout for all to come see. Such episodes would get her labeled as "crazy," and she told me how confusing it was to wake up the next day with a lucid mind and wonder what had gotten into her.

She described her early hospitalizations as a series of episodes, but I didn't remember it that way. In my memory, she was there one day and gone the next, and nearly a decade would pass before she returned.

I told her how bereft I had been when she vanished. Up until then, she'd been a popular, high-achieving high school student, and her sudden disappearance with an illness no one would explain or discuss would make me obsessed with understanding mental health. I revealed that she was the reason that I'd chosen to become a psychologist. I didn't tell her that I was still searching for a cure. I didn't want to get her hopes up.

"There was a year when I was in bed," she shared, "and Mommy came to visit me and was horrified that I did not even get up to brush my teeth."

She attended a seminary in Jerusalem for a time, where she continued to experience manic and depressive episodes. She stayed in Israel for many years, where she attended classes in various institutions and tried to heal. There seemed to be periods of improvement, months that went by without incident. Then she would either stop taking her medications, saying they made her feel blunted and not like herself, or a stressor would occur, and she would end up hospitalized again.

Over the years, she received a litany of diagnoses, but the one that most fit her condition was a severe form of bipolar disorder. There was a cruel reality Shani would discover about the kind of mental illness she suffered: once you begin experiencing episodes, you are never completely free of them. Finally, with the help of competent doctors, and by using her own mind to understand what did or didn't work for her, she found an effective combination of medications and talk-therapy that allowed her to emerge, after years of debilitating dysfunction, as someone who could, on most days, pass for "sane."

In many ways, Shani was simply odd because she was Shani—colorful, funny, exuberant, vivacious. She laughed as she told me about the time she attended a modern Orthodox shul in Israel. There, she found herself among the congregants who socialized after the services, single guys and girls, mingling easily. With her sheltered Hasidic upbringing, Shani was accustomed to men and women always separated by a partition; she pretended then to be at ease, as if it were normal for her. She managed well enough, until a man approached with an innocuous comment. "Are you new to the neighborhood?" Suddenly panicked, Shani blurted out, "I will *not* marry you!"

At age twenty-five, she met Felix, the man she would eventually marry. Unlike the men she knew growing up, Felix had been raised secular in San Francisco. He found religion while attending college in Boston, and by the time he graduated, he was an occupational therapist and a newly minted Orthodox Jew. In Borough Park, Felix would've been considered way too nonconformist for a match with someone in our family, but to Shani, he was wonderful. The two of them shared a love of mountain bikes, hiking, and the land of Israel. Felix's calm seriousness provided the perfect foil for Shani's squiggly personality.

I met Felix when I was a high school junior, days before their wedding. He was standing on a stool, painting the cabinets in their new kitchen a dusty shade of blue. He was ruggedly handsome, lean and tan with blue eyes that twinkled shyly when he talked about Shani. Hindy and I brought touches from Brooklyn, high-thread-count sheets and nice soaps, and laid them out for Shani and Felix's first marital apartment.

Shani and Felix had moved back to the States and into a similar apartment in Queens several years later, complete with their trademark wall of mounted bicycles. Shani taught computers to high school students and Felix worked as a pediatric OT. Things seemed okay. Shani was a colorful sister who showed up at family events in her shiny scarves, little Micki and baby Adam in tow.

Shani decided she would not risk the collateral damage of threatening our family's reputation by disclosing her illness publicly, and so I helped her pick a pseudonym for her writings.

A few weeks later, she published a series of articles about her experiences in psychiatric facilities, and how she survived her terrible illness. Her articles were beautifully written, touching and incisive, with a measure of self-reflection that showed her true character—one of deep honesty and boundless compassion for others.

I felt hopeful for her. She was doing well. Well enough, it seemed, to be my rock of support.

About two months after our movie day, Shani called me on the eve of Passover. She half asked, half informed me that she was in a taxi on her way from Queens to Lakewood, with her infant son. Her elder daughter Micki had stayed behind with Felix, who she had been arguing with and now wanted to leave.

When she got to my house, she proceeded to regale me with the story of her taxi ride, which she somehow managed to turn into a hilarious adventure. She talked nonstop. She had a cup of wine, and then she went to sleep for over twelve hours, while I took care of her baby.

When she woke, we sat around my dining room table and shared childhood stories. We laughed as we mimicked the expression on Hindy's face when Shani visited her home in a skirt slit up to the thigh. "I had tights on underneath!" Shani exclaimed. "But I may as well have been naked. I don't think she ever recovered!"

Shani noticed that I had set the oven at 356 degrees, and wondered out loud, "That's kinda creative of you." I wanted to hug her. We weren't very affectionate, us sisters, so instead I just shared my entire inner dialogue, the whole analysis, kit and caboodle—our version of love.

"Cookbooks aren't the boss of me, I decided. I am just so tired of being told what to do." The words had spikes on them. They came out sharper than I meant them, and suddenly I realized just how controlled I had been feeling, just how powerless.

Shani ate my gooey pineapple upside-down cake, made with my creative interpretation of the cookbook instructions, and teased me, "I think you've discovered an even better way to do this!" I hadn't realized how much I missed that sisterly banter, how my very bones yearned for it.

Over the next couple of days, Shani was exuberant when awake, wanting to do new or fun things, go to the park, hear everything about my divorce drama. But she needed her sleep. I suspected that her medications, if she was on them, made her tired.

Those were my few days of having a break from being a single parent to my own three- and one-year-old. But I took care of her son anyway, because I loved him, and I loved his mom, and she needed me. And the truth was, I needed her, too. She was the only one of my sisters who still acted like a sister.

A few days later, Shani returned to her husband, and all seemed well. And yet, I wondered about whether she was truly stable. I worried that her reality was not quite the same as everyone else's.

I Can Kiss Away the Pain

I no longer sat on the couch and pretended to read the same Orthodox magazine over and over again to avoid going upstairs to my husband. Instead, I watched TV and called Shani whenever I wanted to. I wore my hair in a messy bun and walked around in pajama pants. One evening, I sat on the icy cold kitchen tiles that were close enough to reach my internet cable wire, and I thought, *Fuck it*. I didn't bother to censor the curses anymore. I was pretty sure God had already given up on monitoring my sinful mind.

I opened my pink laptop and I googled until I found what I was looking for: Match.com. I tiptoed up the stairs before going any further. I made sure Avigdor was sound asleep, his blanket moving gently with his soft breaths, one tiny foot sticking out in the dark. I found Shira in her crib, round cheeks smushed against the pink gingham sheet, tiny lips smiling as she dreamed. I was home free. It was my time. I took a deep breath, and then typed and typed and uploaded and typed some more.

I still didn't know exactly what I wanted. *Trust your gut*, I told my clients. Me, personally, I didn't have a gut. I felt the ache in my breasts when I saw newborn babies, the residue of having nursed my own. I knew when my legs were sore from running up and down the stairs to get bottles and then sippy cups and extra wipes. That whole swath of me in between the end of my rib cage and the top of my thighs—it felt like nothing at all. I had given my gut to God in a series of blind sacrifices over the last four years.

The last thing I remembered feeling, before I gave myself away, was her. Dassa.

I wondered if she still felt me, if she remembered holding my chin in her hand, pulling me close. I wondered if she thought about me as she lay underneath her husband, in the desert settlement outside Tel Aviv, miles away from the nearest internet café.

I needed to find out who I was after stealing my body back from God. I watched the little arrow on my screen hover over the button "woman seeking woman." I pressed down, watched the button turn green, and forced myself to breathe. In. Out. In.

I read up on the internet guidance for blind first dates before I responded to Cathy's cheery direct message. I couldn't afford to go into it uninformed. I needed to know what to expect, how to stay safe, and what exactly would be expected of me. The internet said it was important to meet in a neutral location and to get there by myself. In retrospect, I wondered about the inherent imbalance in my dates with Yossi. He had always picked me up in his little green Mitsubishi, and that meant I was stuck until he decided to drive me home. I would not get stuck again. Not ever.

I showed up at a Starbucks off the New Jersey Turnpike right on time, and I spotted her through the tinted glass. She was slight, face leaning to the side, straight dark hair falling over high cheekbones. She looked smaller than me. *Good*, I thought, *I don't have to worry about being attacked.* I exhaled, dropped my shoulders down from around my earlobes, and walked in the door, trying to ignore the thumping in my heart.

Cathy jumped up from her stool, pulled out the one across from her, and looked right at me. I felt the jitters turn to a slight tremble, and then fade away as we talked.

I tried not to be obvious as I scanned her narrow body for signs of a bulging weapon. Nothing. I held my grande blond roast with both hands. I knew better than to let anyone near my drink. The internet said that could lead to being drugged and raped. I started to wonder if the people on Google knew anything about anything when I heard her voice trip over itself. "Thank you for meeting me. I was so happy when I saw your message on Match." She didn't seem like an attacker at all. In fact, she looked a little bit nervous as she ran a delicate hand along her thigh.

"Are you cold?" she asked, and started to pull her own sweater off her shoulders when she saw me look briefly at the ceiling vents. I wanted to answer, but I was stunned and trying too hard not to stare. Her bare arms were smooth, and tan, and I could see the edge of a delicate collarbone swooping, graceful. I felt something come alive in parts of my body I had not yet been taught to name. I swallowed the sensation and found the words, "No, but thank you so much."

I told her all about my children and my divorce. I had learned my lesson. Better to put all of it right out there at the beginning. Yossi never forgave me for the things he did not learn about my crazy family before we walked down that long, predetermined aisle. Maybe I was trying to prevent another catastrophe. Maybe I was trying to scare her away.

Later that night, I sent her an email layered with mixed messages, like a basket of my children's magnet tiles. Little colored pieces with opposing forces fighting among each other and then clamping together, hard.

"My life is complex," I wrote. "I am complex—if it's too much for you, just let me know." I pushed her away and desperately hoped she'd stay.

When her email arrived, a full twelve hours and twenty-eight minutes later, I had to blink the moisture out of my eyes to read it. "It was very nice meeting you too! I enjoyed our face-to-face chat. You say your life is complex, but no, that's not too much for me. I feel the same way—that I'd like to get to know you better." I was not allowed to want, but I wanted so hard that even I, a person grown used to responding robotically, couldn't stop.

We continued to meet in coffee shops and send emails to each other about life and love. I was delighted when she simply asked me about my day and seemed to want to hear my answers. When she leaned close, I felt a thrum in the space where my gut used to be, like the low rumble of a car engine before it started. I imagined what it might be like to hold her in my arms, to feel her skin against mine.

"So, I'm dating someone."

I told Shani about the general scope of it, using gender-neutral pronouns and hearing my own voice shake. "It's a lawyer, which is probably pretty good, right? That means they're intellectual like I am, and our conversations are fascinating." She, of course, wanted to know all about him.

This was Shani, I reminded myself. The one who owned denim pants and wore them when she rode her bike to Queens College, as she worked on finishing her degree. She colored outside all the lines, singing as she did it.

I plunged in so fast, before I could stop myself. "It is actually not a man."

Suddenly, my body was static electricity, bristling with fear. What if this was one step too far, even for Shani? What if this was the straw that made me lose my very last sister?

"Malka! That's fantastic! What is she like? When can I meet her?"

Shani's voice always sounded like there was a bubbling stream behind it, about to spill over with the sheer wonder of living. I let it wash over me, douse my electric panic. Shani still loved me. Even though. Even though I was dating "not a man," and even though that vague confession was my only way to describe my own sexual identity.

Three months into my divorced life, I realized that I was splitting myself in two again.

I had a job at a Hasidic girls' school, among students in plaid pleated skirts just like the ones I wore at their age. There I was Malka, the religious social worker who blended right in, in my long skirt and barely there makeup. I hosted groups of eight-year-olds in my small basement office, where they strung crystal beads while I taught social communication. I handed tissues to mothers who disclosed what was really happening at home and asked me to help their daughters cope. I welcomed teachers to hang out, as we shared plates of pasta and fish sticks from the lunchroom. We talked about the Purim costumes we sewed from scratch for our children, about how we hoped the snow would melt in time for the holiday.

Outside my job, I was Sara, the new divorcée. I bought a new wardrobe of body-hugging sweaters and trendy studded boots. I drove out of Lakewood, scanning the road behind me in my rearview mirror as I pulled some of my own hair from under my wig and then blended the real and artificial strands together with a wide toothed comb. I pulled my sleeves up above my elbows, sprayed Lancôme Trésor on my neck, and drove over the county border to Cathy.

One crisp March evening, I drove us to a rainbow-filled bar in Asbury Park. Cathy seemed at ease, with one elbow on the polished wood bar counter, smiling right at me. When she turned toward the bartender and ordered for us both, I whipped my long wig behind my shoulder and took it all in. There were men in skintight jeans leaning into each other. A woman with tattoos and a baseball cap, who tucked her lover's long blond hair behind a jeweled ear. I squinted in the dim bar lighting, scanned the entire room. No one was staring. No one was stopping them. When Cathy turned back toward me and handed me a green glass bottle, I allowed myself to bend in close. Soft pop music filled the space between us, *you are beautiful, no matter what they say.*

When I spoke, my voice was right on beat. "You. You are so, so beautiful."

She smiled, and I felt light inside my rib cage, almost like I could fly.

Cathy told me I looked really sexy in my skirt. Later, in the darkness of her suburban driveway, she reached for me. Her small block in Central

Jersey was a safe zone, but I still surveyed the street to make sure no errant Orthodox Jews had wandered across the Lakewood town line.

I felt her lips on mine and wanted to stay right there, forever. She pulled me closer, and I felt her toned body fit right into my own slight frame. It was the first thing that felt right in a long time. I felt her move against me under the stars. Her cheek brushed mine, so soft. It had been too long since I felt a smooth jaw, one without rough manly stubble scratching at me. I shut my mind off and ran my fingers underneath the edges of her turtleneck.

I was so caught up in her breath on my face and her tongue behind my earlobe and the taste of mint in her mouth, then mine, that I almost didn't notice what was happening. I felt the edge of her bra underneath my fingers before I felt the inside of me. My gut, the part that had been gone for so very long, it was back. Something inside me was flickering. It moved through me, until my hips were pressed to hers, until I could feel the sparks underneath her skin, too.

Stop! I yelled at myself through the smoky powder in my mind, *Stop.* I couldn't think when I felt like that, and I needed to think. I couldn't remember why. But I made an excuse and got into my car and tried to ignore the pulsing sensation between my thighs the whole way home.

The next morning, I woke up and fed my babies Cheerios at the glass kitchen table. They babbled together, as Avigdor poured his sippy cup of soy milk onto the plastic tray of Shira's high chair. She splashed the runny milk with her pudgy fingers and rubbed it into her wispy curls.

I looked into Avigdor's twinkling blue eyes. "Soy milk goes in a bowl or a cup, *zeeskeit*. Not on a baby's tray." I kissed his round cheek and then cleaned baby Shira over the kitchen sink. I packed bags of snacks in their little knapsacks. Shira was in a matzah and jelly phase. Avigdor got chocolate pudding in his lunch box, as he had every day for the past year.

I walked them to the playgroup building and dropped them off in gender-separate classrooms. Toddler boys in one room, toddler girls in another. They would graduate to segregated buildings on opposite sides of town the following year. I waved to the other mothers in headscarves and wigs, holding their own babies and bags full of formula and diapers and sandwiches. I looked modestly to the ground when the fathers passed by me, rushing with children tucked under their arms, tzitzis strings hanging below their suit jackets.

There were only mommies and daddies. There were no mommies and mommies or daddies and daddies. That couldn't happen here.

Cathy couldn't happen. I replayed the kiss in my mind and painted it black. She was just a girl. A non-Jewish girl at that. Whatever I felt, it couldn't be right.

I knew what the rules were when I agreed to follow them. Technically, Jewish law was very murky around female homosexuality. In some ways, it felt like God didn't believe two women could even have a meaningful sexual relationship. He hadn't bothered to expressly forbid it. I wondered if a penis was required for actual, real sex, since only acts involving a penis were mentioned in the Torah.

I was caught in the odd space again, between my feelings and God's. My longing for Cathy felt palpable, seductive, dangerous. God, I figured, would probably wave a large white hand at us and just say, "Keep it down, girls," and then look away until we were done making love. I didn't suppose he cared that much.

However, even if it was not technically that sinful, where would it lead me? What if once I allowed myself to want women again, I couldn't stop? I could never have a public relationship with a woman. Yossi had made sure to include not only the Torah, the seminal texts of Jewish scripture, but also the titles of giant tomes with add-on prohibitions in our custody agreement, the Shulchan Oruch and the Mishnah Berura. Those books held admonitions against living like the non-Jews, against being immodest, against following desires of the heart and the physical flesh. If lesbianism wasn't expressly forbidden, I was sure that Yossi and the rabbis could find other phrases that applied, that labeled me a sinner. To keep my children, I needed to follow the most stringent version of God's word.

I felt the shadow world brush against my soul, threatening to pull me under. If I deviated, custody would be transferred to Yossi. And it would have been my fault, my choice of fireworks over custody, Cathy over my children. I could overcome this. I would overcome it.

"I'm sorry," I typed into the small email screen, keeping my heart bound in ancient stone. "I don't think we are a good fit. You are truly unique, and I want to give you the respect of valuing your time. Best of luck, truly."

I shut the screen down and it went dark. Done.

Four months after my divorce, I realized that as long as I lived in the beige prefab neighborhood I would only be able to flap my wings up and down in place. The houses were so close that I closed all the blinds before I turned my laptop on, so that none of the black-clad neighbors would notice a blue light coming out of my windows. It was so homogenous that my friend Declan from the psych unit could never pick me up in his truck without everyone thinking I must have become a prostitute after my divorce.

I sold my diamond ring, and it was enough for first and last month's rent on a house at the edge of Lakewood. The house had three floors and a huge grassy backyard and even a fence. It was in a neighborhood where the men and ladies sometimes had Shabbos dinners with other married couples. Where some of the ladies wore a few strands of their own hair outside their headscarves and nobody said anything.

On moving day, I helped nice, muscular men find the garage, where they dumped the heavy mahogany dressers and headboards from my old life. I showed them my sun-filled bedroom, where they put my brand-new queen-sized bed right in the center. It was my small splurge, bought with the leftover diamond ring money. The new bed meant that I was free of the sharp slices of memories that haunted me at night. I would not have to sleep at the edge of my mattress anymore, trying to avoid the parts of it that made my throat close and my hands shake. His rings, ironically, had paid for my freedom.

As the movers put the final slats of Shira's crib together, a man came running up the stairs. His eyes were excited over his fluffy beard. "Welcome to the neighborhood!" He smiled at me, even though I wore a denim skirt and a bright red bandanna over my long wig. "Thank you!" I smiled back, so grateful to be acknowledged. His next words though, they showed me just how far I would ever be from normal, even in the new house. "Where is your husband? I want to say hello!" When I told him there was no husband, that it was just me and the kids, he shrunk back down the stairs and out the front door as if the house were made of flames.

I was still not one of them.

I had made some sin-filled decisions, but I could still snap it back. I had not done anything irrevocable. I always wore full garb within our town limits. The Cathy stuff had happened far away from Lakewood. The clear drinks and tiny bikini happened in a whole other country.

I could get married again to a Jewish man. It was the only realistic future.

I unpacked, bathed the children, tucked them in, and then slid my knees under my birch Ikea desk. No more crouching in the corner of the kitchen to watch TV with the shades drawn. In the new house, I had a proper Wi-Fi connection and several yards of land between me and the nosy neighbors.

I knew that I was not willing to trust a matchmaker ever again. I did the next best thing and created profiles on frumster.com and sawyouat sinai.com, Orthodox Jewish dating websites. I posted a picture of myself on moving day, standing on my lawn in my tight jean skirt that covered only half of my kneecaps. The full-length picture communicated, "I am young and skinny. I flirt with the edges of religion, but I live inside them." I paused at creating a profile name and then it came to me: *aftertherain*. If the guys were smart, they would ask me what the rain was like, and what I hoped to find in the after.

At first, there was a slew of *u up* and *heyyyy* and *hottie* messages. Then a knight in shining grammar showed up. *Sounds like you've been through something,* he wrote. His name was Isaac, and when I learned that he was a doctor, I became even more intrigued. That could work. Me and an educated Jewish man.

We met at a small café in Park Slope and chatted over mugs of coffee, in sentences we soon completed for each other. I felt him checking me out when I stood up to use the restroom.

Ever since my divorce, something strange and thrilling had begun to happen. For the first time, men noticed me. Maybe I exuded whorish-sinner vibes, or maybe I just hadn't looked around before. It happened every time I went out, at the Wawa when I filled cups with coffee, at Rite Aid when I wheeled a double stroller around and bought diapers, and even at day-care drop-off. When a guy friend called me a "pretty young thing," I dared to hope that it was true. I stood straighter and I made eye contact and smiled at people. I knew that the short knit dress I had on was one that got more looks than usual, and Isaac appeared to be no exception to the other men.

He did not hesitate to tell me, "I like you. When can we do this again?"

Isaac planned fun dates for us, afternoon picnics at Brooklyn Botanical Garden, bowling at places that served cocktails, and hookah bars where we sat on embroidered cushions and talked.

As we passed a cherry-flavored bong between us one evening, he shared his dream of building an upscale private practice with some of his med school friends. I told him that I had not dreamed, not in a long time. He nudged, gently, until I remembered. Back in the before, I did have one dream. It was hazy now, covered in debris, miles and years away, but as he put a hand on my thigh and looked at me like I was someone who mattered, I could see the dream again.

"I always wanted a PhD in psychology," I said quickly, and took a gulp of my drink.

"You should absolutely do that," he said, without furrowing his brows or looking around for distractions. His jade eyes met mine, and the chatter around us seemed to disappear until all I saw was him, leaning forward slowly.

I knew he was going to kiss me before it happened. I made a split-second decision to angle my face forward, to put a hand on the back of his head. When his tongue found mine and the space between us disappeared, I felt it. A pleasant sort of rush in my head, a sensation like cotton candy dissolving in my mouth, down my throat. It felt nice.

I was so, so relieved to be feeling nice with a man.

I threw my credit card onto the low table, a move that was more masculine than I intended. I kept my chin tucked into his neck until the check was paid and I grabbed his hand and headed outside. Under the city streetlight, I reached for his biker-thin body and pulled it against mine.

"I want to feel you." His voice was like a low rumble of thunder, too bedroom for the street.

"Me too," I whispered, surprised to realize that it was true—though perhaps not for the same reason as his. I wanted, I needed, to find out if it was just Yossi that made my body shut down, or whether the same thing would happen with all men. I needed to know if I could make it to heaven one day, with less sacrificing than I'd done before.

Later, I was scared to death and so I made the only sane decision I could think of. I scheduled a call with Rabbi Levi. The rules were starting to feel like a maze of death traps. I needed to know that our next moves were sanctioned.

"It's okay, Malkaleh. You may ask."

Rabbi Levi listened as I told him all about Isaac, and how I didn't want to sinfully engage in extramarital sex, and I didn't want to make Isaac sin, but it felt inevitable.

"This is a dangerous conversation, Malkaleh. If I give you permission to do these things with him, will he ever marry you?"

The rabbi was trying. He really was. But he didn't realize that the Jewish men who fit my dating status, diminished by the divorce and the kids, that category of men expected sex. They just did. They wore kippahs and wanted a kosher home, but they also wanted to sleep with the women they dated. If I didn't give it to them, someone else would. And I would never get to stand under another chuppah.

Rabbi Levi heard my long pause, and he sighed a gentle sigh. He gave me the loophole I sought: I was permitted to immerse myself in a *mikvah* before sleeping with Isaac. The *mikvah* was intended for married women, but by immersing before sleeping with Isaac, I could help us both avoid the deepest depths of hell. It was like stealing candy from a store and then putting an identical candy back on the shelf a week later. It was officially less bad, but still morally shaky. I felt like I was deceiving God to save my own soul.

"You are a princess, and you will always be a holy child of God, no matter where you go and what you do. Always remember that."

Rabbi Levi left me with words that brought tears to my eyes. If he believed that, then maybe, just maybe, all was not lost for me, not yet. I had lost so much in the last few years. The respect of my sisters. My virginity. My marriage. The chance to raise my children with both of their parents in the same home. The last thing I wanted to lose, the last thing holding me together, was God. I wanted to believe that he still watched over me.

As I walked down the steps and into the warm waters of the *mikvah*, I prepared to connect with God.

I had a different prayer than usual. I floated underneath the water, made sure not to clench any part of my body so the water could purify every crevice. *Please make him want me. Please make this work. I want to do your will. Please help me. Help my children be untouched by my sins. Help me make a real Jewish home for them.* My tears blended in with the warm rainwater.

"Kosher!" the *mikvah* lady proclaimed. I had immersed properly, and I was kosher again.

I walked my naked, pure, glistening body up the stairs and into the robe she held open for me. She saw the moisture in my eyes.

"Mazal tov!"

I texted Isaac, "Mission accomplished."

"Room already booked," he responded. He knew that I wouldn't have sex with him until I was at peace with the Holy One. And he was ready. So was I. Ready to see if he could fill me in ways that would feel right for once.

I packed the children first. Yossi lived at his parents' home, back among the dripping crystal fixtures and gold-tasseled tapestries. There, the yards of granite countertop were always stocked with chocolate-filled pastries and warm trays of his mother's cooking. Still, my heart crumpled into itself when I pictured little Avigdor in his wire-rimmed glasses wandering around the cavernous rooms of the house. I didn't even want to imagine baby Shira, looking at the faces around her, seeing her grandmother's pinched smile, her grandfather's round red face, and her father's cold blue stare, as she searched for me.

I packed their favorite teddy bears, little ziplock bags with complete outfits labeled "Friday night" and "Shabbos day." I typed a list of feeding schedules and instructions and placed it in the little suitcase and zipped it all up along with a chunk of my heart. *He has visitation rights*, I reminded myself, and if I refused the visits there would be an ugly custody battle, the outcome of which would be out of my control.

I packed my own bag with all new items of lace and spandex, things that Victoria's Secret recommended for the sort of weekend I was about to try. I tasted the bitterness in my throat, the bile retained from the last time I purchased items with which to sell my body. I was not sure how I felt about sex in general. But I was determined not to let him define the whole of it for me.

When I pulled up to the address that Isaac sent, I saw a shuttered house set innocently against the Jersey Shore. My hands seemed stuck to the steering wheel, knuckles protruding. *Just breathe*, I said to myself, gulping hot air through my nostrils. Nostrils. I laughed, shakily, remembering Avigdor pointing to his own little nose and asking what the holes in it were called. When Isaac's cobalt Beetle appeared in my rearview mirror, I shoved the shakiness all the way down and forced a smile. He held up bags labeled with the name of a luxury kosher supermarket, grinned in my direction, glowed in the warm setting rays of the summer sun.

I kept my trembling heart down below the sound of my carefree laugh, my pleasant tone, as we unpacked and settled in and lit the Shabbos tea lights that he had thoughtfully packed. Then we fell into twenty-five hours of each other.

For the first time, I was with a man and my muscles weren't clenched, I wasn't trying to eject his body from mine. I wasn't crying, and there was no pain. I was okay. I was so thrilled to be feeling okay. I climbed on top of Isaac, looked down into his eyes, and watched them turn. Seafoam to dark jade, in sync with the deepening of his breath, the grasping of his arms around my waist.

It was fun to watch him get turned on by me. I glanced at myself in the full-length mirror, afternoon sunlight reflecting off my skin. I was kind of turned on by me too—by the power I had.

It might be enough, I thought, enough to keep me interested for a while, if not forever.

Isaac had also given me a more crucial gift. The blossoming hope that maybe, just maybe, I could work my way back into a normal Jewish life. I could see the vision start to take shape, me in a white gown standing under another holy canopy, sipping wine that had been blessed by a rabbi. My children, being raised in a home with me and a kind, kippah-wearing man, up until they were old enough to find proper Jewish spouses and stand under canopies of their own. Maybe I could clear the weeds that had started to block my children's paths toward heaven.

I Like the Way It Hurts

A little kernel of doubt formed in my mind. Isaac was light and fun. He dotted his i's and crossed his t's with quiet, doctorly diligence. With him, I was light and fun and professional, too. I never told him about the fear that lived in my throat, the way I worried, every day, about losing my children. I didn't share how many times each night I left my bed and peeked into my children's rooms, just to make sure they hadn't been taken away, that they were still breathing.

On my way out of work one day, I texted Declan, a colleague I had grown close to.

Not sure he is deep enough for me, he's just too happy too often.

Then I pulled out of the hospital parking lot.

Isaac called me, moments later, his voice incredulous. "Did you mean to send me that?" I checked my phone, scrolled frantically through the texts, and realized I sent my words about him *directly to him.*

Isaac, who was not even a therapist, called it a Freudian slip. I took too much pride in my own knowledge of the unconscious mind to pretend that wasn't true. By the end of the day, Isaac had decided he needed a break.

Before we hung up for the last time, he gave me one last backhanded gift. "I don't know what's going on with you. You're kind of a mess. But get that PhD. You deserve it."

Between raising two toddlers, training the staff at work, and studying for Graduate Record Exams, I became sufficiently distracted from dating.

I kept a stack of GRE vocabulary flash cards in my car, where I scanned and committed them to memory at stop signs, red lights, and crosswalks. At the side of the road one day, I talked to myself out loud: "Censure: verb. Sara was censured for getting a divorce."

The sound of metal-on-metal crashed through my study session before I felt my head hit the steering wheel. In the stillness that followed, I sat up and scanned my limbs. All intact. I opened the car door and stepped out onto the street to find a small, bearded man waving his hands around, tzitzis strings flailing in the breeze.

"Oy! Don't worry about it!" I could see the front bumper of his car out there on the ground, bearing a tan streak that matched my Altima.

"What happened?" I stared at the space behind the dandruff flakes on his dark suit jacket.

"I thought you were parked; I didn't see you signal," he explained. "Just a little bump, it doesn't matter! Are you okay?" I looked down at my stockinged feet, neat and lined up in my flat shoes. "Yes. I think so." He was right. I forgot to signal before trying to turn. But he didn't seem bothered.

"That's the most important thing. Praise God." He smiled through the beard, bowed his black hat back into the driver's side of his banged-up car and drove away.

Later that week, I sighed and looked for a body shop. The lease on the Altima was almost up, and I couldn't return it in its current state. There were two major body shops on the road leading out of Lakewood, both lots crammed with broken vehicles. It was almost a signal of righteousness when one drove around with dents in our neighborhood. A missing bumper or dented car door meant, *Look at me, focusing so hard on follow-ing God's will that I don't have time for earthly nonsense.* I had been to the body shop on the left side of the road with Yossi, when the taillight on his ten-year-old Buick died. Therefore, I chose the shop on the right, so I would not have to answer questions about where my husband was, and whether he approved the repairs.

By the time I got my dented car down the road, I was tired. The work that it took to keep my feelings shoved into compartments, to keep the information running through my mind, was exhausting. During the day, I ran admissions and supervised a team of therapists who were responsi-ble for helping women heal from abuse. The women arrived at our facility with scrapes and wounds. Some of the damage was visible on their skin, dark spots along their arms and discolored streaks on their faces, from violent attacks by those they trusted. Some of the scars were so deep that they were only visible through worn eyes, dragging feet, shaky hands.

I got home to scars of my own. Children who arrived back from time at their father's looking so lost that it took all I had to hold the pieces of my heart together. To greet them with a calm routine and a face that said, *It will all be okay.* I was so far from okay; I could barely remember what that felt like.

"You wrecked this up pretty good." He looked at me, then at the folded metal along the side of the vehicle, and back at me.

I saw the question mark on his too-tanned face. I ignored it.

"How much will this be to fix?" There was no time for conversation. I needed the car fixed in less than the amount of time it took me to drive down the road to the body shop.

"You have somewhere to be?" There was a quiet consideration in his deep voice. I noticed a kippah on the skin of his reddened scalp. I decided to chance it. Maybe he understood what it was like to juggle too many things at the same time.

"I need this car to drive my kids around. I am a single mother." He moved his lean body closer to me, and closer to the wreckage of my vehicle. He quoted a price. "I'll give you a deal on this." He walked me past the other banged-up cars, past the men in grease-covered clothes wielding metal instruments under the hot sun. He helped me rent a car and waited with me until it was delivered right to the edge of the tarmac.

At some point, he introduced himself.

"I'm Ben. I'm divorced too."

He extended a hand for me to shake. I was too grateful, and too drained, to care that it was a clear test of my religiosity. I shook his hand, with full knowledge of what the gesture communicated, at the edge of Lakewood: I was a Rule Breaker. If I would touch a man's palm in broad daylight, who even knew what I would do under the cover of night?

He texted me later, and I remembered that I had put my number down on the stack of forms that covered his desk. "How r u?" I tried to stay polite and distant. I failed.

A few days later, Ben pulled up at Starbucks, an hour late. I threw my GRE study guide in the slick leather back seat of his car, tucked myself inside the tinted windows, and waited. Instead of an explanation, he had a plan.

The plan landed us at the boardwalk, four plastic cups of vodka-cranberry on a tiny wooden table in front of us. I did the social work thing and asked him questions about himself while we drank. He asked questions in return, but his felt like gentle feathers teasing at my façade. By the time the alcohol seeped through my veins and turned the volume down on my many thoughts, I was already intoxicated. He had cracked the code! He knew how to be Orthodox, and divorced, and still smell the sea salt, still laugh and flirt on a summer night.

We walked along the shore, and he showed me how to break into a private area of the beach. I worried, for one split second, about the loosening of my tight grip of control. But my muscles had been pulled so tight, grasping that control for so very long, that they seemed to have lost their iron-clad strength. I didn't want to fight anymore.

When he put a hesitant arm around my shoulder and waited to see if I would pull away, I leaned in. He smelled like cigarettes and Doublemint gum and escape. I turned my narrow chin into the whisper-soft cotton of his shirt and stayed. When I felt the brush of his lips on mine, I kissed him without thinking about anything but the taste of him. *He's a good kisser*, I thought, before that thought was followed by the cacophony of others until they faded away into the dark and my mind went still. As the midnight waves fell over each other onto the pale sand, I too began to fall.

I walked through the motions of my days. I filed paperwork and ran support groups and wrote admissions essays. I ran home and heated frozen pizza and cut little fingernails and kissed tiny cheeks. Ben became an electric thread through it all. His text messages were microdoses of painkillers.

He showed me NJ nightlife and worked around my babysitter's schedule with no complaints at all. He parked on quiet streets so I could peel the long garments off my body and change into slinky dresses. He entered beachfront clubs before I did, checking to make sure they were safe, free of community members who could report my naked arms and legs to the rabbis. He understood the stakes. He too kept a kippah in his glove compartment, popped it back onto his head when we passed exit 88 on the parkway, one mile before we hit Lakewood.

Like me, Ben had loved and lost, first his religious wife, and then a girlfriend he slipped and mentioned every time heartbreak music played around us, at clubs, on his car radio, and in the music videos that served as constant background in his cabin. The year was 2009, and heartbreak songs were everywhere. I watched Megan Fox engulfed in flames on screens around his home way too often as Rihanna's "Love the Way You Lie" blared repeatedly. My heart was shredded too. With Ben, the fraying edges and the broken parts of me were right at home. We did not have to explain our pain to each other. We got right to work on helping each other forget.

I learned that Atlantic City was a great place to forget. Ben seemed like a sort of VIP down there. He kept plastic casino cards in his wallet: Harrah's, Tropicana, Borgata. They greeted him with free rooms and drinks and invitations to high-stakes poker games in back rooms. When we got back to our hotel rooms after he'd gambled through stacks of chips, we sank into each other. If sex with Ben were cake, it was decadent chocolate brownie soaked in vodka. It slid down through me with no sensation at all. My body felt a pleasant sort of numbness, which allowed me to move and bend and do the things he wanted. In return, he gave me a raft to hang on to amid the crashing tides of my world.

"Let's play Russian roulette," he whispered.

My hands were up against the wall. I didn't know why. It was just instinctual as soon as I saw the gun. I was lying on sheets that smelled like old socks, feeling the little pills of cotton on my naked body. It was dark in his bedroom. Stagnant in a way that evoked years of bodily fluids and cigarette ashes.

He came closer and I felt it against my temple. Hard and very metallic. He bent his head over me and chuckled in my ear. "I'm just messing with you. You can handle it right?"

I paced around inside my head. This didn't feel like play. My breath stuck in my throat, and I felt frozen in place. *I'm such a baby*, I thought. *Real women would know this is hot.* I pictured the movies we had watched, dominatrixes in tall leather boots and shiny red lipstick sending their whips through the air and leaving splotches of pink on bare skin. That must be the kind of thing that excited Ben.

Never contradict a man, the teachers lectured to us in seminary. *Their egos are fragile.* My job was to look at the man, the very tall and muscular man holding a pistol to my head, and use my inner wisdom to help shape him into a better person. *Bina Yeseirah.* That's what they taught me. Or maybe that's just what I heard.

"Nice gun, Ben, very impressive." I covered the shaking in my voice with a casual laugh. My insides were static. On edge. So loud.

"I knew you'd love this." He ran the hard metal from my temple down across my face, my jaw. I tried to act cool, but images of my children flashed inside my eyelids. Who would make sure Avigdor never ate dairy and carried his EpiPen everywhere? Who would hold Shira until she fell asleep at night and then gently tuck her tiny body into her crib? They barely even talked. How would they understand anything at my funeral? At my shiva. At their father's house, where they would be stuck in a life-time of chandeliers and icy distance.

The gun was on my shoulder blade, running down the sides of my rib cage. If there was even a miniscule chance that he would pull the trig-ger, I couldn't afford the risk. So I played. I turned my inside shaking into enough energy to raise my hips off the bed as the metal hit them. "That is so fucking hot, give me more . . ." I moaned out loud, parted my legs slowly. "You and that gun, you're such a badass, you're turning me on," I said in the voice of someone else entirely.

His eyes turned to dark glitter. I saw the nicotine stains on his teeth as he moved above me. "This is the big leagues." He held the gun between my legs. I felt the hard metal against my soft skin. I played so hard, I played for my life. For my babies and their future. I smiled at him, turned my breathlessness into breathiness. "Fuck me now, hard." I looked him in the eye, deep, the way I knew worked on him. He dropped the weapon, finally, and turned me over.

The lines on the sheets blurred as I held back all the panic. The gun was on the hardwood floor, to my right, near the nightstand. He grunted and panted above me. I ignored him. I kept my eye on the floor, which was easy enough. He liked to see me on all fours, so my facial expression was not important anymore. He thrusted. I calculated. He grunted. I strate-gized. He grabbed. I moaned like I had learned from all the porn he kept running on the dust-covered TV. I was a quick study. I picked things up and I used them.

And then I was standing, and his enormous bicep was around my neck and the gun was back in his hand. "That was fucking insane," he said, chapped lips grazing my cheek. I wondered if he was referring to the sex, but that was the farthest thing from my mind. All I wanted was to have the gun far, far away from my body.

My babies were home, in bed, with their overpaid and highly qualified and very religiously devout babysitter. I had left the house with a long skirt over my jeans, told her I was going out with some friends. How would she find out that I was dead? How many hours would pass before she got alarmed? All she had was my cell phone number. Would he answer it, after he buried me underneath the snow and the cigarette butts that littered the deserted backyard of his cabin? It was not a coincidence, I thought quietly, that he lived surrounded by trees. *Don't be dramatic*, I chastised myself, *it's almost over.*

I pressed my narrow frame against the rough skin of his chest. "You don't have the guts to shoot this. Let me see you try." I bit my lower lip and slid deeper into the headlock. Submissive and flirtatious and letting him take all the control. He pointed the gun at my head. I heard a click. No more safety. And then I felt my body jerk at the same moment that the explosion hit my eardrums.

Wait. I was still alive. If I heard the gunshot, I must have been breathing! Unless I was in hell. I looked down and saw a bullet lodged in the floorboards. I picked it up. "My souvenir," I said lightly and watched, wary, as he finally, finally put the goddamned thing back in a drawer full of musty old boxer shorts.

I won. I got him to believe that none of it fazed me. Ha! I was the best actress alive! I deserved an Academy Award! I saw myself in a long, fashion-forward gown with slits up to my hip, posing on a red carpet, flirting with the cameras. The adrenaline turned to thrill, and dopamine, and I felt alive.

I kept that bullet in the coin pocket of the Bosca leather wallet my tante Faigy bought me for my Bais Yaakov twelfth grade graduation present. I didn't know why. I just knew I needed it.

It turned out, my seminary teachers had all the wisdom I would need for this particular man: Do what your husband says. Figure out the needs he has, even those he can't say. Never judge or police him. Just accept him.

How did they know that was the way to keep a man? I was astounded by the brilliance of it. They even knew to warn us: the outside world will tell you there is such a thing as "love." The rabbis would roll their eyes and make us all laugh at that. True love, they instructed, was about giving. The Hebrew word for love, *ahava*, came from the word *hav*, "give." We loved those to whom we gave. That was how we built relationships.

Ben and I spent the weekend at the Tropicana in Atlantic City. Ben sucked on Parliament Lights the whole way down, flicked a cigarette butt out the tinted window every few miles. *Fuck it*, I thought when he offered me one. I inhaled with him, and breathing nicotine into my lungs helped numb the fear that I felt, of being caught in the front seat of his car with my wig off, my hair loose. We continued our rampage to forgetting the moment we parked and accepted complimentary drinks from the concierge. By the time the sun set over the ocean, we were hammered. We wandered from casino to casino, making stops at ATMs along the way so Ben could withdraw more wads of cash.

"I used to hang out here back in the day." His voice was low, rumbling thunder, carrying its own storm within. I looked up at the storefront and through the blur of my drunkenness, I read the neon lights, "full nude" and "girls." Damn. Right near us there were naked curves and skin and soft shapes that I had been trying so hard to block out of my mind. "Let's go!" I said to him, my voice light and jokey, but my heart dead set and sure. "Are you for real?" He turned toward me, swaying just a tiny bit, the edges of a smirk on his lips. "Yeah, I never told you I'm into girls too?" His entire face lit up as the highlighter-pink signs flashed and beckoned us inside.

He sat near me while the sexiest woman I ever touched began to dance. Clementine had waist-length black hair and emerald eyes, and skin that moved through my hands like silk. She glided around me, brushed a smooth cheek against my very still face, laughed, and made the dim cubicle feel full of sparkles. Ben watched me, smiled when I did, and did not seem to care about her at all. He handed her an extra bunch of bills and asked her to keep "taking care of his girl." I caught her eye as she straddled me, flawless butt moving over my thighs, and asked her about herself. I just needed to know everything.

She took my hand, moved it until my fingers were underneath the silver string around her hips. "You can touch me if you want." I did. She was a mermaid, dancing in the air and flipping her waves of hair over my body while she told me that she was a college student, and that dancing was her way to let off some steam. I held on to every speck of attention she threw my way like it was diamond dust, allowing it to cover me until I, too, felt iridescent.

The next day, I put on the red bikini that had been in the bottom of my dresser drawer since Aruba and went to a rooftop pool with Ben and a bottle of vodka. We lay in the late August sun, talking and taking swigs right from the bottle. "That was fucking hot," he said. "I could watch you do that every day for a long time." He told me he had been depressed all summer, until he met me. That this was the first time he'd felt hope in a very long time, since his own divorce. I knew the feeling. I would do anything to keep both of us right there, in that hope.

He threw me a challenge. "I bet you could make out with any girl at this pool." I looked at him, and for the first time, I noticed the shadows behind his smirk. I saw a man who was struggling to hold on to feeling high so that he would not drown in the low, murky waters of his life. I felt lucky to be the person who had helped him stay out of the tangled reeds of despair. We needed each other. And I knew how to make it last.

I turned to the woman on the next chair, offered her a drink, and commented on the music she'd been playing from her speaker. Ben stayed in the background, threw compliments our way, said things like, "The two of you look really sexy right now." It was as if we had practiced it, we were so in sync. I lit the spark, he fueled it, I danced in the flame, he tended to the kindling. When she turned her body toward me and asked for a stick of gum, I knew it was on. We kissed, her lips feeling all wrong on mine, her thick body strange in my bony arms.

This was nothing like I'd imagined. Dassa, Cathy, and even Clementine had offered a delicious sort of intimacy. Every time their skin grazed mine, I felt the soft glow of their touch light me up from the inside. I fought every fiber of my being as it strained toward them. I believed that if I gave in to it, being with a woman would be my absolute undoing.

As the pool woman's orange dyed hair stabbed at my chest under Ben's distant gaze, I felt nothing but mildly repulsed. I guessed it all tasted the same when I was consuming it for the benefit of someone else.

Later, he tugged at the towel I wore around my body, my skin still pink from the scalding shower that did not wash off any part of the afternoon. "You are a fucking badass," he whispered into my neck. "I need you now." *That was so worth it*, I thought, before he plucked the thoughts right out of my head as if they were irrelevant.

"Malkaleh, what happened to you?" I heard Rabbi Levi's voice through the phone and my heart started to crumple. He sounded so worried.

"I'm fine, don't worry." I was on the floor inside my walk-in closet, my back against the hems of so many skirts, fabric that was supposed to be my armor. "I just need permission." I didn't notice how hard I was pulling at the swath of wool above me until the fabric came loose from its hanger and fell over my shoulder. "I need your permission for an ... an—" I gulped and steeled myself. "For an abortion."

"Oy, Malkaleh. I'm so sorry. Who did this to you?"

I willed the tears away and I confessed to my rabbi. I told him everything. How I met Ben and thought he was a nice Jewish boy. The way he seemed like a good match for me because he was also divorced and had a child. I thought it was the right thing to do, that it would earn me a chance at the right kind of marriage.

"I can't tell you to kill the baby, Malkaleh. But I can send you to someone who can help you. He deals with these kinds of things. He's a good man; he knows the law very well." My rabbi gave me a phone number and a blessing for surviving the challenge.

Under the cover of night, I drove to the edge of town, to the renegade rabbi who dealt with questions that came up for those who lived at the very edge of the rules. I was ushered into his book-lined study by a small woman wearing a headscarf around her lined features. The rabbi asked me questions. I protected Ben. I didn't give him the name of the man who impregnated me. Just the information that was needed.

"I'm a single mother. I have two babies." I looked modestly at my folded hands. He looked at me across the dark wood of his desk. "Were you raped?" His Israeli accent made me feel comforted somehow. Like my abba was with me instead of being oblivious to me, to all of it. "No." I was not willing to compromise the integrity of the conversation. I wanted my rabbinic answer to hold up in the eternal court when the time came. He nodded. Gave me the permission I sought.

I scheduled the abortion for a Friday and sat inside a musty clinic office, holding a paper cup with a tiny fatal pill.

I thought about my other pregnancies, about the moments I shared with the growing beings inside me as they kicked against my ribs and poked tiny hands and feet right up to the surface of my skin. I wished I could grow this baby in my body too. I wished I were able to count the weeks until the day when I would drink orange juice and feel the first flutters of the baby's movements in response. I wished I could sing to the growing child within me, sending waves of calm down through my body.

I could just imagine Avigdor and Shira snuggled up against me on the couch, talking to the baby in their own little voices and telling him or her how much love they had to give.

I put one hand on my flat stomach and sighed out loud. The words of my divorce agreement flashed before my eyelids in clear typewriter letters, "*It is agreed by both parties that the children will be raised according to Halacha . . . If it is determined . . . that one party is not raising the children according to Halacha, custody will be transferred to the other biological parent.*" The agreement was clear. If I violated the rules, I lost custody of my children. Having sex outside of marriage was a clear violation of the rules, but not one that anyone could prove.

If I were to walk around Lakewood, pregnant with a child that was conceived through extramarital sexual intercourse, everyone would know. The rabbis would take my children, hand them to Yossi, and I might never see them again. The same rabbis who believed that abortion was a sin were essentially forcing me to get rid of my baby. They were still controlling my body, despite how much I wanted to believe that I was free.

I swallowed the pill before I could feel anymore, before I could change my mind.

Ben stayed with me that night, held me as I grieved the lost life and my long-gone innocence. I had fallen far, so far. Over the next few days, I picked up on hints Ben dropped about other women, and I realized I had been ignoring his darker side in the thrill of our dangerous escapades.

I was too tired to do any calculations. I didn't even feel the sharp blades of my sins slice through me anymore. I saw chunks of myself splattered on the floor. My values. My self-respect. My feelings. They were no longer attached to me. I watched dispassionately as the things that comprised me disappeared.

I was twenty-five years old, and I had been pregnant five times. Two miscarriages. One abortion. Two babies.

I was tumbling, so fast, so hard, just falling through the air, even if no one on the outside could see.

Help Me Unravel

"**M**alk-ah!" Abba greeted me when I entered his Brooklyn warehouse. We walked past his employees, past shelves stocked with piles of prayer shawls and colorful embroidered yarmulkes. He smiled through his beard, and I noticed the new gray streaks and wondered if they were there because of me.

"Avigdor knows most of the Aleph Bais and Shira always shares her toys with the other children at playgroup." I plucked the morsels of good news out of the quagmire of our lives for Abba.

"So, they are the smartest ones in their class?" Abba loved to note our accomplishments. "What about you?"

Genevieve had challenged me to be more real with Abba. To tell him about my struggles. She pointed out, correctly, that my divorce was such a big shock to everyone because I always acted like I had it all together on the outside. "I was asked to supervise a new therapist at work, so I guess they think I'm doing a good job!" Abba's eyes crinkled at the corners. "But it's hard sometimes. I am really tired." I sighed, silently apologizing to Genevieve in my mind. That was the most I could get out. I had already caused Abba way too much pain.

"It's hard sometimes for me also," Abba started, and his face seemed to lose its shield. There was a weariness in the shadows underneath his eyes. "You know, it wasn't easy for me to stay married for all these years." I sat there, stunned, and tried my hardest to keep my neutral therapist face on. Genevieve was right! Maybe I could build a more authentic relationship with him.

"I stayed for you children." He looked at me and I knew, in my core, that it was true. He really believed he had sacrificed his life for me and my siblings. "I was waiting until you all got married off. I wanted to move back to Israel, take care of the business there." It all made sense, looking back. The way Abba always talked about the white stone of the holy land, the fresh pomegranate trees, the thousands of Hasids who sang at the temple built for his rebbe. *You deserve to go and have the life you want*, I wanted to tell Abba. But that was too social work-y. So instead, I said, "I am going to be able to support myself very soon." It was my code for letting him know that I would not stand in his way.

"We still have to marry Mimi off," he said, and then the Abba I knew was back, sitting straight up and opening the metal desk drawer, brisk and sure. The worries that raced around my brain slowed and settled. I was nowhere close to being able to pay my bills or go grocery shopping without Abba's credit card. My divorce agreement left me with all the marital debt, student loans, and six hundred dollars a month of child support from Yossi, which barely covered my car lease and insurance. Since I was the one who asked for the divorce, I deserved to pay the price, I had thought. That was before I realized how it would add up, the cost of Cheerios and babysitters and new shoes for growing little feet.

I felt like I had just taken a whiff of the sharp horseradish that Abba grated from scratch every year for Passover. There was pressure building in my brain, trying to leak through my eyes. A staccato of two competing voices. *How can I ever ask Abba to keep sacrificing himself to take care of me?* And *How will I ever survive if Abba leaves?* Don't worry about that right now, I told myself sternly. I had people to take care of. Immediate problems on my plate, like returning client phone calls and figuring out what to cook for dinner and driving back down the Garden State Parkway in one piece.

In my life plan, I was supposed to go from my father's house to my husband's care, a path that made financial responsibility a superfluous skill. When I disrupted the whole life plan with divorce, finances were the last thing on my mind.

"You know, I give you about one hundred thousand dollars a year," Abba said as he handed me the final stack of twenties and hundreds. "Will you be able to survive when I move?"

"My new job pays well," I told him, not because it was true, but because I wanted him to have the joy he had denied himself through my entire lifetime. I did not give any thought to the actual numbers. One hundred thousand dollars seemed like a whole lot for him to have given me, and I was half sure he was exaggerating.

I barely noticed when bills began to come through the mail slot of our new home. They were addressed to me, with the presumption that I was a person who was adult enough to handle them. I picked them up on my way into the house, balancing knapsacks and holding on to children's little fingers. I saw the bills on the counter out of my peripheral vision, where they blurred together, as I warmed up frozen dinosaur nuggets and asked the kids about their days at school. Sometimes the bills looked orange and kind of neon on that counter, and when that happened it stressed me out, so I threw them in the trash or deep within a drawer to be handled later.

Corporations like PSEG and the phone company seemed like very vague and abstract places to send my meager social work salary. However, the visible people in my life always got paid. The sale of Abba's company, followed by his move to Israel, meant that his money flow became a trickle. My sister Goldy began to manage Abba's funds, which meant that she grudgingly sent me postdated checks for my landlord, along with reminders that

Abba's money was about to run out. The neighborhood grocer accepted checks too, so I was able to buy the children yogurts and cereal and bread. Some weeks all I could afford was a bag of baby carrots for myself, but that was okay too. I was young and healthy. I didn't need much.

The children never knew about the money worries. I made them believe we were rich and lucky. That we had more than enough. We counted the days to Tuesday each week, for Bakery Day, a tradition that we built together. The friendly bakery workers knew us by name, and the women wiped their hands on their aprons as Avigdor and Shira stared into the glass countertops and chose between the Sesame Street cupcakes and fancy pastries. On the good weeks, I got a cheese Danish, my favorite, and we all ate our snacks together in the car on the way home, because why wait when there were baked goods to be enjoyed?

That very car, though, turned out to be uninsured. One of those envelopes must have held the notice about that. Another must have held the warrant for my arrest for unpaid tickets, and the notice that my driver's license was suspended.

I found all that out in a cloud of exhaust on the side of the road.

I was driving down Route 3 in New Jersey, familiar shopping mall strips on either side of the highway, just starting to feel like I had it all under control. I had finally broken up with Ben, which was a huge relief. The children were doing well. Our house was filled with music, with hope, with little dancing feet.

And then I crashed.

There was so much impact that it threw me forward. The lanes before me seemed to freeze. The world went silent and then loud, and I felt the steering wheel hit my chest. As I noticed blue and red flashing lights around us, I remembered that I did not, in fact, have it under control at all.

"License and registration please."

The young officer tapped the rear window. My brain flashed rapidly to the many driving-related envelopes I had received in the mail with large, bright orange labels, stamped *URGENT*. I assessed the officer, neat blond hairline beneath the NJPD hat and black metal items strapped to his heavy belt. I had gotten to know men, in recent weeks and months, to know how human they were underneath it all. I was bad at flirting, but excellent at playing damsel in distress. It was my strongest card, and so I went with it.

"Please, Officer, can you tell me what happened?" I tried to delay the inevitable, but his baby blue eyes remained hard and strict as the driver of the other car was wheeled away in a stretcher. He glared. I stuttered. He demanded paperwork. I fumbled. I focused on keeping my face scrunched up and confused behind the long, highlighted bangs of my wig. Finally, I dug some old squares of documents out of the crumb-filled glove compartment. I handed them over and my eyes pleaded with him, helpless, in the signature move that had gotten me out of trouble on so many roadsides before.

"Ma'am." That one word said it all as he handed my expired documents back to me through the car window. The officer was the "law enforcing above all else" kind. If he called me "ma'am," he would not give me his number and plan to meet for drinks at a dive bar nearby. He would not lean closer to me as we shot a game of pool and then trade a PBA card for a chance to feel my body against his. The games I had played with some of New Jersey's finest officers, they were not welcome here.

"I'll let you drive home, ma'am. This time. But you need to pay these tickets and attend all these court dates." He walked away and left me holding a stack of hard paper that looked like it would bring my bank accounts even further into overdraft.*

---

* Every year, people of color face discrimination and fatal outcomes as a result of interactions —just like this one—with law enforcement in America. I want to freely acknowledge that had my skin been any color other than white, this accident might have resulted in my arrest, the removal of my children, and possibly a threat to my life. The fight for racial equality in America is still urgent. See colorofchange.org for some ways to help.

I wore a pale pink cashmere turtleneck to court in an attempt to look innocent and virginal. It was what I had seen female criminals do during their televised trials. It was several months later, and it was cold and dark by the time I pulled up to the courthouse. I was shaking, terrified of losing my freedom. I was already doing a more than Herculean job raising two babies on my own. That job would be impossible in a New Jersey suburb without a driver's license.

I knew I was in serious trouble when the other driver showed up in the courthouse lobby, purse clutched to her side and a thick cushion around her neck. My lawyer looked at me, his large square face revealing help-lessness and pity at the same time.

"Try one more time, it can't hurt," he instructed me, looking at the gift-wrapped chocolates and apology note I held, purchased in the event that she would come all the way out to the courthouse from her perfect white shuttered house a couple of towns over, just to make sure I was punished. In retrospect, I realized that his legal advice mainly consisted of having me drive to the address listed on the police report to ply the other driver with gifts. As if that would make it okay that I was on the road with no insurance to pay for the damage her back and her car bumper sustained when our cars collided. That was the lawyer I could afford though.

"What's the worst that could happen?" he asked me now. His shirt half hung out over the strained belt of his creased pants. He stood tall and spoke with kind authority, and so I listened and headed toward the other driver.

"No," she said, voice so sharp that I felt stabbed.

When I inhaled again, it was to the smells of my fellow criminals on the line to the metal detector that would lead us back into court. Their cigarette smoke and sweat mingled with the scent of my shame. I threw the wrapped package into an overflowing metal garbage can, watched it land atop old McDonald's fries. I didn't want to see this evidence of my naïveté for a single unnecessary second. This part I could control.

The rest of the process passed quickly, and then I was hyperventilating and handing my driver's license to the clerk. I felt the walls of my safe world falling all around me, falling onto me, and I couldn't breathe.

I drove home in what would be my last legal drive in a year. For the first time since my divorce, maybe for the first time ever, I finally broke. The tears came fast, and they came hard, and snot dripped down my face into the wool of my sweater. I couldn't stop.

I didn't want to admit that I was falling apart, not even to myself. I was stumbling through the world blind, with no direction, no compass, just falling over my own feet. I couldn't trust the gut that led me to Cathy. I couldn't trust the heart that warmed to Isaac. I couldn't rely on the twisted part of my mind that got me into Ben's headlock, with a pistol pointed at my head. I was so lost; I had forgotten where I was trying to go.

Isaac was right though. My mind still worked. I had graduated from Rutgers University with honors. I knew I could handle the academic rigor of a doctoral program. Besides, I hated the way my marital status preceded me before I even walked into a room, when I was introduced as Ms. instead of Mrs. I could avoid all of that if I went by Dr. instead.

I studied the Princeton, Columbia, NYU, Fordham, and Rutgers websites. I learned which programs offered stipends and scholarships. I read the research published by those who made admissions decisions. I drove to Barnes & Noble and purchased books about applying to PhD programs in psychology. In a world of chaos, it was the one thing that felt right.

After my car crash, I opened my bills and read them. I lay awake in bed most nights, running numbers and finding out that no matter how many times I did the calculations, I did not have enough money. I tried to apply for a credit card, and I found out that my credit score was in the red section of the credit graph, hovering at around 402. I visited the social service office in my town, scanned the long lines for any clients of mine, and then kept my head pointed down at the scratched linoleum while I told the caseworker that I couldn't afford my grocery bills. I was denied aid because my earnings put me just above the poverty line.

I never wanted to rely on a man for support again.

In the darkness of my bedroom, while my children slept, I googled and googled and googled. I wrote admissions essays and asked my kind Rutgers professors for letters of recommendation. Dr. Merritt, whose class I left during LGBTQIA+ education day, wrote a glowing letter and mailed it to all the addresses I sent her way. Professor Jozef, who taught me to question whether women really needed to be silent, wrote a letter that recognized the real me, the one he saw behind the bangs of my wig.

When I got my first rejection letter, from an Ivy League university with a less than 10 percent acceptance rate, I was crushed. The whole time, I believed that I was smart enough to compensate for everything else—my failure as a wife, my failure to give my children a stable childhood, my failure to be a good Jew. At least I was smart, I thought. I imagined that as soon as the admissions directors saw my personal statement about helping the Jewish community, and my passionate words about psychology, they would just quietly move my application to the top of the pile.

As I sat on my red sheets and refreshed my emails, I was blindsided by the letter. They didn't even offer me an interview. Just a form letter for a standard type of applicant who does not meet their criteria.

I switched tabs, to my Wells Fargo account. My balance was $4.32. I knew that my TD bank account was even worse—that one was in overdraft by over two hundred dollars. It was still two days before my next paycheck. Two days to drive local roads and hope I didn't need more gas. Two days to make do with bread sandwiches for the children's breakfast, and macaroni for dinner. When I deposited my paycheck, my account would go back up to eight hundred dollars, after the overdraft was paid off.

It would seem like a lot, for the first day of the two-week period before my next check. I would splurge on yogurts and maybe a new sweater from Nordstrom Rack. I would fill the tank to the top. Then I would have to make my car payment of over three hundred dollars. I would get an envelope in the mail with a PSEG electricity bill. One of the children would need a check written out for a school trip. I would be in overdraft again, before my six hundred dollars of child support came through, before my next paycheck came in.

I didn't just want a PhD, I needed one. I didn't know how to take care of us on my social work salary. It just was not enough. Even with Abba paying my rent, through checks that came on the eighth of every month, after my landlord knocked and sent several emails. Even with that extra help, I was not making it.

I refreshed my emails between client sessions for the rest of the week, and in the car while I waited in the carpool lane, and outside the bank before I deposited my check. Finally, the next two universities responded. They, too, were elite universities, ones I chose because they provided their PhD students with financial scholarships and a stipend for living expenses.

They, too, rejected me. *It's not personal*, I tried to tell myself, but it sure felt personal. I was a person, and they didn't want me. I was not worthy. *Maybe I am not all that smart*, I worried. But I had no idea who I even was without my intelligence.

I didn't want to cry. There wasn't time to cry.

I felt the fear return, the sharpness in my chest, the staring up at my bedroom ceiling all through the night. How would I keep it up, groceries and housing and clothing and bills, without a better income? I couldn't live from overdraft to overdraft forever.

I prepared emails for the admissions departments asking if there was anything I could do to strengthen my application for next year, and I waited until the sun came up before I hit send. I couldn't have them seeing my sleeplessness, my anxiety, my signs of two a.m. mental breakdowns.

I learned that I needed a research internship. I was so grateful to get one, under the supervision of my former Rutgers professor Dr. McMahon, whose class I fell asleep in back when I was a brand-new mother, what felt like eons ago.

I applied to seven programs a few months later, some PhD, some PsyD, and one DSW—a Doctor of Social Work—program. I was invited to three interview days. I visited campuses, walked through the wide green lawns and inhaled the scent of academia, and felt right at home. I listened to grad students talk about their grueling schedules, and all throughout my smiling and chatting with professors, I calculated. Forty hours a week, plus travel time, plus research time, plus two children, plus full-time job to support two children—any way I sliced it, it would be impossible.

I was rejected by six programs and wait-listed for the seventh, my least favorite, the DSW program. I kept thinking my research experience wasn't extensive enough. I'd only had a one-month internship, and unlike many other applicants, my name was not listed on any published research articles.

Finally, I applied to Capella. I called the phone number, completed a very easy application, and got accepted nearly overnight. I felt like I was cheating, because it was an online university, even though they officially called themselves a hybrid program. I knew it would be seen as an "online degree." I needed something flexible, though, because I could not do in-person school while raising two little children.

I calculated and realized it would take five years. I kept calling the academic tracking advisors to ask, "Can you make this go any faster?" They told me, "You are already moving at the speed of light."

I stacked as many classes as possible on top of my already full workload. I was running, sprinting toward the finish line, but it was still not nearly enough.

PART III

Something Wild

Where Do Broken Hearts Go?

"**M**alka, I need your help."

I rolled over in my bed, disoriented by the unnatural speed in Shani's voice. Her words hurtled through my phone, and in between bursts of incoherence, I made out one solid and alarming fact: her husband, Felix, she said, had tried to choke her. She wanted to travel to Israel, where she and the children would be safe. But at the moment, she was on the side of a highway with a packed suitcase, both children, and no airline tickets.

I heard sounds in the background. A radio crackled. Fast cars whooshed past.

"The police are here." She sounded scared, so scared.

"What?!" My body jolted upright.

For a brief moment I felt conflicted: I worked at a domestic violence shelter, and I knew that when women disclosed the details of an assault, they should always, always, be believed.

And yet, I knew my sister's illness, her impenetrable mind, in turns brilliant and mad. I heard the story change as quickly as she spoke it, a blur of contradicting facts in a single frenzied run-on sentence. I did not think she was lying. But when her illness took over, sometimes her truth was not the same as reality.

I thought of my very caring brother-in-law, Felix. I was under no illusions—even the most gentle people could snap. Felix was a lovable sort, even if slightly odd. He wore mismatched socks with open sandals to family bar mitzvahs. He would bring a gift of one whole pineapple to Shabbat dinner, instead of the traditional chocolate or wine. I didn't want to believe that there was a side to him that I hadn't seen.

"I'm coming." I didn't bother to hide the weariness in my tone. She was too far gone to hear it anyway.

I lifted my children out of their beds and placed their sleeping bodies gently into the car. I put the address she gave me into the GPS.

I had no idea what I would do when I got there, and so I called Hindy. Hindy, the biggest sister of us all, the person who never seemed lost, who had practically been the mother of our family for as long as I could re-member.

"Malka, where are you?" I heard the sleep in Hindy's voice, but also the full and immediate lucidity, and I told her what was happening.

"You aren't old enough to remember all the incidents." Hindy knew Shani's illness better than any of us. It was Hindy who shared a bedroom with Shani when she first began to see eagles flying through the walls of our childhood home. It was Hindy who listened as Abba spent hours on the phone discussing promising new psychiatric cures discovered by cutting-edge medical science.

"I think I should bring her back to my place to rest." The doubt crept through my clenched vocal cords.

"Malka, you have enough on your plate." I heard the crack in Hindy's voice through the distance that separated us, and I felt a moment of sad-ness for how our relationship had deteriorated. Our daily phone calls about recipes and children had morphed into occasional stilted conver-sations, with so many words left unsaid between us. Hindy had not for-given me for getting divorced. I had not forgiven her for siding with my husband while I clawed my way to freedom. Still, there was love between us. I heard that love, just underneath her instructions. "Call Felix. He will come and get the kids. You don't have to handle this by yourself. It's okay."

I was still gripping the phone and trying not to cry when our call ended.

The GPS led me to a cottage-like building illuminated by the letters POLICE. I carried the heavy weight of my children up the concrete stairs.

Under the fluorescent lights in the entrance, my six-year-old niece Micki sat quietly, her little face pale, a female police officer beside her. I put on my cheery-aunt voice, and said, "Look who's here to visit!" Micki stood up, the pink ruffles of her little skirt in eerie contrast to the fear and confusion in her dark eyes. The police officer stood up with her, and I watched her take me in with all my trappings: the toddler on my hip, the car seat under my elbow.

"You must be the sister." I put the car seat down and shook her hand. It was important that she knew I was the normal one.

She guided us all to a back office, where Shani sat near a car seat of her own, rocking it back and forth with one foot while she wrote. I saw pages of handwritten notes piled on top of each other. She spoke quickly, loudly, every sentence a burst of exclamation.

"You're here! I'm writing my statement! Adam fell asleep! Micki is probably scared! Tell them I'm safe to go! We are gonna have the best time at your place! I can't wait to shower! I have a suitcase with clothes, don't worry!"

Then she leapt up and hugged me.

The police officer brought us a Tupperware of green grapes. "It's all I have, I'm sorry. The kids must be hungry." She gave us some space and I tended to everyone, gave whole grapes to the big kids and cut some in half for the little ones. I got crayons and papers and passed them around. In the seconds of stillness that followed, I met the officer in the hallway.

I hated myself a little bit as I took a select few facts and parceled them in the sort of laymen's terms that I knew were beyond questioning. I said I was a social worker, that I'd worked on an inpatient psychiatric unit. I disclosed Shani's history of severe bipolar disorder. I knew the necessary jargon, and I saw her expression begin to shift. She nodded, her dimpled chin moving sharply over her dark uniform collar.

When the medics arrived, Shani's eyes flashed at me in shocking disbelief. The voices slipped and slid inside my head.

See? The medics know she is manic.

Still, I should have protected her.

Beneath all the voices and all the facts, I knew that I had betrayed us both.

It took only a moment, and Shani's voice changed. "I know you're doing what's best," she said, as the EMTs led her out of the police station. "Please take care of my kids. I love you!"

I stayed with the children long after Shani was led away, attempted to keep them calm. I read to them from the tattered children's book the officer had found. Finally, at four a.m., Felix showed up, his face haggard.

Micki ran across the entryway. "Daddy!" She threw her arms around his long legs. I strapped baby Adam into his car seat, passed the car seat to Felix.

"Thank you," he said, his face a blend of resignation and anguish.

I pulled my headscarf back over the strands of hair that had fallen around my face, during the long night of trying not to come undone. I loaded my children back into the car. For the first time all night, I noticed how cold I was. The chill was in my bones, under my skin. My knuckles felt like icicles bent around the steering wheel. Dappled rays of morning sunlight came through the bare trees, and their branches seemed to poke at me, accusatory: *you betrayed your own big sister.*

I knew I would go home and do all the things I was supposed to do. I would take the day off and let my babies rest. I would make pancakes and then dinner. I would let Hindy know how it all turned out. I would call Abba and give him a glossy version of events that ended with, "I made sure she got to the nicest inpatient unit in all of New Jersey, where they can really help her."

But as I drove through the residue of night, all I could see was a dark, empty road ahead.

Several weeks later, Shani appeared to go back to normal. She took her children to Israel for the summer, with Felix scheduled to join. She called me to talk about the new sidewalk cafés she discovered, the friends she was visiting, the summer camp that taught Micki to speak Hebrew. She asked how I was doing and reminded me to "have some fun, Malka! It's a beautiful world!"

As the summer wound down, Shani told me that she didn't think her marriage would last. Soon after, my sisters and I got news of her and Felix's decision to divorce. She decided to stay in Israel, where she felt safe and supported by a network of friends. Her two children, beautiful seven-year-old Micki and baby Adam, stayed with her, and she poured her fierce love into raising them as a single mother.

Her reasons for divorce made sense to me: she and Felix fought a lot; they had begun to make each other unhappy. It was simply no longer working.

To my other sisters, however, a woman who chose divorce was likely experiencing a mental breakdown, and they made their position clear in ways large and small. Shani, like me, began to feel the chill of Hindy, Dina, and Goldy withdrawing their affections.

In the meantime, I continued to work with survivors of domestic violence and sexual abuse, at a progressive clinic north of Lakewood. At my new job, the offices were painted in soft shades of pastel and the boss was a modern Jewish social worker, a feminist with short hair and warm smiles and wonderful clinical supervision skills.

"See you next week," I said to a client as she left my office. I swallowed a bite of granola bar and glanced at my phone, my two-minute check-in before the next client arrived.

Then I saw it. Nearly a dozen missed calls from Shani. Every worst-case scenario ran through my mind.

I pictured Abba, crumpled on the floor of his Jerusalem apartment, being rushed to the hospital in a diabetic coma. My abba. Just when he finally realized his dream of moving back to Israel, blocks away from his rebbe's shul, where he and thousands of other men in black silk robes gathered each week to sing and pray.

I saw Shani, on a white stone sidewalk, telling an Israeli police officer, "My sister in America will tell you I'm not crazy," as she tried to pluck invisible grapes off invisible bushes.

Stop catastrophizing, I told myself. I tried to remember that Shani had been stable, rational, and under the care of excellent doctors since she moved.

Everyone is safe, I repeated to myself. Still, the powder-blue walls blurred around me, and I felt the dizziness before I noticed that I was holding my breath.

I don't have time for this now, I reminded myself, and shoved the phone back in the desk drawer and slammed it shut along with my worry. If I didn't see my clients, I would not get paid, and if I didn't get paid, I would not be able to afford groceries. I sat up, smoothed the creases in my worried face, and smiled when a six-year-old girl popped a curly head into the doorway. "Morah Sara! Is it my time yet?"

At the end of the day, as I got into my car, the icy feeling of fright returned. There were more calls from Shani by then, and I took several deep breaths. Then I called her.

"Malka, they took my kids!" she screamed, sobbing, barely able to catch her breath.

"Shani, breathe," I said, as I struggled to find my own air. But she couldn't stop, and the urgency of her sobs filled my car, and then I finally heard what she was saying.

"They took Micki and Adam away from me!" She broke down again into frightful wailing, sounds in sharp waves, rapid, hitting me one after the other after the other. "They came, a whole bunch of them, guys in black. They grabbed the kids so fast and left, and I don't know anything. I need you to find out where they are. I already called everyone. No one is telling me anything!"

I listened, the panic in my chest rising, engulfing me. I imagined the Hasidic men she described, bursting into her apartment in Jerusalem, grabbing her children, then disappearing into speeding vehicles.

"They were so brutal. Micki looked so scared, Malka. Her little face." Her voice broke, and I felt its stab in my chest.

I put the car in drive because I still needed to make it to school pickup on the other side of town, and I dialed Hindy. I didn't have time, never had time, but my sister was breaking, and my niece and nephew were in danger, and I had to take care of it even if that meant swallowing my every tremor as I attempted to drive in a straight line.

Hindy's voice helped for a second. She sounded calm, measured, the opposite of Shani. I stopped at a red light and breathed through her first few words. But then I started to understand what she was saying and the dread set in, hard and dark, throughout my body. Hindy wouldn't say who, but someone in our family had decided that Shani should not be her children's caretaker anymore. Hindy was vague, mentioning the names of distant uncles, a rabbi, and a religious psychiatrist. "They're fine," Hindy said to me in a tone that belonged in a lullaby, not in a kidnapping report. "Felix is flying them back to New York."

She told me that Felix was the stable one. "He was begging to stay married," she said. That, to her, meant he was the parent with better judgment and better values.

I put a foot on the gas and screeched into the parking lot of my children's yeshiva. I half expected the teachers to tell me they'd already been picked up. That some men in black came on behalf of their father. That I could call someone else to find out what happened to my babies. When I saw Avigdor's puffy coat in the corner of the playground, I threw my car into park and I ran, as fast as I could, until he was in my arms and the velvet of his yarmulke was smushed into my cheek.

"Mommy!" Shira ran up to me and grabbed my leg. "I baked!" She showed me a tiny foil pan and it felt like an absolute miracle.

"You baked! I love it! I love you!" I bent down and hugged her birdlike shoulders between mine, inhaling the scent of child sweat and cinnamon.

I buckled both children into their car seats and drove home stiff with fear, glancing into the rearview mirror every few seconds to make sure they were still there. I still had my own children. But that did not mean we were safe.

After the children were tucked into their matching polka-dotted sheets, I sat down and googled. I needed to find out how children could be taken from their mother without any law enforcement intervention. The more I read, the more my muscles clenched, and my jaw felt wired shut with tension.

On the *New York* magazine website, I read a detailed article about another mother with a similar experience, just a couple years earlier, a mother who did many things I did, and I grew more and more alarmed as I read.

Gitty Grunwald, a twenty-one-year-old woman, was raised in the Satmar Hasidic community in Kiryas Joel, New York, but left her husband, taking her toddler daughter with her, and tried to forge a life outside the community of black and white. She wore pants out in public (so did I), she stopped keeping kosher (I still tried, but occasionally failed), and she hung out with other ex-Hasidic rebels (just as I had). I retraced my steps as I read through her story. We were not so different, she and I.

Gitty's husband, a devout Hasid, arranged for a group of men to grab his daughter from a day care center, then had an attorney argue for him in court that the mother was unfit, demanded that Gitty take a hair follicle drug test, which she failed. In her words, "I smoke a joint two months ago and that gives them the right to take my daughter away?"

I scrolled back up, holding the tiny screen of my Palm Pilot right up to my nose, looking for other reasons for this mother to have her three-year-old kidnapped from her. I had worked with many child protective services cases, and I knew better than to believe that a single hair follicle test would, under ordinary circumstances, be enough to determine custody of a child. I knew that was not how it worked. I had treated women with track marks up their arms, signed documents attesting that they came to session, and watched as they walked through the doors of our transitional housing center holding their children. That happened even in cases where their children were born addicted to cocaine and heroin, even when fetal alcohol syndrome was evident in their misshapen skulls, their delayed grasp of language.

In Gitty's case, it wasn't hard to imagine the story between the lines: Hasidic leaders cultivated strong ties to local political leaders, and they held sway over judges by threatening to grant or withhold the votes of a powerful election bloc. They were also deeply resourceful and able to raise funds easily for the shrewdest attorneys, which Gitty could never have afforded on her own.

I felt paranoid when I started to imagine Hasidic men planting bags of white powder in Gitty's car. I wanted to believe that my fear was irrational, but I knew that many in the Hasidic community, once they believed a child's soul was in danger, that the child might follow a rebelling parent out of the faith, would go to any lengths to keep that from happening.

I remembered the joints and bongs I smoked on my weekends away from my children. I thought back to the casinos and bars and clubs, scanned my memories: Were there security cameras that could have recorded me? Community spies who may have seen me?

I dialed Shani, wondering what evidence my own Hasidic family used to get her children taken. Did they get ahold of her inpatient records? Call one of her doctors and pretend to care, only to retrieve her personal medical information?

"Malka. I spoke to Micki."

Shani sounded far away, speaking one heavy word at a time. She needed more contact with them. If she couldn't hold them close, she needed to at least see their faces. "Can you arrange a Skype call maybe?" she asked tearfully.

I promised her that I would reach out to Felix, make a plan for her to see her children, and to let her know that they were okay.

"You will?"

A flicker of hope flashed through the phone, and I tended it as best I could, tried to keep it alive. I knew that she was at higher risk of a depressive episode than ever. If she fell down the well of emptiness and landed in another inpatient unit, she might never see her children again. And so I distracted her with strategy talk—when I would see her children, how to best explain everything to them, how to assess their emotional states without scaring them.

Shani began to have regular video visitation with the children over Skype. She worried, though, that they weren't able to be fully honest with her, with their father always present. When she asked if I could arrange for the children to have a more private space when she spoke to them, I promised to arrange it, and I called Felix and insisted that he provide my sister that little shred of comfort.

I talked to Shani every day, until the day that Micki and little Adam arrived at my house for Shabbos. They were so wordless. Small faces staring up at me, Micki hiding half of her heart-shaped face in the collar of a plaid coat that was at least one size too big. Adam clutching his backpack with both hands. I threw all of mine and Shani's planned conversations to the side and served them warm chocolate cake at the kitchen table. My children's chatter filled the still space around them.

When Adam yelled, "Avigdor got more cake than me!" and then Micki's mouth turned up into a tiny smile, I knew they were starting to feel safe.

For the rest of the weekend, that was all that mattered, I decided. I would find words to calm Shani later.

"You seem exhausted," my new therapist, Henry, said from his folding chair in the clinic that took my insurance. Before I could respond, his eyes drifted shut, shaggy white eyebrows reflecting the early afternoon sun. I didn't blame him. My life was so exhausting that I, too, would have liked to curl up and take a nap.

During our next session, right at the top of our session hour, I told Henry, "I don't know why I kept this." I held the bullet that had been in my wallet ever since Ben shot his gun right in front of me.

"Is that what I think it looks like?" Henry was not nearly as alarmed as a therapist should be when their client was holding ammunition. But at least he leaned forward in his chair a bit, and his eyes were open. I had learned that it was best to present shocking, dramatic things to him all in a row, like little grenades all lined up and ready to go off. That way, he stayed awake through most of my session.

"Here." In a rare moment of helpfulness, he tipped a trash can over toward me. "You don't need to hold on to that anymore."

I tossed the bullet into the can, heard it roll around and then settle. I felt weirdly naked. The bullet was my evidence of badass-ery, my proof that I was a survivor. Henry was right, though. I had survived traumatic events, but I was moving forward. I was keeping kosher again, even when I passed Starbucks and really wanted a brownie. I wasn't drinking the weekends away in dim casinos anymore. I was ready to leave the darkness behind.

God Bless the Broken Road

I already knew that my rabbis and seminary teachers were right: the Hollywood version of love did not exist. I was tired of pretending that it did. And so, when a colleague offered to set me up with his friend, an Orthodox Jewish man from Long Island, I said yes.

When he picked me up for our first date, I assessed him as he drove. I noticed the way his pale cheeks flushed before he spoke, the small razor cut under his neat, trimmed beard. He seemed nervous all the way through the Lincoln Tunnel. I chatted about the weather and our mutual acquaintance. I wanted to be attracted to the shape of him, broad and sturdy in his tailored blazer.

But I knew that would never happen on its own.

I had watched too many scenes that featured Callie and Arizona on *Grey's Anatomy. This is not for me*, I told myself every time they kissed, or their bodies touched, or when they just looked at each other in that magical way. And still, every time, my fingers, as if on their own, would hit pause, then rewind, and my body would thrum like the inside of a guitar, and I'd watch the whole thing all over again.

My body, left to its own devices, would never react that way to a man.

When Eli excused himself during our dinner to answer his son's phone call, I studied him, wondered if I could manufacture feelings for him. They said that was possible, my mentors. That feelings came from the mind, and that the heart could not be trusted.

"The Band-Aids are in the bathroom cabinet," I heard him say, in a teddy-bear soft voice. "I'll be home soon. I love you. Call me anytime."

By the time he ended the call and looked back at me, I knew he was worth trying to love. I felt like I was flicking a lighter at the base of my heart, trying to make a flame last in the wind. I knew how anxious he had been to impress me, and yet he still took his son's call during our date. *Flickering sparks.*

He was the sort of parent that I was, the exact sort of father I wanted for my children one day. His eyes were crystal blue, just like my son's. His right cheek dimpled when he smiled. *Flick, sputter, tiny flame.*

"I think full sleeve tattoos are so hot and if I weren't religious, I would definitely get one," he said shyly. *Flame growing, catching, holding steady.*

After our date, he exited the car in front of my house, came around to my side and held the passenger door open. He asked if I would like to see him again and I said yes before I could hesitate, before the ember could go dark.

When I told Eli about my pursuit of a PhD, he became my most enthusiastic cheerleader. When I passed my comprehensive exams, he had a vase of a dozen long-stemmed roses delivered to my door.

"You will do this," the enclosed card read. "You are one of the most brilliant people I have ever met. I believe in you and can't wait to watch you succeed. You got this, and I got you."

He stuck around, found my wounds and sewed them up one by one. *He might be a man*, I told myself, *but he loves me.* He showed up like a superhero bearing a portable heater when there were power outages in the cold winter. He taught Avigdor to tie his shoes and he joked around with Shira until she giggled out loud. He showed me off to his family and friends, dusted me with the glow of his admiration and made sure they saw me as golden. He was the perfect kind of Jewish; he kept up appearances of following the rules on the outside, but when we were in private, he dropped the restriction against touching before marriage.

After several months of dating, Eli became the most solid thing in my entire world. When my grief for Shani mingled with my own desperate fears, I let him hold me. He pulled me against his firm chest, and he let me fall apart all over him. I cried and dripped and cried and gulped and sobbed. He never stopped holding me, not once.

He told me it was going to be okay, and he meant it. "I'm right here. I'm not going anywhere." His soft beard skimmed the top of my head as he kissed me softly. He let me collapse against his warm body all night in my messy bedroom that could not possibly be as comfortable as his own glass-walled penthouse.

It was such a relief to be able to let go of the burdens, the old heavy boulders I hadn't even realized I was holding. That feeling, I just wanted to live inside it forever. I was tired of holding so much all by myself on my narrow shoulders that threatened to cave in.

"I heard you're seeing someone," Hindy said, trying to hide the hurt in her voice, not entirely succeeding. I hadn't asked her to vet him, and that was a demotion. As it turned out, though, she had done some vetting anyway, via our cousin Tzipora, who had attended summer camp with Eli's sister.

"She says she was a very nice, normal, fun girl."

To Hindy, that was important, because his family mattered as much as he did.

"I think the family has money," she said, "but they don't really talk about it."

I thanked her, my words polite and my tone gentle. I knew she meant well. Also, it was kind of nice to have some vestige of her sisterly care, even if a bit misplaced. And so, I ended the call before I blurted what I really thought. *You think I care about YOUR opinion? Do you not remember what happened the last time you vetted a man for me? Seriously?*

Once Hindy mentioned it, I saw signs of Eli's family wealth in places I hadn't looked before. When we visited his sisters, I noticed that even though they did not work outside the home and their husbands were unemployed Torah scholars, they lived in three-story houses on plush lawns. I realized that Eli was always available to run to my service because his job was so part-time that it barely existed. I didn't know much about money, but even I knew that that sort of job could not possibly yield enough to pay for his penthouse, his fresh-off-the-lot car, and his son's private school tuition.

I was not about to walk down another wedding aisle with skeletons in my closet. I didn't want to worry about what would happen if he discovered the real me. And so, I told Eli everything. Almost everything.

We were parked on a side street in Clifton, at the end of one of our dates. I kept my gaze fixed at the brick wall outside the car window as I told Eli about my family's history. I blinked the emotion out of my eyes and tried to sound matter-of-fact about my mother's descent into darkness, about her disconnect from reality. My voice wavered when I talked about Shani, and the years of confusion about her illness, my constant fear of becoming ill like her.

I looked into his eyes and waited for his rejection, but he pulled me close and held me, and he gave me his reassurance without needing to say the words. That was not all though.

"I'm not as innocent as I look."

I explained that I had a history of battling attraction to women. That I suspected I was bisexual, but I had it under control.

"Were you scared to tell me that?" He was slow, careful. I turned around and saw his eyes soften, his movements gentle, as he shifted himself into place around the shape of my fear.

"I just don't want you to feel deceived," I said, and hoped my sincerity was convincing. "You might hear rumors about me sometime. I wanted you to hear it from me first."

Eli, in alignment with his warm values, reassured me that he was not going to run away anytime soon. Eli, a product of the same culture as I, also believed that women could not be truly, biologically attracted to other women. He determined that my experimenting with women was just that, an experiment.

"You probably just wanted to try everything after getting out of your marriage," he said. I agreed, because that was the easiest thing to do in that moment.

They say that once three Jews know something, it is public knowledge. More than three Jews knew of my pants-wearing, cigarette-smoking, smudged-eyeliner self who frequented strip clubs and poker tables. The only way to be me and get a good Jewish man was to get ahead of the story and spin it just a bit.

That was his spin.

I was being honest, but I was also calculated. Never far from my mind was the knowledge that the rabbis granted me custody of my children only conditionally: that I must keep to a strict Orthodox lifestyle, or they would take them from me. I vowed that I would never let that happen.

And so, I needed to be a good Jewish wife to a good Jewish husband, and Eli fit the particulars. I loved who he was as a human being, even if I felt indifferent about his human body.

By May of 2012, Eli and I had been dating for a year and a half, and he had been so in love with me the whole time. I kept wondering, though, if he was ready, whether he wasn't too fearful, after experiencing difficulties during his first marriage.

I knew that if Eli and I were to get married, I would move to the Five Towns, his neighborhood in Long Island. Given that our religion mandated we could not live together until after our wedding ceremony, at which point we were expected to immediately share a home, things would happen quickly. My kids would have to switch schools and get adjusted. I told him that unless we made plans soon, I couldn't make that happen for the upcoming school year.

In the least romantic move of our entire relationship, Eli took me out to a kosher steakhouse. A regular, Jewish, date night. When it was time for dessert, the waiter brought a champagne glass that was pre-engraved with the words, "Malka, will you marry me?"

I said yes, because I loved him, and yes, because I was drowning, and he was my raft.

It would hurt to admit it later, but I knew, even as I said yes, that it was for the wrong reasons.

Most of me was ready to leave temptation behind, but a small piece of my old self needed to do one last thing before committing to a lifetime with Eli.

One Saturday night, I dug my first pair of Fossil jeans out from the back of my closet, fastened them to my hips with a gauze belt, drove through the Lincoln Tunnel and into the West Village, and headed to the Cubbyhole, a tiny dive bar coated in rainbows.

"Hi, I'm Miriam," a woman said as she sat down on a ledge near me and looked right into my eyes. Hers were dark. Bedroom dark. I smiled and offered my hand, the hand that was not holding a cigarette. It was a motion I had practiced at similar street corners in my previous lifetime, the wild one.

It was my last time, I swore. And then I was inside, and the women were just so intoxicating. Women, packed wall to wall, women who were checking each other out, flirting, searching. Rounded asses in tight pants, cleavage peeking out of casual tops, long hair, spiky hair, tattoos, glossed lips. My gut reacted to each scent, each glimpse. *That's the devil*, I said to my weakening spirit, *you have to ignore it.*

I couldn't kiss anyone. I couldn't take any phone numbers. If I chose to do things that a true Jewish woman should never do, then I would lose it all. The divorce agreement that I signed two years ago was still in effect, and it always would be, forever. *If it is determined that I am not raising the children according to Jewish law, custody will be transferred to their other biological parent.*

Jewish law mandated that I be straight. I was straight.

As the night turned hazy with the sweet scent of so many mingled perfumes, the smooth taste of vodka soda, I felt beautifully engulfed. I caught sight of Miriam's buzz cut moving through the crowd. I could tell she felt it too, as she turned sideways and maneuvered toward me. Katy Perry's "I Kissed a Girl" came on and the whole bar came alive, whistles and cheers and voices that sang along. I felt Miriam's hips against mine, moving to the beat. She reached up, cupped my jaw in her delicate hand. All I could think was, *Stop it. You are not attracted to her. Not. Attracted. Not.* I pulled away.

Why did women always know to touch my face when it was something Eli had not done once in the hundreds of times he had kissed me? Sigh. Stop. Sigh. I pushed past the butches with short hair flopping over their smooth faces, past the studded ears and the long hair and the plaid shirts tied around waists. Until I was outside in the spring air. *I don't need that anymore*, I lectured to myself. *I can pass the test. I have passed it. I can be straight for as long as I live.*

I didn't want to search for a woman's touch at the cost of my children, my family, my future. I refused to be another pretty face seeking comfort in the drunken night. I leaned against the streetlight, watched a crowd of women as they stood in groups, shared cigarettes, kissed in ways that involved their entire bodies. I told myself I felt nothing at all.

I drove away and back to the suburbs, showered it all off along with the memory of myself. The self that came alive at the sight of sin. I shoved that self deep into the corners of a closet that I would leave behind when I said *I do* to Eli, and to the promise of a shore on the other side of the turbulent waters.

As I packed my boxes and got ready to move in with Eli, I felt ready to shed all the parts of my life that weren't working anymore. Things had gotten so bad, I often had to choose between paying the electric bill or buying food for my children. I would lie awake at night, crunching numbers, never finding solutions.

As I threw my children's old toys into trash bags along with my expired face creams and threadbare bath towels, I envisioned the upgrade: beachfront penthouse, a father figure for my children, better schools.

It all felt heart-poundingly real. It was not my first time promising myself to a Jewish man, getting ready to stand under a wedding canopy. I tried my hardest to forget the scars of it, the thin stretch marks on my body, and the fear in my heart.

I zipped a simple eggshell gown, from J.Crew's bridesmaid's rack, up my spine. I looked down at my hipbones, like bent wings, poking through the satin. I was vaguely aware that sometime in the previous few weeks, I must have stopped eating. All dressed up in my hotel room, I couldn't seem to find everything I needed. I had the vague sense that I was misplacing a bobby pin or wallet or lacy lingerie for later.

Eventually, I climbed into a cab and watched the blurred shapes through the window, the smoke shop where we stocked up on cigarettes, the Starbucks where we got our morning coffees, the kosher Dunkin' Donuts on the corner of Rockaway Boulevard. I'd been a visitor to those places, but they were going to become my neighborhood spots. By the time I got to the wedding hall, gown trailing behind me, pink Coach bag over my shoulder, wheeling a small suitcase with a wig box balanced over it, I was met with Eli's raised eyebrows. I was late to my own wedding.

There was time for a couple of quick photos, me standing like a bronzed twig in a gown, him in a traditional white linen robe over his suit. Rabbi Shalom helped me sign the marriage contract, and one more document, a controversial one that I insisted on. A prenuptial agreement that was binding by Jewish law, a relatively new religious innovation that had spread through the Modern Orthodox world. In it, Eli agreed that should we split up, he wouldn't ever withhold a *get*, a religious divorce. The prenup still carried a stigma, and I told him I needed it as a political statement, a show of support for all women. I told myself that, too, as I stood before the rabbi and signed my name.

Abba had flown in from Israel for the occasion, and I was relieved to see him standing tall in his traditional black satin coat and fur hat, looking as regal as ever.

"I barely recognized you," he said, gesturing to my cream blond wig, having transformed from a brunette with highlights.

The wedding did not require much of my presence; it happened around me. A ceremony, where Rabbi Shalom sang blessings and passed silver cups of wine. Then a cracking of a plate under Eli's heel and voices shouting "mazel tov" into the air around us. There was some dancing with new friends and old friends and some pausing to stretch my lips into a smile for the photographer.

I scanned the crowd of women on my side of the leafy dividers, and there were my sisters, standing off to the side of the ballroom. I broke away from the circle of people around me, pulled them in. I embraced them one at a time, thanked them for coming. Hindy and her husband, Meir, drove down from their upstate summer home, leaving any number of children and grandchildren behind for the night. Dina and Ezra made the journey from Flatbush, leaving their six children at home, the older ones babysitting the younger ones. Goldy and her husband, Shragi, were there too, a fleet of their own little ones with friends or neighbors in Borough Park. Mimi, our only single sister, was on the side of the ballroom, serving fruit cups to my children and making sure the juice didn't drip onto Shira's little gown, Avigdor's new tie.

We did not talk about the missing sister, Shani, who was locked behind the doors of yet another psychiatric unit. We did not talk about our mother, sitting in the shadows of her mind, alone in our childhood home. They showed up for me, despite our many disagreements, and that was all that mattered.

When the music stopped, Eli and I sat together at the head table while Rabbi Shalom clinked a glass and spoke beautiful words about us in a melodic voice, and even quoted my abba's Hasidic rabbi in his talk. Abba smiled, a wholehearted one this time, nodded at me and Eli, and his eyes seemed to say, *This is different from what I'm used to, but I think you will be okay here.*

Eli noticed his son, Josh, fidgeting in his suit, sitting between uncles. There were no children present other than our own; it was a second wedding after all, and that was not something our siblings wanted their children to emulate. Eli waved Josh over, and then Avigdor and Shira were in my arms, and we looked at each other and made the split-second decision to make our own rules. We asked the waiters to bring some chairs and plates, and then we had a head table that included all of us. Me, Eli, Josh, Avigdor, and Shira, all in fancy clothes, eating off fancy plates, and for the first time all day I felt like I was home.

Our friends and family felt it too, and the slight edge of trepidation faded off their faces. They nudged each other, turned to us and smiled, tables full of wigged women in long-sleeved cocktail attire on one side of the room, and men in dark suits around tables on the other side. We were a real family, complete with a husband, a wife, and children. The Jewish version of a Hollywood happy ending.

We did one more nontraditional thing. The waiters passed dessert plates out, brought one with sparklers over to our table, and the band paused their Hebrew music to play, "Happy Birthday to Avigdor!" Avigdor's narrow face flushed, his blue eyes lit up, and we all clapped for him as the sparklers filled the air. He turned seven on July 5, 2012, and that, too, deserved a celebration.

Landslide

The Five Towns was a place to be Orthodox Jewish, but in an updated way. Many of the adults were college educated and worked as professionals in mainstream America's workforce. It was perfectly acceptable to own a TV, to attend sports games, and for husbands and wives to have opposite gender friends and acquaintances. On the spectrum of Jewish identities, from Hasidic (the most right wing) to secular (far left), the Five Towns was somewhere in the middle/right, what some described as "Modern Orthodox."

For the most devout, there were yeshivas for boys and Bais Yaakov schools for girls; those were where my children were enrolled. For those at the other end of the religious spectrum there were co-ed Hebrew day schools. The more modern a school, the more likely they were to have a robust general studies program and learning centers for children with individualized education plans.

The Five Towns was also known for its affluence. Not all were wealthy, but many were. Lawrence, the most moneyed of the Five Towns and the third wealthiest city in New York State, was home to the families whose names glittered on the façades of Jewish institutions across the country.

It was an upgrade, and I was anxious about the move. I worried that

Borough Park and Lakewood had stamped themselves indelibly into my personality, and that would make me a hick among sophisticates. But I knew that I had enough skills to pretend. I had always been good at shaping myself to the expectations of others.

I dressed carefully for my debut as Eli's wife at the Village Shul, where he had been a member for years. I teetered on the line between trophy wife and modest-enough-for-shul. I had begun to wear dresses so tight that they required thongs underneath, shoes so tall that walking required careful balance. On my way down the empty suburban blocks, I checked my makeup in the reflection of shiny car mirrors. Then I swallowed hard and opened the double glass doors into his world.

I forced a smile as I watched scores of Modern Orthodox Jews mill around in the synagogue lobby. They were not like any observant Jews I had seen before.

The Hasids in my hometown of Borough Park clung to the laws of modesty in their strictest form. Orthodox law mandates that women wear clothing that covers their elbows, collarbones, and knees, and that married women cover their hair. In Borough Park, the Hasidic women added fabric to the letter of the law; their dresses and skirts landed a solid four inches below the end of their kneecaps, and their sleeves were no shorter than mid-forearm. One would never, ever, catch a glimpse of a clavicle in the women's section of shul. Married women wore wigs that looked, well, wiggy. Helmetlike. Stiff, straw-like hair that did not flip around, did not flutter in the breeze, and definitely did not extend past the shoulder. Men were required to wear two head coverings as a reminder of God's constant presence above their thoughts. In Borough Park, they wore velvet yarmulkes and tall fur hats. They respected the traditions of their European ancestors, and wore long black coats and unshorn beards, to distinguish themselves from the non-Jews.

In Lakewood, the rules were several degrees looser for Ultra-Orthodox

Jews. Women still covered all of their skin, except for their necks, faces, hands, and perhaps a mere few inches above their wrists. Some women wore wigs that had visibly separate strands of hair, wigs that extended partway down their backs, and occasionally had hints of subtle highlighting. Men wore dark suits, ties, and a double head covering of yarmulke plus black felt hat. Some trimmed their beards, and some were clean-shaven. They would still stick out like meticulous aliens in any non–Jewish American settings, but just slightly less so than their Hasidic counterparts.

Among the Five Towns Jews, the rules were more like general guidelines. Women wore necklines that hovered around the collarbone area, some above it, some dipping just below, some revealing just the very edge of cleavage. They stood tall in delicate stilettos, in dresses that draped over their bodies effortlessly. I saw kneecaps in the synagogue lobby, sometimes bare of stockings and tanned to perfection. The wigs were different too. Supermodel hair, some with visible, bright highlights, waves that fell to the middle of slender spines.

The glamor was so thick; everyone appeared to be coming from a Hollywood red carpet and heading to an afterparty. I caught whiffs of expensive scents as they walked by, nothing like the heavy sweetness of the Victoria's Secret body lotion that was on my skin. Their diamonds twinkled in the light of the shul chandeliers, as they leaned toward each other and the various men who milled around with and between them, in the very same room.

I searched the crowd of bespoke suits for Eli and caught sight of golden cuff links on monogrammed cuffs, silk ties under clean-shaven jaws. The men wore belt buckles with designer brand letters, flashing in the morning light, brass capital *H*s and interlocked lowercase *A*s. They smelled like the inside of a luxury hotel lounge. They looked like they had custom leather shelves at home, of hair product and exfoliating facial soaps and manicure kits.

And then I saw Eli, eyes sparkling as he caught mine, rushing through the crowd in his pressed gray suit until his arm was around my waist. He didn't seem to care that my eyeliner was too thick or that the seams of my dress were just a bit too misaligned for this crowd, or that my heels were a tad too chunky to blend in. He looked at me like I was the answer to every prayer he had ever uttered. I felt my shoulders uncrunch just a bit as he gave me the rundown, told me who was relevant and who didn't matter, and which man was in trouble with his wife on that Shabbos morning.

"You should come to us for lunch next week!" a woman's honeyed voice wafted toward me, framed by hanging emeralds the size of quarters.

I looked at Eli, tried to telepathically communicate my panic. Lunch? I did not know what lunch would look like in Long Island's Hollywood, but I was pretty sure I did not have the wardrobe for it. He scanned my face, still smiling like he'd won the lottery, but his soft eyes registered the wide-eyed fear in mine in microseconds.

"Thank you!" he said, smooth and warm. "But we have the kids next week, all of them, and we're still figuring out our schedule. Can we check in with you later in the week?"

I can do this, I told myself. *I will find a way to make us fit in here*, I promised myself as I followed the crowd to an outdoor tent, where waiters bore trays of canapés and shot glasses of liquor.

Eli and I had anticipated that we would need the summer months to help our children get adjusted to our new blended family. He kept his work schedule even lighter than usual. He said that nothing gave him greater joy than watching me, textbooks scattered on the bed around me, typing thoughtfully into my dissertation outline. For the first time in years, I did not have a job. And it was okay. Eli casually placed supermarket orders that arrived in several large boxes. He booked flights and cars for our family vacation. He drove me to Bloomingdale's and insisted I leave *Pretty Woman*–style, with so many bags of lavishness. He found out that I had never watched *Pretty Woman* when he saw my blank face at his reference, and we watched it together, cuddled in our bed.

After a couple of months of marriage, I found that I was equipped enough to be a stepparent. I had treated enough children in similar situations; I had witnessed the paintings of enough stick figures moving from one house to another. More important, I knew what it was like to be a child who felt like the world was shaking on its axis.

I was also very well educated on the fine art of being a wife. Despite the failure of my first marriage, I still had notebooks filled with my own handwriting, about how to serve one's husband. They contained details such as: always put his plate down on the table before your own, never contradict him in public, encourage his Torah learning, but do not pressure him.

There were the occasional moments where Eli raised his voice in a way that alarmed both me and my kids. He hollered things like "WHERE ARE THE KEYS?!" instead of just asking if we'd seen them.

"He is a cantor," I told my children. "His voice is just naturally louder."

This is a small glitch in an otherwise impeccable system, I told myself. *Don't make it bigger than it is.*

The only wifely duty I struggled with was *mikvah*. The first time I counted seven days after my period and entered the ritual bath building, my body froze. I lay in a tub designated for the purpose of female purification, in a private room with marble tiles and full-length mirrors surrounding me. I fought the flashbacks, vividly streaming in my mind. My ex-husband's body on mine. His chest hair. Me crying. Him ignoring me. Taking from me. Lines on pregnancy tests.

I did all the grounding and breathing things and forced myself to press the call button and follow the *mikvah* attendant down a hallway. I removed my robe and dipped my naked body into a small pool of rainwater while she watched. I prayed, begged God, *Please come home with me, please help me do this, please enter my home and make it holy.*

When I got home, I forced a smile at Eli, took a quick shower, and put on the outfit he found sexiest: an oversized men's button-down. I opened our glass bedroom doors and headed to the balcony, hoping a cigarette would calm my body. He found me sitting on the balcony floor and crouched down next to me, lifted my chin until he could see the droplets in my eyes.

"We don't have to have sex," he said, and sat back, waited for my cue.

"We do," I said. "I already said the blessing."

I had read the blessing for *mikvah* night off the laminated card on my way out of the ritual bath, and if we were not intimate, that would be a blessing made in vain.

"Can I hug you?" He waited until I nodded, and then wrapped his arms around me, held me while I hyperventilated against his chest. "I love you," he whispered. "We will do this when you're ready." He held me until the flashbacks faded, until the breath came back into my lungs, until I remembered that it was him. That my feelings mattered, with him.

As the months passed, I learned to see beyond the luster of my town. I dropped my children off for playdates in storybook mansions with circular driveways, where uniformed maids welcomed them inside. I got a part-time job at a local psychotherapy practice, and I began to see the soul of the town, in the clients who entered my office with real worries and traumas. I met parents who prioritized their children's therapy over their own vacations, who wrote careful checks and took even more careful notes on how to do better.

I learned that there were many families who struggled to make ends meet, and that the reason they never stood out is that their bills were often quietly covered by the privileged members of the community. The more I saw, the less I stressed about my own clothing and status and fitting in. I was back to doing what I loved most, witnessing the courage of my clients and helping them to see it for themselves.

Shira got through the adjustment period and started to light up from the inside again. She was loved by her fellow first graders, and her teachers reported she never made anyone feel bad, even though she was in the popular group.

Avigdor had a harder time in second grade at his yeshiva, where the boys played sports during recess and called him weak when he stood on the side of the yard. I wished that Yossi, his father, was slightly less devout, just enough to own a soccer ball, to kick it around in the yard with his son. I was endlessly grateful when Josh saw what was happening and played basketball with Avigdor for hours after school, building his confidence. They would come inside sweaty, Avigdor's dimples showing, as they became brothers.

I found out that Josh left his middle school classroom during the day and visited Avigdor at lunchtime. He found the boys who were bullies and threatened them, "You better leave my brother alone." They were both laughing when they told me about it, so I laughed with them. The bullying stopped, and Avigdor got invited to be a part of lunchtime basketball games.

When Hurricane Sandy hit Long Island in October of 2012, three months after our wedding, Eli and I sent our children to stay with relatives who did not live on the beach. We stood at our balcony railing and watched as the ocean swallowed the first two floors of our building and then rushed forth to swallow the houses down the street. We watched as Eli's car, custom leather seats and all, floated down two whole blocks and into a wire fence. We were alone in our apartment, and it felt like the honeymoon we never got around to planning, a gift of days that suspended in time. We didn't mind lighting candles at night, or cooking popcorn on the gas stove, or losing power on our laptops.

We created entertainment of our own, moments of lying face-to-face and talking about what it was like to blend our families, about our community and its drama, and about how amazed we were at having found each other. I loved watching his face shift when I climbed on top of him, as his blue eyes took on shades of the storm outside. In his gaze, I saw a reflection of myself that surpassed anything I had ever seen in a mirror. Through him, I saw a version of me who was not limited by surviving through a single moment in time, but a me who could think big, bigger, until I broke through the edges of what I believed was possible.

When I pulled my shirt over my head and leaned down to kiss him, it was because I wanted to lose myself in him. I wanted to forget the existence of our bodies and plunge ahead to where all that mattered was disappearing the space between us. It was heated, the way we fused. He held on to my waist like I was his salvation, and I fucked him because he was mine. I watched him spill over in a primal release, teardrops in my eyes, in wonder at what we created together. It was bigger than love, or sex, or the skin we inhabited. It was goddamn cosmic.

When the storm subsided, we dragged ourselves out of isolation and took a rental car to a local lot, where Eli signed a lease on a sleek luxury SUV. In his excitement at the upcoming reinstatement of my license, he encouraged me to test-drive a coordinating sedan. Instead, I found a lot on a nearby street and signed a lease for a burgundy Honda Civic. It just felt more me, and I wanted to hang on to as many me things as I could.

Several months later, Shani's number showed up on my phone, just as I was parking my car outside a nail salon in the hour between my last session of the day and my children's school pickup time.

"Malka! How are you! I miss you! How is the Five Towns?" She always started with the questions, and I believed she genuinely wanted the answers, but she never waited long enough to get them, not anymore.

"I have a plan," she started, as I put quarters into a meter and walked past the Infinities and Lexuses and Acuras that lined the streets. "I am moving back to America! I think I can get my old job back and I have a friend I can stay with, and I am getting my paperwork ready, and I can't wait to see you."

I listened to my sister's voice, sounding alive for the first time in months. I wondered whether she sounded too alive. Whether the sudden liveliness was the mania that often followed her depression.

Still, as I entered the salon and picked out a pale pink polish, I was just about ready to encourage her, to be excited along with her. Then her tone shifted. The words were still speeding, one after the other after the other, but there was an unsettling fervency in her voice.

"I need you to talk to my kids in person," she said. "Maybe on Sunday. Ask them how they'd feel about it, without telling them it's really happening. Maybe you can record the conversation just so I have it."

I interrupted her. "I don't know if that's a good idea." I put one hand in front of a manicurist and held the phone in my other.

"Relax," the manicurist said, trying to bend my stiff fingers.

I didn't expect Shani to understand that I was already overwhelmed with school carpools and making playdates and attending the almost weekly occasions hosted by Eli's eight siblings, bar mitzvahs and weddings and brisses, all of which required my presence. I couldn't tell her that my shiny new life was too demanding, not while her life had been shattered. Instead, I offered another truth,

"I don't know if I can talk to your kids about this. What if it doesn't work out?"

I could already imagine her daughter Micki carrying another crushing disappointment on her ten-year-old shoulders. I could picture her bending down to comfort her four-year-old brother.

Against the soft classical music of the salon, Shani's voice sounded like so many pounding off-beat drums. By the time my nails were filed, and it was time for polish, my fingers were shaking so hard that the manicurist held them down with one hand while painting with the other. Shani begged me to do more things, like have her children draw pictures and then send them to me for analysis.

Back in my car, I felt guilty all the way home, as Shani kept talking and asking for things, with an urgency that crept through my veins, my chest, and then all of me, until it was just too much, and I was desperate to hang up.

When I finally got off the phone, I dove right into carpool lines and homework time and refereeing between my children and their step-brother.

In the days that followed, when Shani called again, and again, and again, I sent the calls to voicemail. It was just too much.

I was stirring milk into my coffee when the call came. Eli wiped his hands on the checked kitchen towel and threw it over his shoulder as I showed him my phone: "Hindy Cell."

"Hindy? What does she want?" he asked.

I shrugged. We had barely heard from my sister in the entire year we had been married. I left Eli ladling food onto plates, calling "Josh! Avigdor! Shira! Come get your dinner!" I knew it wouldn't be a *just calling to say hi* kind of conversation. We had already lost the casual sort of sister love, and all that remained was the weighted kind. I took the call in my bedroom and closed the door behind me.

"Malka," Hindy started, her voice sounding strained, "you know Shani had a very hard few months. She was very depressed."

Why was she telling me? Did Shani need help?

"Malka, she didn't make it."

I stared at the blank TV screen in front of me.

"She jumped off the Plaza Hotel in Jerusalem, from the eighteenth floor."

I noticed that my hand lost its grip on my phone. It fell to the floor, and I dropped to the floor beside it. Everything in front of me seemed fuzzy and unreal, and I wondered how I might push Hindy's words back into the phone.

I could hear Hindy's voice, still speaking, but I couldn't listen any longer, and besides, nothing she said mattered anymore. It was too late.

Beyond the Door

I parked outside Felix's small Queens house, the one he used to share with Shani. When Felix opened the door, his eyes were watery, his chin shaky.

"I didn't know what to do," he said. "I just told them she died. I don't know what else to say."

I had to be with Shani's children, and I was trying hard to think coherent thoughts, something to say to Micki and Adam.

"It's okay," I told Felix. "Of course you had to tell them."

Felix gestured vaguely around his living room. I saw little Adam putting blocks into a puzzle cube on the floor. Micki slipped into the room in a striped summer romper. She looked at me with so much darkness in her eyes, confusion on her thin freckled face.

"How about a walk?" I said, and she followed me out the door, walked around the city block with me, her small sandaled feet matching my stride.

Then she was in my arms and sobbing, her tiny body shaking against mine. I held her as tight as I could, and we stood together on the sidewalk. I felt the tears well in my eyes, the grief rise through my chest. I measured, thought, calculated the merit of her seeing my human reaction to the news against the risk of further traumatizing her. *It's okay for her to see me hurt over this*, I decided just before the tears flowed down my face and into her hair.

"What happened?" She stopped and looked up at me with deep brown eyes that were the same shade as mine, the same shade as her mother's.

I repeated the lie I'd been told for eons. "She was sick for a while, and I think at the end her heart gave up, and the doctors couldn't save it." That part, at least, was true in some ways.

Micki looked skeptical. She knew that Shani had been sick in ways that were not physical. She knew that I knew that too. We were both at the police station when Shani was escorted out by medics. We had both seen Shani race against her own mind and then fall into bed for weeks.

My answer wasn't enough for her. It wasn't enough for me at her age, when I was missing Shani. But I didn't know what else to say.

I'm sorry, Shani, I whispered in my heart. *I promise, one day I'll tell her who you really were.* I felt the spirit of Shani right there, embracing me, forgiving me, understanding that the lies were all I knew.

For the shiva, the seven days of mourning, I returned to my childhood home, where we, the sisters, would observe the week of mourning. Abba would sit shiva in Israel.

When Hindy opened the door and I took my first steps into the house, what hit me first was the silence. I forgot how quiet the house was, a stark contrast to the loudness of the home I shared with Eli and our children. No electronics playing in the background. No footsteps or murmurs or even the sound of conversation. Just dead air over the parquet dining room floor, which was buffed to a flawless shine.

Hindy examined my black zip-up hoodie.

"Good," she said, "you ripped on the right side." Then she furrowed her brows, and an unfamiliar vulnerability appeared. "Do you think anyone will notice I ripped the wrong side?" She tugged at the safety pins. "Or will it look even stranger if I have two rips?"

The law mandated where we ripped our shirts, how many inches across our hearts, and those were the shirts we would wear for the next seven days of shiva. I thought, *Is this really what she's worried about now?* Then I reminded myself, *She has a right to grieve in her own way.* Out loud I said, "We should get that book, with all the laws for mourners, just so we have it."

She nodded, though I couldn't help seeing, in Hindy's concerns, a symbol for all the airlessness of her world. She was worried about what people would say when we mourned our sister. I was worried about things like, *We will never get to see the glint in Shani's eyes as she tells us another one of her creative plans. We will never get to watch her kiss her children and dance with them in her arms. We will never get to pick out a fortieth birthday gift for her.*

The house started to sound familiar again as a long wail came through the walls. I tried to ignore it, like I had ignored so many strange sounds in the house before. But the wailing pierced through my ripped shirt, through my heart, and I felt it reverberate inside my body. *She just lost her child*, I realized, and I wrestled with myself until I remembered that I was an adult, and her strange moods could not hurt me anymore.

I took careful steps over the worn linoleum of the red kitchen floors. I stopped at the door of her bedroom, watched her feet, in house slippers, one over the other at the edge of her bed. I steeled myself as I entered the room, shoved my own tears down, back into the locked base of my skull. She looked at me and the wailing continued, softer, a series of anguished cries. I sat down on the bed across from her, looked into her sunken eyes. She gulped for air.

"Malka?" she sobbed, and looked at me, wrinkles like ashes through her skin. I sat with her because she was my mother. I sat with her because I knew that she did not mean to live inside of tombs, that she did not choose to have a mind that was shrouded by demons. I sat with her because that is what Shani would have wanted, for our mother to know she was not alone.

We did not mention years that had passed, the children I'd had that she never met. We both knew that she was not strong enough to face the next generation, that her psyche had crashed too many times before, that it was just better for everyone if we stayed estranged. I wanted to believe that leaving me alone to live my life was her way of saying *I love you.* I wanted to believe that she would be devastated if I died too.

In the absence of words, we shared the touch of our identical bony hands, grasped together. Her knuckles and mine both white, her breath and mine both trembled, her eyes and mine both spilled over, flooded down our faces.

As the shiva days progressed, something bizarre happened. The sisters who raised me from birth shifted in their chairs and looked to me for answers. Maybe it was because I was a therapist, or because I acted the role of someone who had it together.

I still didn't know if it was one of my sisters who had made the decision to have Shani's children forcibly taken two years earlier, before her final round of hospitalizations. I wanted to believe that whoever made that decision had information that I did not. Maybe they knew, from Shani's friends in Israel, or from Abba, that she really wasn't managing, that she was starting to unravel again, that her children needed more stability than she could provide.

There was a lot that I would never know. However, I did recognize the shape of love. When one of us broke, the others winced; when one of us faltered, the others held her up. The sisters in the shiva room were the ones who taught me what to do when I got my first period, the ones who kept lists of everything I would need for my wedding, the ones who opened their homes to me and my children. And although we never said the words out loud in our family, I loved them, too, with my entire heart. So I listened to their questions.

Dina asked, "Why, Malka? Why did she do it? Why now?"

Goldy asked, "What is the best way to talk to my kids about this?"

Between visitors, I shared insights garnered from my patients and my schooling: bipolar disorder could be so painful, that sometimes all the person wanted was for the pain to stop. It was nobody's fault. On the psych unit, I had treated people from the most supportive families who just couldn't take the pressure in their minds anymore. Shani had over forty inpatient hospitalizations. It was the disease that killed her.

I believed some of my words. At the same time, I wondered what could have been. What if our family had truly supported Shani? What if we had listened instead of judged? What if I'd invited her to my home that night at the police station, instead of calling an ambulance? I wondered if my other sisters had regrets, things they were afraid to say out loud, ways in which they failed her. It might have been the bipolar disorder that broke Shani, but we could have patched her together. We could have at least tried.

Dassa called me, her voice an octave deeper than it used to be.

"I had to," she said. "I just had to."

I imagined her looking out onto the dry desert sand on the other side of the world, finding an international calling card, breaching the oceans that kept us apart. She did not make any of the usual, impertinent shiva comments. With her on the other end of the phone, the tight knot of my grief unraveled, and I cried. She was there through the guttural sounds of my brokenness, through my hoarse, incoherent descriptions of what happened to Shani.

When my breath came back into my lungs, I changed the subject. "Does it have to be this serious for us to talk?"

She talked about her husband, how he joined the Israeli Defense Force, and how sometimes they moved bases at a moment's notice. They didn't always have phone access. The army was unpredictable like that. I heard the words underneath the ones she spoke out loud, *I will always care about you, but we cannot be in touch.* She sounded proud, purposeful, and I heard traces of joy as she talked about defending the borders of the Holy Land. I thanked her for giving me the only bit of comfort I had felt all week. "I knew I could do that for you," she said, and her old low chuckle returned, just for a moment, and then she was gone. I held on to the traces of her love, packed them away in my heart, and returned to the shiva room.

I went home to my children each night, sat down with them, told them little bits of what had been happening.

"Her heart was too weak," I explained, the lie tasting like sand in my mouth.

"Mommy, is your heart gonna get sick?" Avigdor looked at me over the top of his neon glasses and asked a version of the very same question that I had asked myself for the last twenty years. Shira curled her body into mine, her small head tucked under my arm.

"My heart is healthy, don't worry. I am perfectly healthy. I promise."

I distracted them with Elmo cupcakes from the local supermarket, treats I had delivered to mark Bakery Day, our own family tradition.

"Next week we will go to the store again," I promised, because weekly bakery trips meant that I was okay, that they would be okay, that we would continue to survive.

As the shiva days passed, we stumbled into some joy in the memory of her. We sat in our mourner's chairs and laughed together in the midst of our sadness. Mimi huddled close to us, watched us, not wanting to miss a word. For her, it was the first time we were all together, in our childhood home, being sisters.

"Remember the way she only ate the crust part of pizza?" Goldy was fourteen when Shani disappeared into the phantom world in her mind. She looked at us, sea-blue eyes large in her pale face, voice thin and unsure.

"Yes!" Hindy was emphatic, sitting straight up, deep dimples breaking through the sorrow on her face. "She used to sit there and wait, and wait, and stare at my pizza until I finally gave in and ripped the crust off."

"And fries," Dina added, her delicate voice rising over ours, with the certainty of one who was closest to Shani. "Fries and crust. That was her meal."

Dina's face melted again, tears skimmed over her porcelain skin, down her narrow chin. Goldy passed tissues and wiped a sleeve across her own eyes. Hindy put a hand on Mimi's shoulder, squeezed. I wished for a red-checkered cardboard container of hot french fries, and for the presence of Shani, just one more time, so I could give her the whole thing.

"How about when she said she didn't need a wig! And I just didn't believe her."

We already knew the story, but we let Hindy tell it again. How she purchased a custom wig, brought it all the way to Israel in her carry-on, gave it to Shani before her wedding. Shani had laughed, put the wig box in the back of her closet, and left it there for years.

"For actual years!" Hindy said, her indignance laced with amusement.

She wasn't one for artificial hair, our Shani. Instead, she wore head-scarves in shades of ombre or tie-dye or patterned with paisley. For special occasions, she had silver-threaded scarves tied in intricate knots, framing her large dark eyes, her glowing olive skin. It was Hindy's turn to break apart at the retelling, and her face creased in anguish, her hands gripped the arms of her chair as she wept. We passed the tissues back to her.

When I got back to the penthouse at the end of the shiva week, I was bone-tired and dry-eyed and guarded within an inch of my life. I needed to take a hot shower, lie down in my bed, and stare numbly at a wall for days or weeks.

"What can I get you?" Eli asked, stepping around me as if I were a china doll at the edge of a precipice. He came up next to me and tried to look into my eyes.

"Just talk to me," he pleaded after hours of my blank silence.

I had no words left inside me. None at all.

In the week after shiva, I returned to work. Between sessions, I collapsed onto the carpeted floor of my office, against my wall of diplomas. They didn't seem at all connected to me. The pain felt so deep, like a pitch-black abyss that I could fall into at any moment if I didn't hold on tight. The edges of the pain were enough to leave me curled up on the floor, heaving, as streams of tears hit the carpet.

Eli shrunk to the side of my grief. I didn't have words to communicate what I was feeling, and I kept it inside as we coordinated dinner for the children and shared carpool schedules and talked about who would pick up cash to pay the housekeeper.

After I was back at work for a few days, acting like a version of the me I was before, Eli asked, "Will we ever have sex again?"

When he saw the look on my face, his broad shoulders turned inward. He looked seven years old, and he rushed to correct himself. "I don't really mean that, I don't care about the sex, I just want to know if it's because you are going through something or because you are mad at me."

For the first time since our marriage, a clear, unwanted thought popped into my head: *a woman would never ask me that.* I tried to shake the thought. I was never going to be with a woman who looked at my face and saw beneath my defenses and held me before I knew I needed to be held.

I reassured Eli, "I just need some time. It's not you, I promise."

I went on vacation with Eli a month later, because we always spent the holidays in Miami, and I had supposedly pulled myself together. But everywhere we went, I saw tall buildings with porches, and I kept picturing Shani falling through the air. We drove to the Bal Harbour Shops, where we used to browse designer clothing and shoes.

When we parked our car, I had a panic attack at the railing of the parking garage. I looked down to the ground, to the palm trees four stories down, and all I wanted to do was jump. I held on to the metal railing and forced breaths to come out of my mouth and nose, and I felt my body shake so hard that I sank to the concrete floor. I wanted to die. I just wanted it to end.

When the breath came back into my body, I told Eli, "It was nothing."

When we returned home, I googled and learned that those who survive a family member's suicide are five times more likely to attempt suicide. It was the first time I said the word out loud to myself. Suicide. I googled some more and found a support group in a local Temple.

I told the group about wanting to hurtle myself through the air. The kind couple who ran the group advised me to seek therapy. I was in therapy, I said. The pain was too deep for therapy, because when I touched the surface of it, my insides cracked and fell apart.

I kept those unopened voicemails from Shani on my phone for weeks. I sat in my therapist's tiny office and trembled as I hit play. Turned out, they were just a series of beeps and tones. She was trying to reach me, but she didn't leave a message. I felt cheated, robbed of my last bit of Shani.

In my grief, I shut Eli out. It was the one thing wrong with me that he would never be able to fix. I tried not to wonder whether our relationship was hinged on him fixing the broken parts of me. He tried to check in with me. "You seem so distant," he said. I lied. Every day I lied. I put my heels on and strode out the door, acted like I was more than fine. I was not sure which one of us had thrown it, but suddenly there was a machete right through the foundation of us.

I didn't want to keep thinking about Dassa and the way she knew exactly what to say when she called me during Shani's shiva. Deep down, I knew that I was not giving Eli a chance. I never talked about the way my heart still felt torn up inside. I wondered whether it would be easier for me to bare my raw edges to someone who cupped my face in her hand, someone more like myself. Maybe the grief was too enormous, too engulfing, to share with anyone.

At night, after Eli fell asleep, I scrolled through Hulu until I found a show that made me forget the midnight days: *The L Word*. I pictured myself living among the lesbians in Los Angeles, where it seemed normal for women to immerse themselves in one another, and then walk the streets with sex-mussed hair, hands in the back pockets of each other's jeans. I wanted to be them. I wanted to send a sultry glance across a crowded café and wait for a woman to meet it. I wanted to show up at her door with a single flower. I wanted to hear about her goals and then help her achieve them. I wanted to see her number show up on my phone and then feel my entire body flush.

I woke up in the mornings at the edge of the bed, Eli's body pressed against mine.

"I love you," he murmured as the sun came through our window. I hated myself for taking a breath before saying it back. It was a selfish breath. A space of a few seconds, just enough to leave him staring up at the ceiling as I hurried out into my day.

Everything is great, I said to myself as I typed lines of statistical data into my computer and ran analyses for my dissertation study.

Be grateful, I yelled inside my head when I came home holding a briefcase stuffed with research surveys and found my children sitting around the kitchen table doing their homework, Eli bent over them to sign tests and help solve equations.

I am so lucky, I reminded myself when I deposited stacks of client checks at the end of each week, when the number on my account got so high that the bank representatives started talking to me in low, respectful voices and ushering me into meetings with their wealth management team.

"I am stressed, and I don't know why," I told Dina through the phone as we peeled and chopped and caught each other up on our weeks with synchronicity borne of a lifetime of sisterhood.

"Maybe it's because you have everything you ever wanted, and now you are afraid of losing it," Dina said, pausing as our blenders whirred at the exact same time.

We were miles apart, but we still cooked potato kugel using her recipe each Friday afternoon. We talked more after Shani's death, sharing our lives and some of our pain, planning family get-togethers for Shani's children.

"I'm fine, really," I said, because I didn't want her to worry. Our family had enough worries.

When we got off the phone, I scrolled through my contacts for the one labeled *G.* Genevieve. I left a message.

"I don't know if you remember me. It's Malka. I just wanted to come in for a few sessions."

Two weeks later, I was back in Genevieve's basement office thirteen blocks away from my childhood home in Borough Park.

I told her what happened to Shani. That my brain replayed a movie of Shani's body falling through the air, all the time. How I felt like everything around me could collapse at any moment.

"That sounds a whole lot like PTSD," she said, leaning back in her cushioned chair. "Just breathe. We can get you through this."

Post-traumatic stress disorder. That made so much sense. I couldn't believe that I, a trauma therapist, had not considered it. My brain was a frozen glob, activated only during business hours, and only for the benefit of others.

"I'm not sure if this is a symptom," I said slowly, not daring to hope. "Since she died, I keep having thoughts that I wish I didn't have. Remember, I was always a little bit bisexual?"

Genevieve squinted at me, and her eyes hit the surface of my kneecaps, exposed beneath the hem of my slinky pencil skirt. She looked back up at my face quickly, but not before she looked above it, right where I had pulled some of my own hair over the part of my wig and clipped it back, with a look that begged the question, *Is she or isn't she covering her hair?*

"Malka," she said slowly. "That's not related to the loss. You have always had a tendency to self-sabotage just when things are going well for you."

I wanted to tell her about the thoughts, the way they crept up at night as I lay near my husband, listening to him breathe. I wanted to describe the way they intensified even more when Eli and I fought. I held it all inside, the way I kept wanting to lean in, put my cheek against the soft skin of my imagined woman. The way I wanted to be enfolded, to pour myself into the shape of someone who felt more like me than like the man in my bed.

Her therapist sound machine roared in the background, as always, but it sounded louder. It sounded like thunder inside my head, crashing against my skull, blocking out the sounds of her words. I watched her mouth move in ways that suggested she was saying that same-sex attraction was not real, that it was a diversion, that I was deliberately trying to destroy my happiness.

I drove home with my knuckles clenched around the leather of my steering wheel, and I knew that I never wanted to see her again. I couldn't articulate exactly why, it was just as if the forces joined from within my body, fire and steel and resolve, and they combined to say, *No.*

Only Human

In the wake of my own grief, Eli fell into darkness.

"I can't do this anymore."

He stood on the porch, outside the master bedroom of our newly rented beach house. We were exhausted with trying to squish our two separate families together in a penthouse designed for a bachelor. We did not quite fit into the beach house, either, but at least it was a fresh start for all of us with two floors, a large dining space, and a game room for the children. That was how it seemed to me. Eli, however, had been dissolving since we moved in.

"You don't care about me."

He tossed the accusation across the balcony, paused so I could refute it. The pause lingered. *He is not wrong,* I thought. Something had changed in the months since Shani died. I just kept thinking about how much I wanted to run away. In my dreams, I was a bartender serving umbrellaed drinks at an oceanfront bar in Aruba. I joked with the patrons through long afternoons, laughed easily when girls wrote their phone numbers on my wrist for later. In my dreams, I was alive.

One Saturday night, I sat on the front stairs of our beach house, browsed the news to catch up on what I'd missed over Shabbos, and read the latest on CNN's website:

> *In a landmark opinion, a divided Supreme Court on Friday ruled that same-sex couples can marry nationwide, establishing a new civil right and handing gay rights advocates a historic victory.*

The colors on my screen felt like lasers, blinding me. I saw the White House glowing in rainbow lights, fuchsia and cobalt and garnet reflecting off the north lawn. My thumb raced up and down my screen as I read the whole paragraph several times in a row.

I was vaguely aware of Eli flicking a lighter and saying something about getting coffee from Dunkin'. I scanned the article again, swallowed the words with my eyes as fast as I could, before he could realize that I was no longer there. I read about the weddings that took place earlier that afternoon, scrolled the photos of women in suits and dresses, kissing each other on the lips, of men in floral wreaths holding each other's hands.

I wanted to catch the next train to Washington, DC, and dance in the streets with all of them. I wanted to smear rainbow glitter across my cheeks and wave colored flags in the air and twirl around in joy. President Obama agreed that love is love and that it had taken too long and that we deserved equality, finally.

"What?" Eli asked as he leaned over my shoulder.

I looked down at myself, at the skirt that had ridden above my bare knees, at the diamond on my finger, glinting in the light of my screen. *This celebration is not for me*, I reminded myself. *Not anymore, not ever.*

"The news," I said, my voice uneven as I became very aware of the rainbow emanating from my screen, into my world of black and white.

I watched his eyes go sideways as he read the words, "Equal dignity in the eyes of the law." He looked at me, I looked at my phone, and our whole world stopped. I knew what the shadow in his blue eyes meant. I knew him enough to recognize the fear, the one he felt already and had voiced to me at least once a week, *What if you stop loving me?*

I had been laughing it off, trying to convince us both that I had found my true love, and that it was him. We almost believed it. I was not about to let either of us down, and so I clicked some links on my phone and found a particle of news that seemed less threatening.

"Check this out!" I said, putting the bounce back in my voice, hoping he didn't catch the tremor. "Ben and Jerry's came up with a new flavor just for this!"

Eli and I bent over the tiny image of an ice cream pint labeled "I Dough, I Dough," and took turns looking for the small OU symbol that would indicate it was kosher.

"Ben and Jerry—they're probably so gay," Eli joked.

I forced a laugh. My laugh meant that our lives were just fine, nothing bad would happen to us. That Eli's fear would be diffused before it grew into something I did not want to be around for.

After the Supreme Court's landmark decision, my body couldn't stop buzzing. It felt like a drill was planted at the base of my spine, always on, always sending tremors through me. I found myself googling tattoo artists, wishing I were allowed to lie down and have someone drill into my body. Wishing that just for a moment, the noise outside me would be louder than the thrumming inside.

Week after week, Eli watched me take screenshots of tattoos on models and actors. The pilled butterfly poem on Megan Fox's shoulder. The dark birds on Shailene Woodley's collarbone in her role as Tris in *Divergent*. The wings that seemed to cradle Rihanna's small breasts.

"I can cut that patch of skin off when you die," he offered, a morbid reference to the Jewish Law that absolutely forbade tattoos. Our tradition was such that once we died, a devout Jew would scrub our entire bodies clean, from our toenails to the skin of our scalps. If that assigned Jew discovered a tattoo on a dead body, that body was not allowed into a Jewish cemetery. Instead, it was buried on the outskirts of the cemetery, along with the bodies of those who died by suicide, another cardinal sin.

The rabbis had found an exemption for Shani's suicide. Maybe it was the mental illness, or maybe they decided falling from the eighteenth floor of a building could have been an accident. She was buried on a hill in Jerusalem among our ancestors. Maybe a part of me wanted to take her spot, on the outskirts. To mark the burial spot that would have honored her pain, would have acknowledged her suicide, instead of covering it up and painting it with a more palatable narrative. I was so over shoving entire parts of the human experience under the rug, out of sight.

I still fasted and prayed on Yom Kippur, covered my hair and body when I left the house, said the Shema prayer with my children each night, and talked to God each morning before I began my sessions. Somehow though, I felt no guilt at all when I completed the online form for a consult with Scarlett Johansson's tattoo artist. In the place of fiery shame or fear or visions of God striking me down with a sharp bolt of lightning, I felt complete calm.

Late one Saturday night, Eli drove us into Manhattan's East Village. The stillness in my bones and in my veins lasted through our entire drive.

"Something with wings," I said to the slim man whose work I had studied for weeks.

"How 'bout I sketch something for you?" He tucked shoulder-length strands of hair behind his ears, revealing earlobes pierced with rings the size of quarters.

I felt a nudge in my side and remembered Eli. He looked around the studio as if it were the scariest place he had ever been, blue eyes wide, fists tight against the sides of his jeans. I followed the direction of his stares, and we both took in the people lying on paper-covered tables, the tattooed arms of artists running machines over skin.

When I saw the artist's drawing, delicate birds flying upward in a curved formation, I knew I needed it on my body. I stood in front of a carved mirror in my red bra, as Eli lifted my arm up and down, pointing out the exact spot on my rib cage that would be the least risky place for a tattoo. We figured that if I were out among modern Jews in a bikini, I would want the option of clamping my arm to my side to hide my forbidden ink.

I lay down on a paper-covered table and allowed a needle gun to pierce my skin. I felt the blood rush through my body, and for the first time in a very long time, I felt alive. It was just me, the tattoo gun, and my own blood.

It was days before I ran my fingers over the rough skin on my birds and counted them. Even though I had projected art therapy drawings from my laptop onto the walls of several large rooms and shown my trainees real-life examples of the importance of quantity in art, I seemed to have forgotten one of my most crucial lessons: when people draw the same object several times, always note the number. A child who drew four apples on a tree turned out to have four members in their family. A mother who drew three flowers in a field of grass turned out to have three children.

I should not have been that shocked to find that without even thinking about it, I had gotten seven birds inked into my skin. Somehow, despite all my mixed feelings about my family, I had Yanky, Hindy, Dina, Shani, Goldy, Mimi, and me all represented on my rib cage. *They are a part of me, like it or not.*

In an effort to cement the cracks in our relationship, Eli and I decided to buy a new house and tell ourselves new lies.

In the new house, Eli wouldn't be depressed.

In the new house, I would have a fresh start after my loss.

Eli's parents were supremely wealthy, and they owned city skyscrapers and buildings that were national landmarks. They believed that renting was a bad idea. "Why rent when you can own?" I didn't fully grasp the logic of the rich. They would never know what it had been like to skip dinner so I could have enough slices of bread for my children. To feel like money was a transient commodity, one that would never truly last.

In autumn, just after Shira began fourth grade, we took the kids to see the new house.

"Is it for permanent?" Shira asked as we toured our new backyard for the first time, stepping around the custom stone edges of our in-ground swimming pool.

"Are we allowed to invite friends?" Avigdor asked, as he bent down to peek underneath the patio, where full-sized rafts and tubes were stored in a neat pile.

"Yes," Eli announced, spreading his arms wide, toward the garden of purple-leaved trees and neat shrubs, toward the sloping roof of our wood-paneled house. "We own this!"

We stopped at the front door, took in the country club across the street, so close that the realtor had warned us about errant golf balls that might whiz onto our lawn. Shira's eyes stopped at the tennis courts, green squares all in a row.

"Yes," I said, hardly believing it myself, "we can sign you up for tennis with the other girls on the block."

Avigdor and Josh stood under the basketball hoop in our new drive-way, looking back and forth between the hoop and the vehicles—Eli's shiny Volvo and my new Audi. "Can you park in the street sometimes, so we can play?" they asked.

I answered questions like someone who knew what she was doing. I walked through the sun-soaked living room and talked about paint colors like a grown-up who'd signed stacks of documents stating that I co-owned what felt like a real-life mansion.

"We need neutrals in here, and shelving on this wall," I said out loud.

Don't get too attached, I warned myself internally. *You never know.* I had lived enough to know that nothing was truly permanent. I also knew that even though our names were on the papers, and we would be paying the mortgage, it was Eli's parents who had wired the half a million dollars for our down payment. His relationship with them was full of spiky hills and fiery pits. His relationship with me felt similar, some of the time. However, in the excitement of our granite fireplace, five professionally designed bedrooms, multiple plush couches, and the promise of summers at the side of the pool, I started to believe that we could overcome all of it, that we could create a future that was deserving of the house.

I had been cracking down on my PhD research, through the nights and between clients and in place of manicures or exercise.

On the day of my dissertation defense, I reviewed my PowerPoint presentation. I held my breath and tried to calm the shaking in my fingers as I scrolled through my diagrams. I was terrified that they'd decide my quantitative research was not executed correctly, that despite the over two hundred in-person surveys, it was inadequate, and I needed to start over.

"I was raised without any access to media," I told the reviewers, as background for the essence of my study, on the Sexualization of Women in Popular Media.

"Are you able to describe the term 'no media,'" one of the professors asked, face blank and turned downward, pen moving over a notepad.

"Well, my home had no TV, no screens at all. I watched my first show when I was twenty-four."

The reviewer's face snapped up toward me as she asked for details. I heard chuckles when I described my shock at watching my first episode of *Grey's Anatomy*, and even more laughter when I talked about how shocked I was to see so many beautiful women on the screen of my Dell Inspiron.

They scribbled as I moved through my prepared slides. They listened as I reviewed the correlational analyses. They were impressed to learn that I went deep into the closed community of Hasidic Brooklyn and found a control group of young women who had never been exposed to media. I reviewed charts with clear results: women who were exposed to TV and movies tended to score lower on measures of body image and self-esteem.

When they congratulated me and called me "Doctor," it felt like a win not just for me, but for Orthodox Judaism as a whole. I had proven our ideals were worthy, through the evidence gathered in my scientific research.

I arrived home to Eli holding balloons and our children hugging me and a table set for our celebratory dinner.

"You said you would be a doctor when I was in fifth grade, and it was true!" Avigdor exclaimed.

I kissed the top of his head, the blue velvet of his yarmulke. "Remember, you can do anything you aim for," I said, and his cheeks dimpled as he answered, "I know."

For the rest of the week, my children called me "Doctor Mom," their way of claiming the achievement with me, of recognizing that we had all gotten to the other side. We weren't the single-parent family at the edge of town anymore. I was not the person who shoved bills into drawers and lay awake at night with fear crawling through my veins. I was a doctor. We hadn't only survived, we had risen.

After I successfully defended my dissertation, Eli helped with every aspect of furthering my career. He supported my attendance at conferences, and when I needed to work late or go out of town, he covered the household for me.

When I first met Eli, I was a social worker, employed by others. Eli helped me start my own practice. Through his marketing company, he assigned a team to build my branding and website, and he was by my side through months of renovations and permit acquisitions for my new office.

At our opening-night celebration, I welcomed the professionals who had rented and decorated offices within my brand-new practice, respected therapists with established reputations for trauma therapy and couples' work. They stood near me for a group shot by a local news reporter, placed arms around my waist and then leaned in for hugs and excited whispers, "Great turnout!" They supported my strategy for breaking into the therapy marketplace as a hot new practice: *don't compete, collaborate.*

I was twenty-nine, one of the younger professionals in the room, and I had achieved something that many of them would never attempt. I allowed myself a moment of pride as I stood before the crowd and welcomed them to our vision of a safe, warm, family-centered practice.

I invited them to walk around, to look at the small cottage that my interior designer had turned into a psychotherapy haven. The walls were painted in soothing tones of mint and tan. The original terra-cotta floor tiles had been glossed and regrouted. The soft leather couches and abstract art accomplished the precise vibe I had been going for when I told the designer, "A combination of Anthropologie and Free People," my way of ensuring the space felt more like an upscale bohemian living room than a sterile office. I showed the visiting therapists my custom-built sand-colored shelves, filled with miniatures that would soon be held by little fingers and placed in the nearby sand tray.

As I scanned the space to make sure I greeted each attendee, I saw Eli slip out the back door. As he glanced back at me, I saw something different in his eyes. It passed so quickly that I was not sure what it was.

Later that night, as I removed my heels back in our bedroom, he asked, "What happens when you don't need me anymore?"

He turned away from me, became a large, huddled figure at the edge of the bed. I felt his fear seep through me as I stood in the shower and washed the evening off. I was the face of the Wellness Center, but how good was I if I couldn't even make my own husband feel secure?

By 2017 I was the director of a vibrant team. My employees had full caseloads, and some kept waiting lists, like me. I led multiple training sessions, and other professionals in the area came to my cottage offices to learn our formula for success. I began to train others in trauma, expressive therapies, and how to communicate with parents of child clients. I was able to finally contribute to my household in a financially meaningful way, to the mortgage, car, and vacations.

On most days, I still sat back up in my therapist chair at the top of every hour, nodding and listening and blinking the tears back. I felt my clinical bandwidth stretch and expand to hold deeper layers of pain than I had ever been able to hold before. I brushed my own fear and abuse and trauma to the side so many damn times that it was almost second nature. I was not at all prepared for the grief; for how fresh it was, even four years later. It was visceral, through every muscle and limb in my body, through every fiber of my heart, through every moment of my day.

I wanted to leave the office and drive to Shani's children and take them home to live with me. I wanted to fly to Israel and search the hotel room that was the last space where Shani breathed, looking for a note, a hint, anything that would tell me what had been going through her mind. I wanted to look out that window and see what she saw in her last moments. More than anything, I just wanted to talk to her one more time.

Eli seemed surprised when I mentioned my grief. He didn't quite say it, but he turned his head to the side, looked down, and waited for me to stop talking. He seemed at a loss for a response, and so after a while, I spared him the whole interaction. During our busy days, it was easier to push the thoughts to the side, the image of a woman on the other side of my texts, a woman who would simply write, *I'm here*. At night though, the illusory woman returned in my dreams, brushed a hand over my cheek, kissed my tears.

Despite my PhD in human psychology, I kept doing all the things that hadn't worked before. My inspiration was derived from my Jewish theology classes, where I learned that sometimes it was more effective to channel our evil inclinations than to quash them. For example, if one felt a strong urge to commit murderous violence, he was encouraged to become a *shochet*, one who slaughtered livestock. If a Jewish woman felt the need to pursue a career in music, she was encouraged to perform for small audiences of other Jewish women. The logic was something like: take the edge off in a way that is not sinful.

I inferred that my desires for women could be managed through finding small, not-sinful outlets. To that end, I read blogs on websites where women posted their fantasies; female student falls in love with sexy female professor, woman cop finds a female suspect irresistible, college roommates reach for each other in the night. I wore an Aviator Nation hoodie with rainbow stripes to our Shabbos lunch table. None of it helped to take the edge off. I still lay near Eli at night, holding my phone and scrolling through the app store, trying not to download lesbian meetup apps.

One day, as we strolled through a nearby mall, Eli and I noticed the brass letters above a brand-new storefront: Peloton. We'd heard about the luxury spin bike from our wealthy friends, and we entered the store, wanting to see what the buzz was about. The next thing we knew, we were signing paperwork and planning a delivery.

I began a routine, spinning every day when I got home from work, cycling until my body felt peace. On the bike, I was distracted by the view of impossibly toned instructors and the sound of pop music and the movement of my legs. I woke up early on Sunday mornings to take live classes, where I chased other riders on the leaderboard as we all built strength. My children learned that when Mom was on the bike, they were not allowed to disturb her under any circumstance, unless someone was bleeding or had a bone poking through their skin.

The energy I exhausted on that bike felt like a remedy for my increasing thoughts about women. Within a few weeks, I spun so hard and so fast that my quads ached.

I booked a sports massage at a local massage therapy center, just like the ones I had seen my spin instructors post on their stories.

As I walked through a darkening local parking lot to my appointment, I thought about the fact that Peloton hadn't taken the edge off at all. It made the edge sharper, so sharp that I could feel it against the inside of my body, trying to cut through. If a woman touched me, the temptations I had been holding down with all my might, they might escape my control. I didn't want to think about what that could entail, and so when I entered the massage parlor, I asked for a male masseuse. That, I thought, would be safe.

"What are your tension areas?" Rick asked, as he stood in the corner of a dim room and took notes on a clipboard.

I told him about spin cycling and my sore muscles.

He nodded, lit a eucalyptus-scented candle, and left the room so I could change. I placed my clothing on a chair and lay down underneath a thin white sheet on a massage table.

Rick moved his large body around the table, sat down on a stool, and started rubbing my scalp. He murmured, almost to himself, as he moved his hands down my shoulders, down my chest. He touched my breasts so casually that for a moment, I thought that must be part of the protocol. But as I heard the pace of his breathing change, I realized that something was not right.

As he moved alongside me, tossing my sheet to the ground, I felt myself lose control of my body. I was distinctly aware of the ways in which my psyche was falling apart, of being violated, but could not will myself to put up a fight as his body broke through mine.

Despite my very extensive trauma vocabulary, I was stunned, at a loss for words.

I don't have time for this. I shook myself out of it and went home, kept my face smooth, and tucked my children into bed. I showered, knowing I was washing away valuable evidence, and also not knowing what I was doing at all.

"It was fine," I lied, when Eli asked if my muscles felt better.

I tried to move on. I woke up. Had coffee.

I took the dark shape of what happened and shoved it beneath my tailored blazer. I could feel it scratching at the surface of my skin, trying to show itself to the world.

A few days later, Eli and I boarded a plane to Miami with our children for their winter vacation. Somewhere above the clouds, while my children watched a movie several rows back and I could no longer see the shape of New York through the narrow window, I crumbled. The tears fell and I curled up, knees to face in the vinyl seat.

On our vacation, I french braided Shira's hair and helped Avigdor pick out a hat for our first Miami Heat game, where we ate hot dogs and cheered along with the crowd. I joined Eli for morning runs on the boardwalk. I snapped photos of our children eating ice cream and I purchased books for them at the Bal Harbour Shops. I waved to neighbors from our town who shared our school vacation schedule and our affinity for North Miami Beach's kosher pizza store.

The entire time, I did not wear my wedding rings. I thought about it. But the thought of putting the platinum bands around my finger made me feel both disloyal and chained. So, for the first time in four years, I kept them off.

After Eli and I returned from Miami, I went back to sitting in the director's chair in my corner office, back to leading clinical meetings and seeing clients. I continued to slide behind the wheel of my Audi at the end of each day and help Eli serve dinner to our children. I continued to furiously Peloton several times a week. I continued to press my body close to Eli's in bed at night, to burrow into the warmth of his chest.

I did not tell him about the sexual assault. I did not tell him that I was disintegrating, that I shook in the shower, and I couldn't stop smelling eucalyptus and man sweat, that my food wanted to come back up my throat as soon as I swallowed it.

"Sure," I said, when he asked if I was in the mood for sex. "I'm just a little tired," I said, when he commented on the limpness of my body in the sheets.

"If we can change the chatter in our heads, we may change the trajectory of our entire lives," Christine said.

I was at an in-person workshop in Manhattan one Saturday afternoon, led by Christine, a spin cycle instructor I encountered on the Peloton. When I first noticed her, she looked different from the others. *This will be good for me*, I thought, as I clicked the ride featuring a woman with wide curves. I was getting tired of looking at tanned six-pack abs, the kind that were inaccessible to my post-childbearing body.

Christine, who inhabited her body like it was a muscular power tool and talked about her size as an asset to her athleticism, made me feel reassured. Between songs, she would look right into the camera, wink one large blue eye, and command, "Sit down!"

I knew there were hundreds of other people taking the class, but it felt like she was talking directly to me. I felt it start in my gut, a twinge that grew into a throb and then a longing. I wanted to reach through the touch screen, ask her out for coffee, and walk her home through the darkening streets outside Peloton's Chelsea studio.

When I noticed a social media post about Christine's in-person Saturday workshop, I convinced Eli to make a weekend of it. "We can just get away," I said to him, adding about the hotel I found in Chelsea, and the time we could spend in pj's relaxing. I slid the words about the workshop in between the others. "It'll be grounding for me, it's just an hour."

Right before the workshop, as I waited for the group to gather, I met Bex, a woman with fire-engine-red hair in a teen-boy haircut, silver rings on every finger, and arresting green eyes. We chatted for a bit, and I told her about my work as a therapist. Bex told me about her asset management company. *This is the kind of person I belong with*, I thought. Someone sexy and accomplished who looked at me in an appraising, hungry, appreciative sort of way. Someone whose sports bras revealed just a hint of cleavage.

Christine leaned forward, the sleeves of her blazer rolled up, light eyes ethereal through her glasses. She seemed even more wise in person than she did on the spin bike, and I was ready to sink into her words, believe in something again, maybe even in myself.

Throughout the workshop, I felt Bex's eyes on my face. I thanked myself for wearing dykey combat boots, for the way in which my slouchy top slipped off my shoulder.

I volunteered to stand up in front of the group and read my intention out loud.

"I will be more authentic," I said to Christine's encouraging nod and to the camera that live-streamed to the Peloton Facebook audience.

By the end of the hour, we all knew some things about each other. Morgan was in from Connecticut with her boyfriend and their child, who were waiting at the Hilton. Dmitri was an accountant from uptown, and a road rider who took Peloton classes to build stamina. Bex had an ex-wife.

The group accepted my suggestion that we get post-workshop drinks at my hotel. We walked across the street together, chatting and exchanging social media information easily.

"You attract great people," I told Christine, who grasped my hand in hers and nodded in acknowledgment.

We settled around a long table, all of us sharing stories and wine through the afternoon. They liked me, the cool city Peloton people. Even more fascinating was how much I liked the Peloton Sara version of me. I felt the frisson in my gut, like string lights were turning on inside, one after another, setting me aglow.

More lesbians joined, people who had dinner plans with someone in the group and were pulled in, setting their parkas aside and pulling beanies off their short hair and ordering whiskey on the rocks. Bex asked gentle questions, sat back while people shared their answers. She had

Christine explain each of her tattoos, the words we could glimpse but not quite make out on the home screens of our bikes. Then I lifted my shirt to show off the birds on my rib cage, laughed at the on-brand compliments, "abs by Peloton!" and the light whistling.

There I was, abs out in the middle of the bar, women laughing and half-empty glasses on the table, when I saw him out of the corner of my eye. Damn. I almost forgot. I clenched my jaw, felt the muscles hit their familiar pattern. *Act natural,* I told myself as I waved him over.

"This is my husband!" I told the group, and I saw them do the same split-second adjustment that I did. They looked at me, ring-less and moto boots and tattooed. They looked at him, bearded and kippah-wearing and huddled in a puffy coat.

"You didn't tell us you had a husband!" they said lightly, pulling out a chair for him and waving the bartender over.

After the hugs goodbye and the promises to stay in touch, he turned a furious face toward me.

"You weren't wearing your rings!"

I rolled my eyes. It had been six weeks since I decided to remove my rings, six long weeks of leaving my rings in their box and holding the pieces of myself together with the bare force of my will. He hadn't seen me at all, the whole damn time.

That's when I reminded him that we were beginning couples counseling in two days. "Let's just save it for therapy."

More Than I Should

Nancy's office was in the very back of a maze of mismatched doors, shag rugs, and flickering lamps. She led us onto a velvet couch that took up the better part of a narrow room, where scented candles and crystal stones littered every surface. Eli planted both polished oxfords on the floor, both hands at his sides, eyes staring straight ahead.

"We have both been in marriage counseling before and ended up divorced," I explained, watching myself from behind an imaginary notepad, as I tended to do when I was in therapy. *Patient seems to feel responsible for husband. Codependent?* She crossed her legs, wide rips visible in her acid-washed jeans.

"Slow down, hun." Nancy waved a hand over a small tray and the scent of sage wafted through the already laden air. She placed cat-eyed frames on her nose, scanned our intake paperwork, and sat back in her armchair. "Why don't you tell me what is bothering you?"

I heard Eli's voice cut through the vanilla and honey and herb. "I think my wife is a lesbian."

I felt my brain freeze, and then start up again, rapid thoughts, one after the other. *Why would he say that?* And *He knows I'm bi* and *I promised I would be authentic* and *Fuck it.*

I looked at Nancy, at the dark brow arched above her highlighter glasses. I looked at the sweat stains on Eli's pale checked shirt, spreading. I had never even said it to myself. But Eli and I had the events of the past weekend fresh in our minds, and I knew they weren't random. I was tired of fighting so hard, of lying awake in bed at night and longing. I was worn down from years of lying to myself and to everyone around me.

I heard words that sounded too small and too far away to be coming from me.

"I think I am gay."

For a moment it felt like relief, to have the words out there. But I could see the reverberations of them bouncing off the walls, back through Eli's shoulders as he turned toward me. I could see the next words on his face, the ones that would result in me being a single mother once again. *I can't*, I told myself, and the workshop people in my head. *Authenticity is too dangerous.* They would never understand that the cool psychologist in designer jeans and a rib cage tattoo was bound by ancient tradition. That the moment I decided that I was not straight, I violated the agreement I signed in the court of Jewish law.

> *It is agreed by both parties that the children will be raised according to Halacha as stated in the Shulchan Oruch and the Mishna Berura. If it is determined by Rabbi Turkel of Lakewood, NJ, and Rabbi Levi of Jerusalem, Israel, that one party is not raising the children according to Halacha, custody will be transferred to the other biological parent.*

No matter how much the string lights inside me begged not to be doused, I was not willing to risk custody of my children. I needed the illusion of my marriage to stay intact.

And so I turned to Eli, with the sincerest expression I could muster on my face.

"You know that you are the only man I would ever be attracted to, right? You are my one percent." I saw the panic in the rapid blinking of his eyes. "We talked about this."

I turned to Nancy, who was looking back and forth between us, mouth agape. I explained that Eli and I had both known I was bisexual for a while. I said I might have realized that I leaned more to the women-loving side of the spectrum lately, but that I had no desire to be with anyone other than Eli.

The rationalizations sounded thin in the tiny chamber; they seemed to dissipate as they hit the air.

Eli was shaking by the time the session was over, and he stood on the side of the road with small bits of spit coming out of his mouth, waving his car keys in the air.

"How could you do this to me?"

There were sobs inside his voice, like broken thunder. He was so loud, I worried that we were disturbing the sessions inside the small cottage, several feet away. I wanted to call an Uber, but then I realized we would both end up at the same destination anyway, and so I climbed into the front seat and stayed still the whole way home.

We postponed our next therapy session, and we both tried to relegate my words to that office miles away, in Oceanside, where they could remain abstract. I repeatedly told Eli the opposite of *I think I am gay.* He said things like, the Torah doesn't even think it is a sin for women to be gay, because how do women even have sex anyway. I laughed with him, tried not to envision all the ways I wanted to be with a woman, all of the naked limbs entwined in mine.

"You are the one I love," I said.

"But are you in love with me?" he asked, and then I distracted him, with deep kisses and spontaneous sex and plans for the future.

My body kept it up for a couple of weeks, the performance of physical intimacy without me there. Then one day, as Eli leaned on his elbows above me and looked into my eyes, he saw how very blank they had become. "I feel like I am raping you," he said. "Where are you?" His words were casual, like one would say, *I don't want dessert today, how about you?*

I heard "rape" and my blankness faded and I pushed him off me, my thin arms like toothpicks against his chest, until he noticed and dropped down and watched me curl my knees to my chest and dig my head in between them. "Jesus," he sighed. "Is that a trigger word now?"

And because I was tired of him making light of my triggers and because suddenly it felt like a lot to be holding inside my rib cage all by myself, I just said it, my voice cold and hard.

"I was raped."

I wanted to hit him with it the way I was hit, to watch him break the way I couldn't. And he did.

He sat up and put two hands on my shoulders and pleaded for details.

I told him to step the fuck back from me. I told him it was recent. I watched the shock wash over him as I dropped the story out of myself and into the space between us.

"What was his name?" he asked, his voice an animal howl.

"What are you going to do? I don't want a big deal. I can't."

I held the massage rapist's name to myself, heard it echo in the darkness of my mind. Rick. Rick. Rick. I saw the cotton-draped table, flashes of my body, the stickiness I wiped off my back with a towel, the way I slid my ring into my purse when it was over and never put it back on.

We stayed awake through the night, taking cigarette breaks on the deck outside our room. I imagined what it might feel like to lift the thick cover off our pool, slide beneath it, and sink into the icy water. I put the thought out fast, ground it down like a cigarette butt before it could catch fire. I had children sleeping in their designer bedrooms upstairs, children who would need me to pack their snacks and kiss them goodbye before they boarded school busses in the morning.

"Have I been hurting you all this time? Every time?" Eli asked, distraught, as he lit his next Parliament off the butt of the last one and huffed into the cold air.

I thought about the years of lying still, the years of being mounted and thrust into, the many times I stood up and washed stickiness off my legs and kept moving. It was twelve years, since the first time, back in the bridal suite of a Brooklyn hotel with my children's father. Hundreds of times after that, of exiting my skin as others had entered it.

"It wasn't you." I told him how I didn't know how to say no, or when to say it. I saw the tears fall from his face, down his parka, onto the dark mounds of leftover snow.

I tried to reassure him that what we had between us was real, that it always had been, that I loved being close to him. I stopped talking when I realized that with every word, I was no longer talking about the previous few weeks of our sex life, I was talking about the entirety of our relationship, devaluing it all.

For the next few weeks, Eli and I held on to the wild, tempting hope that it was the assault that caused our marriage to splinter. That it was fixable. It would be something I could get treatment for and then turn back into the shiny blond wife I was.

There were some holes in the theory though, and I realized how ridiculous I sounded when I sat with my new therapist, Jacques.

"It's the trauma of the assault that has me just being over the whole idea of being with a man," I explained.

He nodded his slow, silver-streaked therapist nod and waited, and then very gently asked, "Have you *ever* wanted to have sex with a man?"

I was stunned. I could not believe that I had never asked myself that question before. "I guess I never really thought about it in those terms," I admitted. "That's a really good question."

"I'm healing from what happened," I told Eli when he asked about therapy. "I need time."

Eli saw me look past his shoulder, out the double glass doors of our bedroom. "But can you just talk to me?" he pleaded, peering at my face, his forehead crumpling. "Where do we stand? Do you still want to be here?"

"We're fine," I said, but the edges of my façade wore thin and my struggle poked through, and of course Eli could tell that nothing was fine.

"You don't love me!" His accusations scorched my skin, and I sat near him on our bedroom couch in frozen stiffness.

"Talk to me!" he begged, his cantor's voice vibrating through my chest, loud, louder.

The more I froze the louder he got, until the words that emerged from him, they felt nothing like Eli at all. His voice filled with fury.

"You think I won't tell people what you are? That you're a bisexual . . . or a lesbian or whatever you are?"

Somewhere in the middle of his rant I chose strategy over compassion. I pretended to check my messages while swiping carefully through my phone and then hitting record on my voice memo app. I knew from my years of helping clients through litigious divorces that it could be useful to have his threats in evidence.

When he stormed out of the house and I heard the angry squeal of his tires leaving the driveway, I forced myself to press play, to listen to his words again. Without him looming over me, I heard something else in his voice. Underneath his words, was the sound of a person shattering. I heard someone who was deeply in love, desperate to say or do anything he could to hold on to me. I felt a tingle of jealousy snake through my spine, up to my skull.

I wish I loved someone enough to lose my fucking mind, I found myself thinking. I was tired of dragging my heart behind me, forcing it into standing positions, squeezing it behind the zipper of tight dresses. I just wanted to feel in a way that took over, in a way that made my body want to move on its own.

My rainbow side existed in just a few places, but the list kept growing. My therapist. Our marriage therapist. Some Peloton people. Eli. Dassa. And recently, Leora, a divorce attorney with whom I had consulted. I could have shut it down at any time, and just acted straight and stayed where I was and stopped creating problems.

I considered that as I hit the buzzer outside Yakira's office. I was not sure why she asked to meet with me, and even though I had hired her as my child's therapist, I still somehow felt like I was being called to the principal's office.

"She's very well spoken, your Shira, very polite." She smiled at me in a way that was meant to be encouraging, but I saw the shadow behind it, the way her eyes hadn't crinkled at all. "I'm just worried about her restricted affect."

"Can you say more about that?"

I sat straight up, clenched a hand around my notebook, scribbled as if I were the therapist, because I sort of was. I always was. Especially when I was nervous.

"It's just that she never fully expresses any emotion. She seems guarded. Like she is afraid to feel things."

I heard the words and they hit that space beneath my therapist shell, and then suddenly I was telling Yakira that I was thinking about getting divorced. I explained that I was on guard too, all the time. I asked a question to which I already knew the answer, "Do you think she is picking up on the walls that I keep up?"

Yakira just looked at me, and her eyes glistened.

I felt the drops of my heartbreak slide down my face, off the same pointy chin that my Shira had. I could see it, her silent little face as she walked up the stairs and to her bedroom, where she spent hours alone. I saw her splashing in the backyard pool with her friends, her face still and serious. I tried to remember the last time I heard her laugh, the last time her eyes sparkled, and I couldn't. I hadn't seen her cry either, not in years, not since she was five years old. She was ten. What had I been doing to my child? I sobbed, ugly gulping sobs, snot mixed with tears, my notebook forgotten, as my fingers gripped the edge of the couch and then the tissue box Yakira passed to me.

I didn't know what I would do, not yet. But I did know that my Shira deserved to live in a home where her mother danced in the kitchen and struggled out loud and loved with open arms. A home like the one I had created, before Eli and my stiff shoulders and my perfect blown-out wigs and my literal clenched butt cheeks over legs balanced on stilettos.

I wanted to hear the burst of my daughter's giggle hit the air. I wanted to see wonder on her face. I wanted to watch her reach for things, knowing she was safe enough to aim beyond what either of us could see.

I just wanted her to feel alive.

Even if that meant I, too, needed to find a way to live again.

Back at home, Eli and I both pretended everything was normal. He apologized for his meltdown, promised that he would never try to hurt my reputation. I pretended to accept his apology. I pretended that in my mind, I hadn't already started to leave.

I slept curled up inside his arms, felt the love come through every pore of his body and enter mine. I soaked it all in, into the spaces within me that had gotten used to feeling satiated. I knew it wouldn't work, the same way I knew that no matter how much I ate before the fast of Yom Kippur, I would still lie on the couch with green-tinged skin by the end of it. I overfed on his affection anyway, knowing I would need to be strong for the steps I was about to take.

I felt his lips meet the top of my head in the night, a move from beneath his consciousness. I stared at the wall, my eyes dry, hating myself the entire time. *How can you do this to him?* I thought, even as I nudged my body closer to his, as I pulled his arm around me.

As the moonbeams filtered through the skylight of our oversized bedroom, I realized that I had never allowed myself to be fully naked with a woman. I had dreamt about it. I had felt the burst of light in my gut as women stroked my face and my body and warmed my skin with their own. I had kissed and touched and teased and coveted women. What if, when I actually slept with a woman, without placing any restrictions on my heart or my body, I realized that I was not gay?

I thought about my children's lives. The trauma they had already experienced, the times I upended everything and packed us into boxes and moved across state lines. How could I rip their lives apart once again? How could I do that without even knowing if I would be more whole on the other side?

Weeks later, I was on the dance floor at the Stonewall Inn on a Saturday night. I wore the skinny jeans I kept in the back of my closet for airports and vacations, and my eyes were set with glitter and liner. Eli was at home, back on Long Island, with my sleeping children and the illusion that I was attending a trauma conference for the weekend. My wig was in the bottom of my suitcase a few blocks away, at a Chelsea hotel. I was aware that the lying should have caused stress, but I could breathe, in the room that swirled in colored lights and the scent of so many perfumes mingled together.

I sat on a bar stool, turned sideways through the shoulders clad in leather and lace, and ordered a drink. I sipped and met the eyes of women with short barber haircuts, women in baggy cargo pants and bare belly buttons, women who smirked back at me, welcomed me, dared me.

"Wanna dance?" A caramel-skinned woman leaned close to my ear.

I let her pull me up as if it were a normal Saturday night for me, as if her hand around my waist was the most natural thing in the world. I felt her hips against mine, and her gentle movements made my legs seem almost graceful as they stepped with hers.

Surrounded by rainbow flags and the sound of Lady Gaga, we danced. She rose to her toes to reach my face, to pull my lips toward hers, and then I was tasting her, being tasted by her, until we consumed each other in a space beyond the bar, in a space that felt something like heaven.

"Whooot whooot!"

We came back down onto the wooden floor, back into the mass of pheromones and round asses.

Her face flushed. "Ignore my stupid friends," she said.

I spun around, put my hand out and introduced myself to the friends.

She tugged my arm, whispered, "Let's get out of here."

In my hotel room, we poured drinks and tossed snippets of conversation around, coy and warm and laden words. For about two minutes. The force that had been drawing us together all night, it took over in the dim light of the private room. I felt my body move on its own, my fingers on the button of her jeans, my elbows shrugging out of my tank top, until there was nothing between us. I felt her mouth on me, as her tongue drew rivers from between my legs, and matching streams came down my face, as my entire being let go. Finally. Blessedly. I was in my body with someone else and I felt every breath and pulsation and every desperate grasp of skin. I tasted the sea salt on her stomach, down the inside of her legs. I heard the pleasure in her coarse breaths, in her visceral moans.

All through the night, we consumed each other. We drifted off into naps and woke up glimmering in desire, submerging within one another. There were words, too, *you're so beautiful* and *I want to feel you again* and *don't stop*.

When dawn broke through the window curtains, we pulled the blanket over our naked bodies. My hand on her ass and hers around my rib cage, we looked at each other for the first time in hours, without speaking. We allowed the awe to wash over us, to coat us, just like we had coated each other.

I was gay! I was thirty-two years old, and I finally knew. One million per-cent. I was gay. I wanted to scream at the top of my lungs. I wanted to run through Chelsea in the morning light and twirl around with my arms out.

A small part of me wished I had known, before I gave my body away. Before I choked down stardust, year after year, numbing the rough shards as they moved through my body. I wished I had known that I was drawn to actual stars, that their effervescence matched mine, that when I swal-lowed starlight, my skin glowed from the inside and my heart did back-flips. The knowledge had been inside me all along. I just wished I had been allowed to look for it.

I thanked her over brunch at Westville. I talked about how busy my schedule was, and friended her on Facebook for later, sometime during the summer maybe.

Then I headed home, my mind clear. I knew what needed to happen.

Lose You to Love Me

I waited until our children's duffel bags were loaded onto trucks, until we waved goodbye through the windows of the busses that would take them to sleepaway camp for the summer.

Then I talked to Eli. I told him the truth, without sugarcoating anything.

We walked the Long Beach Boardwalk and talked as miles of strangers passed us by, in their jogging shorts and specialized bikes. I told him about my weekend away. I explained that I needed to be sure before wrecking our life.

He cried, his body shaking in the sun, sweat and pain dripping down onto the wooden slats.

This time, I cried too. We stood with our arms around each other, and we wept, heaved against one another as the tide went down and the waves turned navy and lapped against the shore behind us.

Eli's voice got loud again, but it didn't scare me. I was no longer sacrificing my body for God, and I felt different. Stronger. I felt Eli's pain in my chest. I caressed him instead of shutting him out. I listened, really listened, and heard how sorry he was for all the ways in which he'd failed me. I said that I was sorry too, for lying to myself for so many years, for thinking I could overcome who I was, for giving him a love that was so much less than what he deserved.

We walked back to our car, spent, exhausted, and for the first time in our entire relationship, I felt unweighted. We headed home, where Eli moved his stuff upstairs and insisted that I take the master bedroom until I could find a new place to live.

"I can't just turn off the love switch," he said, as he left me the better toothbrush charger, the fluffier pillow.

He turned around, waited at the door. "Is it okay . . . ? Can I?"

I nodded. He crossed the floor in seconds and wrapped me in his arms. I inhaled the Cartier Sport and dried sweat and faint nicotine. The scent of Eli. I missed it already.

"I know," he responded to the words I hadn't said out loud. "I know."

After a couple of days passed and we were able to look at each other without one of us breaking down, we set up a meeting with a mediator. We agreed to keep our own assets. I would sign away my ownership of the house. He would not claim any part of my practice. I would leave him with everything except the Peloton, which he said he never wanted to see again; too many bad associations of losing me.

For a moment in time, it seemed like everything might be okay.

Then the round of challenges began. It was easier, the second time around. I knew what to expect. I was not surprised when the blows struck, but they still hurt.

I drove to Monsey to meet with Rabbi Levi, who was in America for a fundraising visit. He welcomed me, as always, with a gaze filled with warmth and the offer of all the time I would need.

"I want to be honest with the rav," I started, looking at the one man who had supported me through thirteen years of trying and failing to stay on God's path. "I am gay."

He regarded me for a moment. Put a hand to his beard, stripes of white through what was once auburn, fourteen years ago, back when I took careful notes in his Jerusalem classroom.

He reached for a response. "But, but you slept with so many men!"

I thanked him for always being there as I held the pieces of myself together, waited until I was back in my car to shudder and try to shake the words off. *He tried*, I told myself. *This is a lot for him.* Rabbi Levi had already given me more grace than I deserved. I had already pained my rabbi too much for one lifetime.

I didn't get to tell him that denial of my sexual orientation was what led me to act in opposition to myself. For me, this meant marrying and sleeping with men. Each time I was with a man, I quashed the feelings in my own body in order to try to feel what I thought I should. Once I stopped forcing my body to be with Eli, I was able to feel the numb parts again. One day, while doing crunches, I felt the muscles in my abdomen stretch and contract. I realized that for my entire life, I followed the instructor's guidance on how to crunch my body, but I just ignored prompts like "feel your core," because I thought my core was different, I just couldn't feel it. That was my level of self-imposed anesthetization.

Days later, I stood in the pristine, white tiled shower letting the water run over my body. I heard the echo of a bell chime through the large, empty house. I ignored it, let the soap run down the lean muscles formed by months of running and cycling through the pain.

It didn't let up, the chiming. I sighed and toweled off, zipped a hoodie over my body and reluctantly stepped over the pale hardwood floors. Past the wall-length windows facing the glittering pool, past the granite countertops that hadn't seen a crumb in weeks, and I pulled the heavy wooden front door open. Shit. My sisters. Dina and Hindy stared at me, somber, as they stood on my stone patio in their long black skirts, out of place in the manicured neighborhood.

I stared at their reflections in the mirrored foyer.

"We had to come," Hindy said.

"Why are you doing this?" Dina asked. She looked at me with tears in her beautiful gray eyes, as she sat awkwardly on the edge of a decorative chair in my formal living room.

"I have a few students over the years who come from broken homes. These children, they are so sad to see. One girl I want to tell you about, she ended up on drugs in seventh and eighth grade. Is this what you want for your children?" Hindy's words gushed out, one after the other, as if speed alone would catapult them into me. "Your kids will never be able to get married, Malka, never!"

My heart twinged as I thought of the way my sisters must have planned their words on the long drive from upstate New York. I ached as I pictured them in the back seat of the van driven by Hindy's husband, looking for ways to change my mind.

"I know you must feel like you're watching a train crash—" I started to say, before Dina cut me off.

"No," she said. "No, Malka. You don't get to tell me how I feel. This, this is not a train crash. This is us losing another sister." Her shoulders slumped back onto my white leather armchair and her chin trembled, not unlike mine. It had only been four summers since we all held on to the edges of our broken world, a world that our Shani chose to leave forever. I hated the way my hands shook, and my own eyes filled.

"I'm still me," I tried to say, but my voice was so small I was not sure it even reached across the room.

I wanted to get out of the formal parlor and sit around the kitchen table with mugs of tea and tell them everything, about the years of trying to be straight, and how I just couldn't do it anymore.

I wished I could give them the chance to think about it, to ask questions about when I knew, to try to understand what I was going through during my marriages. If they knew that I was gay, even if they didn't believe being gay was a real thing, at least they would have known there was some logic behind my broken marriages.

I couldn't though, because of the provision in my divorce agreement. If I were up-front with my sisters, I would not merely lose custody, I would in effect have *given up custody*. Dina still had Yossi over at her weekly Shabbos table. Hindy's husband, Meir, called Yossi to wish him a happy new year every Rosh Hashana. If my sisters told Yossi I was a lesbian, he would have immediately gone to the rabbinical court and been awarded my children.

"I'm sorry, Malka," Dina said as she stood up. "I don't know who you are anymore."

Hindy followed, dusted her skirt off with the back of her hands. It felt like she was dusting me off.

When the front door clicked shut behind my sisters, it felt final.

I talked to Hindy one last time, more by necessity than by choice.

I was in my dentist's waiting room, flipping through a magazine when Abba called.

"Malk-ah! How are you?"

I realized with a start that no one had told him about the divorce. "How are you feeling?" I asked, as I always did, ever since his angioplasty last year.

"*Baruch Hashem*." His voice was a warm rumble, one that I wanted to curl up inside.

"Abba, I have to tell you something," I said, and stepped outside the immaculate wood and leather waiting room. I told him that Eli and I had been struggling, and that we decided to separate. I figured it was better to start with the idea of separation, to break the news slowly.

I didn't expect my lion-strong Abba to audibly cry. I heard his voice fall apart as his words came through the sobs. "Malk-ah, I beg you," he cried, "don't do this."

I listened, wishing I could take it back, wishing it weren't true, wishing my whole life were different and that I didn't have to hurt him this much.

I didn't want to hear my abba's sorrow, his anguish. I didn't want to hear his next words. "My heart can't take this. Please— Please— Just stay married. Please—" His voice cut out and I heard gasping on the other end of the line.

I steeled myself and called Hindy, who, God bless her, picked up on the first ring. "Abba's having a heart attack and I don't know his address in Israel, please get someone there right away."

"Okay, okay, don't worry," she said, and I heard her whip out an address book and look up the Hebrew-named street in Jerusalem. Later, she called to tell me that she sent one of our nephews over and he stayed with Abba until he could breathe again. No heart attack.

Still, I didn't want to risk my abba's life. I called him back and lied, "Eli and I are going to try to work it out, it's okay, I am sorry I made you worried."

I heard his relief. "What can I do to help?" he asked, as he had my entire life.

It was my turn to help him, I decided, as I thanked him and turned the conversation to our family's newly born babies. He was so far away, across the ocean. He didn't have to know.

I moved into the next stage of my divorce entirely isolated, as if in a vast white chamber, like the bottom of the World Trade Center Oculus afterhours, with not a soul in sight. I was alone. No mother. No father. No sisters. Just me, trying to walk bravely ahead into the blank white future, trying not to sink to my knees and give up.

I met with a realtor and looked at apartments and basement rentals in the country club neighborhood. Each one just felt like a grimy downgrade from the mini mansion. Then she showed me a shuttered cottage on Atlantic Beach, one block from the shore, with cozy furnishings. It had a 1980s wood-paneled kitchen and three bedrooms, all on the same floor. It came with a wide denim sofa, full beds, and a real working fireplace. I could see us, eating dinner on the patio through the fall, roasting marsh-mallows in the winter. I could see us healing.

When I picked my children up from their camp bus stops, I told them they had twenty-four hours to rest before we left for vacation. I watched them walk across the mirrored foyer, past the formal dining room, and heard their innocent relief at being back in what they thought was still home.

"I missed this shower so much!" Shira said. "Wow, I forget how good it smells in here."

I packed them back into the car the next day and drove miles up the highway.

Avigdor, who had turned twelve over the summer, was excited to be legally allowed to sit in the front seat near me. He flipped through radio stations and put his sneakers up on the dash and casually asked, "Is Daddy going to drive up later?"

I distracted him with questions about camp and requests for music stations. Then we were all distracted by a uniformed concierge who of-fered us a menu of services for our stay: private tennis lessons, swim in-struction, on-site fitness classes, and massages.

"Nice, Mom!" Shira slapped me five.

I was deliberate about the choice of hotel. I wanted my children to know, in their guts, that their mother could afford to take them away on her own.

We unpacked, had dinner at a local deli, and were walking back to our car in the deli's parking lot when I said, "I need to talk to you guys about something when we get back." Both children stopped in their tracks.

"That sounds bad," Avigdor said.

"Just tell us now, Mom," Shira insisted, her face already paling.

"Okay," I said, not wanting to drag it out any longer. I led them to a grassy strip on the side of the parking lot and sat down facing them. They looked terrified. Avigdor put his hand out to Shira, and she grabbed it.

I began my prepared speech about how sometimes adults had problems getting along, and it was nobody's fault. I got half a sentence into it, "So, you guys noticed Daddy wasn't home when you got there—"

"Are you getting divorced?" Shira asked so quickly, too quickly.

"Yes. The short answer is yes. We are going to be okay. I promise. Everything will be okay." I tried to talk, but I looked at my children and I saw their eyes well up and then we were all sitting on the narrow strip of grass and sobbing. They held each other and I held them, and the tears kept coming. Their bodies shook against me, their thin shoulders shuddered in my arms.

"I knew it," Shira said. "You think I didn't hear you fighting all the time?"

"What?" Avigdor sat up, his blue eyes raw, the kind of raw I had never seen on him before.

"Yeah," Shira said, "you're lucky your room isn't over theirs." She told him about the slamming of doors and how quiet I was during the arguments.

"Mom," Avigdor said, "I didn't hear the fighting, but you just never looked happy." I was stunned. The whole time, my children had already known something was wrong.

"What are you going to miss the most?" I asked, once the tears died down and we were all plucking shoots of grass, not ready to leave our spot.

"The house," said Shira.

"The father," said Avigdor, and my heart broke all over again.

We spent the rest of the week in Glen Cove, just processing the news. We bought sketch pads and pencils at Barnes & Noble and spent some time drawing each day. We lay on beach chairs and listened to music. We talked about the future, about what the children would tell their friends. I reminded them how much fun we used to have, in our old house in New Jersey, when it was just the three of us. We reminisced about that time, pulled up old pictures and laughed at the memories. We headed to a local mall and picked out house scents for our new home, Moroccan spice for Shira's room and vanilla for Avigdor's.

When it was time to pack up and head back to town, I saw the children's minds starting to adjust. We spent the drive home planning our new dinner menu, one that didn't have to cater to so many palates. We decided to have breakfast for dinner on Sundays, Hungarian Goulash at least once a week, and pizza every Thursday.

I knew the road to freedom had only just begun. There were legal battles ahead. Probably a whole lot of therapy, too. Still, as we rolled the windows down and blared "Cake by the Ocean" out the car window, I felt a hint of something new. The tendrils of the me I had been before it all began, before the weddings and the divorces. The me with light eyes reflecting in the sun, the me who sang out loud even though I knew I was totally off-key, the me whose heart was open. I could see her, the old me, in my rearview mirror, hair loose and eyes crinkling, and my God, she was beautiful.

I Don't Even Know If
I Believe

The children and I moved into our winter rental in Atlantic Beach, the surfer-dude sibling of the Five Towns. It was just a short drawbridge and less than a mile away, but the vibe was completely different. Sandy beach bars instead of upscale restaurants, pickup trucks instead of luxury SUVs, and families who grilled hot dogs on Saturdays instead of having formal Shabbos lunch. It was close enough to my children's schools, and far enough from the prying eyes of our friends and acquaintances.

We spent a week hanging art on our new walls, visiting the local farmer's market, and making sushi from scratch for dinner.

On the first day of school, I dropped Avigdor off at his all-boys yeshiva wearing a new cobalt polo shirt and high-top sneakers. This would be the final year of casual clothes; next year, in eighth grade, he would dress like the high school boys and the teachers, in a white shirt, dark pants, and a black felt hat.

I dropped Shira off at her all-girls school and watched her walk toward a circle of other sixth graders, all in different versions of the same Adidas sneakers and plaid uniform skirts.

"Bye, Mom." She waved as I lingered in my car. I drove away, but I didn't stop worrying for the rest of the day. I knew how cruel kids could be about things like divorce. I hoped the rumors weren't bad, that people weren't speculating about Eli and me, wondering if either of us cheated or went crazy.

I worried through my day treating clients. I worried while answering emails about my new lease on an office space I would share with colleagues in Manhattan for one day each week. I ordered new business cards with an eye on the clock.

At the end of the day, I sped across town to Avigdor's yeshiva. I knew something was wrong from the way he made a beeline for my car. I could tell by the defeat in his shoulders that he was not okay. He barely shut the door behind him before he said, "I never want to go back there again."

I asked him what happened, and he begged me to just drive, fast. He held up a sheet of paper lined with Hebrew words and his own doodles.

"This is what we'll be learning the entire year."

He passed me the sheet and I pulled over. The page was filled with text about the Jewish laws surrounding divorce. There were details, such as how God shed a tear when a couple decided to end their marriage.

Later that night, with Avigdor's permission, I called his rebbe, Rabbi Blum, and asked him to be sensitive around the divorce topic. I told him we had a very recent divorce in our family, and that Avigdor was trying to be brave, but he was in pain.

Rabbi Blum responded empathetically, and he thanked me for telling him. "Nonetheless," he said, "this is our curriculum for the year, and we cannot change it."

At that moment, as I stood in the backyard of my cottage house, I realized: I may have freed myself from a future that would have continued to crush me. But my children—they were still not free.

Over the next few weeks, I grew even more uneasy about Avigdor's schooling. His school days began at seven a.m. and went until late evening. He began to speak about hating the Gemara, the set of texts that would comprise his

Judaic studies for the better part of each day, for the next five to ten years.

When he brought home tests from his language arts lessons, I was stunned to find comments from his teacher that were patently incorrect. His math teacher, Avigdor also told me, was a rabbi, and it made me wonder about the faculty's qualifications.

I worried about how it would all affect him when he got to high school in two years. His stepbrother Josh was older than him, and so I knew what the next years could bring. By high school, the boys were often smoking weed and hiding alcohol in the ceiling tiles of the school bathrooms.

One night, I took Avigdor out to a restaurant for us to spend some time together, and he told me he wanted to take that Gemara and write a big *X* over it.

"If the Gemara were made of glass, I'd just drop it on the floor."

I could tell how much pain he was in, that he was being pushed over the edge. I didn't want him hating Judaism. I wanted my son happy and able to make his own choices.

I thought about our old life, when I may have said things like, *Your rebbe is trying his best.* But I was no longer sure I believed that. When he got in the car each day and reported whatever new thing his rebbe said, I began to ask him *his* opinion.

"My rebbe says, listening to secular music is like putting your soul in the deep fryer," he said, and I asked, "What do *you* think about that?"

He was surprised the first few times, looked at me, checked to see if I really meant it, and then he got used to speaking up.

"I mean, the deep fryer? That is, like, so stupid. Does he think we're idiots?"

I could see his dimples flash and his shoulders straighten in those moments.

As the school year progressed, I tried to make our home the safest possible landing spot for Avigdor at the end of his grueling days. I bought a basketball hoop for our driveway and built it with my own bare hands, even though the instructions suggested that at least three men would be needed for the task. I didn't care. I couldn't wait for men to show up and save us anymore. I poured my fury and my protection into the drilling of screws. I was beyond proud when I only chipped one hot pink fingernail and produced a working hoop.

Avigdor dribbled and shot hoops for a while, and then came back inside, barely having broken a sweat.

"I'm good," he said. "Thanks for the hoop."

It was days before he admitted that basketball just wasn't the same without Josh.

"I just didn't want you to feel bad," he said, my sweet boy who was being made to feel bad every single day at school. He still had it. The sweetness. I wondered how long it would last.

One day, Avigdor came home from school and told me that his rebbe called him out of class to talk to him. Apparently, Avigdor had been passing notes to another boy with divorced parents, in a mutual effort to block out the lessons.

"If your father died," his rebbe asked, "would you cry at his grave?"

His rebbe was teasing him, Avigdor said, hinting that, now that his parents were divorced, he must no longer care about their concerns.

Even more ominous, his rebbe had ended the confrontation with, "I see right through you. Go back to class, but know that I'm not done with you."

I emailed the entire middle school faculty and requested an immediate meeting.

The next day, I strode into the office of the seventh-grade dean, Rabbi Shapiro, in my blazer and heels, and the secretaries greeted me by name. "Dr. Sara!" They were used to seeing me in their hallways, advocating for my clients, setting up behavior plans and meeting with the school counselor.

In a conference room near the dean's office, Rabbi Shapiro gestured to a chair at the long table, and I sat down to face four men on the opposite side: the dean Rabbi Shapiro, Avigdor's rebbe Rabbi Blum, the school counselor, and the associate dean. I used my best therapist tone to make my points. I didn't want to be combative. I just wanted my son to feel safe at school.

"I am sure no one means to make Avigdor uncomfortable," I began. "It's just been a hard year for our family."

"We appreciate your call," Rabbi Shapiro said. He added, "It's usually we who have to ask parents to come in." I broached the broader subject of the year's curriculum. I explained that the divorce had been difficult, that the Gemara they were studying made it even more painful, and that Avigdor was uncomfortable being asked personal questions. Rabbi Blum's round face flushed over his beard.

After some back-and-forth, the faculty all concurred. They could not change the curriculum until after Passover, in April, months away. I did, however, get permission for Avigdor to skip the morning prayer services and to start school at nine in the morning, instead of seven. It was a small win.

But it was far from enough.

"Welcome, mothers and grandmothers, aunts and sisters, to this very special evening!"

I sat in the school auditorium, waiting to see Shira onstage for her bat mitzvah play, to mark the occasion of the sixth-grade girls becoming official Jewish young women. The principal described how hard our sixth graders and their teachers had worked to prepare their performance. When she stepped down from her podium and the lights dimmed, she walked past my seat, squeezed my shoulder, and stood behind me for a moment. She knew that I was alone. She made it her business to know. To sweeten the tough moments.

Then a row of girls in long-sleeved black shirts and long black skirts filed onto the stage. Somber musical notes filled the auditorium. The girls lifted their arms, almost perfectly in sync, revealing golden wings the length of their entire bodies. I started my cell phone video, identified the shape of my Shira, and felt the pride well up in my eyes. She looked so regal, her thin face serious and her toe pointed.

"I can't believe she is almost twelve," I whispered to the woman near me, who dabbed her own face with a cloth napkin.

The next group of girls filed onto the stage. They were dressed in colorful hats and vests. One girl stepped to the front of the group, put a hand on her hip, and sang:

I hate my army uniform! The colors I oppose.
Why must I wear such boring clothes?

I grinned in the dark, so thrilled to see the girls singing about individuality. My grin faded when three girls came up behind the first one and placed a camouflage jacket around her shoulders while singing:

Poor, poor soldier he'll never win
It's really quite bizarre
Why despise the badge of honor
That makes us who we are?

I looked around the room, at the round tables of women, wigs nodding and hands clapping to the beat. The fabric on their bodies fell below their kneecaps, and I seemed to be the only one saddened by the sea of conformity that was about to swallow my daughter.

When Shira found me in the crowd, I kissed the top of her head, and told her how well she performed. We posed for some photos, my arm tight around her shoulder, clasping her to me. I watched the other families file out of the building, girls in the same black mini Uggs, mothers in ballet flats or short heeled boots. Among them, there was not one man or boy. Not one pink or yellow or white sneaker. Not one tattoo. Not one short-haired butch lesbian. Just a wave of chatting, smiling, congratulating servants of God, all in uniform.

Several weeks later, I attended a parent-teacher conference at Shira's school. I arrived in my longest skirt and full wig, notebook in hand, ready to hear how she was doing.

"She is so smart," the Judaic studies teacher said, as she brushed her own short wig out of her eyes. "I just don't know why she keeps missing the test questions."

I mentioned that according to Shira's IEP, she was supposed to have testing accommodations.

"What IEP?" the teacher asked.

An IEP is an individualized education plan based on a student evaluation, which details specific accommodations a student might require. The teacher's response struck me as preposterous. I'd already had this discussion, at the beginning of the school year when I spoke with the middle school faculty to discuss how they might help my daughter access her strengths and overcome her challenges. Shira was gifted in many areas, but she needed the right kind of environment, such as quiet rooms for test taking, to access those gifts. Her teachers, having not been made aware of her needs, wrote her off and assumed she just hadn't been trying hard enough.

It was unbelievable. Unbelievable enough that I was certain the school faculty would deny it later. I slid my phone out of my purse and hit record.

I walked through the large auditorium, to the next teacher's table, and had almost an exact repeat of the conversation. "Nobody told me," the teacher said. "And anyway, I'm not sure how we can change things. This is just the curriculum."

By the time teachers number four and five said they did not usually provide academic accommodations, I was furious. I knew I sounded harsh when I said things like, "It's not a matter of preference, these are things my daughter is legally entitled to." I got the responses recorded each time.

I listened to the recordings on my drive home. I felt bad for the young teachers. I was a teacher at their age too, back when I held all the naïveté and a seminary certificate at eighteen years old.

When I got home and asked Shira what had been happening at school, she shrugged and said, "It's fine. I'm just not that smart." And that, I knew, was untrue, and it broke my heart most of all.

Shira shared other incidents that made me uneasy. On Chanukah, her teacher invited the class over for a party at her home, and she instructed them to wear their school uniforms, even though it would take place after school hours. She explained to the girls, "I don't want my husband to feel uncomfortable."

I was disgusted. My daughter was eleven years old, and she was already being taught to cover up, down to her ankles, to keep a man comfortable.

Another teacher stomped through the classroom and slammed the girls' books onto their wooden desks. "The way you just jumped in fear— imagine how much more fear you will feel when God is the one punishing you!" She shrieked for effect.

Shira again was upset. "Mom, I don't know how no one else comes into the room to stop her. It's really loud, so loud."

I was glad to see her questioning, but I was not happy with what she was being taught.

While married to Eli, I never contemplated a change in the children's schooling, even though I often thought it was inadequate. Eli's son Josh was in the same school as Avigdor, and it made sense to keep them to- gether. I was also a more distracted mother while with Eli, as I worked to keep the peace above all else.

I was not ready to come out openly as gay, because I hadn't worked out how to be out of the closet and maintain custody of my children. Still, some- thing had changed in the years since I married Eli. I had established myself on firmer footing. I no longer carried the same terror of Lakewood's rabbis.

I wanted my children to know who they were on the inside, or at least to have the space to figure it out. I thought back to my entire childhood, when choices were made *for* me. By the time I was old enough to make choices for myself, I couldn't see out of the box anymore. I married the man I was told was best for me and was stuck with consequences that would last my entire lifetime. I didn't want that for my children.

Even more vital, I wanted my children to be able to go to college, and for that, they needed to be better prepared. My college degrees ultimately paved my path to freedom and gave me options beyond the world in which I was trapped. I wanted my kids to always have options too, to have the ability to live their lives on their own terms.

I knew that change would require a battle, a final showdown, with Yossi, with the Lakewood rabbis, with the whole structure that placed the Sword of Damocles over me. I was finally ready to fight.

For years I had helped other people's children feel safe, supported, and comfortable at school. As the director of the Wellness Center, I sat in offices within almost every local school and met with teachers and faculty to explain the results of educational evaluations, to set up behavior plans, and to advocate for children experiencing family or personal difficulties. I worked with attorneys and child advocates in divorce cases, and I testified at trials where education was at issue. In each instance, I pictured the children under discussion, their little face in my play therapy office, and I used my training and the credibility of my credentials to find the words that they did not know how to say themselves. I took their, "I hate my teacher," and combined it with the results of their testing, classroom observation reports, and parent sessions to figure out what needed to change, and to help make it happen.

It was time to take everything I had learned and use that knowledge for my own children. I identified three middle schools that had both the right sort of learning support for Shira and better curricula for Avigdor. I completed six separate applications, attached the required fees, and dropped them off personally with secretaries I already knew by name.

The schools I identified were under the umbrella of Orthodox Judaism, although they existed toward the far end of the umbrella, just underneath the outer spokes. They had separate classes for boys and girls, but in a single shared building. They asked parents to disclose things like which synagogue they attended, and to pledge that their homes were kosher and Shabbat-observant. That was a far cry from my children's current schools, where those questions did not even need to be asked.

Each time, I informed Yossi via text or phone call, hoping against hope that he might agree to one of the schools I chose. For one of the schools, he sent me a flat-out no within a couple of hours, in a series of bizarre text messages.

> Him: *I got inside info on the school . . . abt 90 percent of mothers go with pants, very Zionistic . . . not an option*

> Me: *90 percent? Where is that information from? I treat many religious families with kids there.*

> Him: *Spoke with a lady working there*

I was frustrated to be having a conversation about the clothes the mothers wore instead of the services provided to students.

As it turned out, though, the schools did not have room for one or both of my children, or they lacked necessary academic accommodations. I applied to a fourth school, one in which boys and girls shared classrooms, and this time I didn't tell Yossi.

A few days later, I called to follow up on the application.

"Oh," the secretary said, sounding confused. "Your children's father said you were withdrawing the application."

This time I was shocked. Yossi had been sleuthing, becoming proactive, and I was afraid of what that meant.

We had co-parented our children for a decade. He took charge of dentist appointments. I did doctor's appointments. We sent update texts, like, "Shira grew an inch and a half," or "Avigdor has a cavity." He had never once done anything to undermine my role.

He was no longer just staying in the background, telling me his opinions. He was making moves of his own. I got the sinking feeling that he had started to consult with his parents, maybe even with a lawyer.

In 2018, I came across an article in the *New York Times*: "When Living Your Truth Can Mean Losing Your Children."

> *The questioning went on for days. Did she allow her children to watch a Christmas video? Did she include plastic Easter eggs as part of her celebration of the Jewish holiday of Purim? Did she use English nicknames for them, instead of their Hebrew names?*
>
> *This grilling of Chavie Weisberger, 35, took place not in front of a rabbi or a religious court, but in State Supreme Court in Brooklyn, during a custody battle with her ultra-Orthodox Jewish ex-husband after she came out as lesbian and decided to leave the ultra-Orthodox fold. The stakes could not have been higher. In fact, the judge, Eric I. Prus, eventually ruled that she should lose custody of her children, largely because she had lapsed in raising them according to Hasidic customs.*

I felt like I was overreacting when I printed the *New York Times* article and brought it to Leora, the local attorney who had handled my divorce from Eli. Leora brought the whole team in for my meeting. Paralegals and partners took notes around the conference table as I passed the article around.

I watched as they all read the piece and looked up at each other aghast.

Weisberger's ex-husband was given sole custody of their five-, seven-, and nine-year-old children. For five years, Chavie was only allowed restricted visitation with her children. Five years. She won them back eventually, when the ruling was overturned on appeal. Nonetheless, even the Appeals Court affirmed the lower court's ruling that the children would continue to attend Hasidic schools, per the father's wishes.

"How do I know this is not going to happen to me?" I asked, trying to be brave, blinking fast, passing around copies of my own divorce agreement, with a very similar religious upbringing clause.

"Sara," Leora said, frowning at the papers, "I don't know about this whole idea of changing your children's schools right now."

It was disheartening to hear my attorney be so doubtful of my chances. But I was not ready to give up.

As I sat with some of the most experienced family law attorneys in the Five Towns, I found that I was very clear about what I wanted. I felt it in the palms of my hands, the edge of my manicured fingernails as they pressed into my flesh. I had fought for myself. I was ready to fight for my children.

Later that month, I was on a dinner date with Kyle, a woman I had seen a few times. I told her about my fears of coming out of the closet, how devastating the consequences could be. She tilted her head, and her short hair fell over an exquisite, sculpted cheekbone.

"Will they actually *take* your children away?"

Her tone was heavy with skepticism. Kyle was a strategist at a tech company, and I could see her weighing my fear with her analytical mind. I forgot how crazy it all sounded, how literally unbelievable.

"I'd give it a ninety percent chance of never happening. But it's the other ten percent that keeps me up at night," I offered lightly, then changed the topic. My centuries-old religious community and their hold on me did not make for easy banter in social situations, and I promised myself I'd keep a better lid on the darkness.

But there were those who did understand. Those who'd been through it, or who'd seen it happen to others. One of those was Elle, a woman I met at a creative arts therapy conference. She was in a backward baseball cap and low-rise jeans, restocking tables with glitter and paint. I walked around with business cards, trying to network with city colleagues.

"Are you with this practice?" I pointed to the sign on her table.

"Nah," she said, and looked at me like I had just cracked a joke and she wanted in on it, "I'm just the supply dude." Dude was code for, *in case you're into women, know that I am too.*

"Hey, supply dude, I'm Sara," I said. I put out my hand and she took it in both of hers, brought it to her lips, and kissed it gently.

We spent the rest of the night at the bar next door, talking. Turned out, Elle was from Brooklyn too, raised Orthodox. We stopped and stared at each other when we realized that we grew up just blocks away from one another. For a year in the nineties, we even attended the same girl's high school on Fifteenth Avenue in Borough Park.

Days later, I was with Elle again in another Brooklyn bar, this time being introduced to her friends.

"She's one of us," Elle said, as she pulled me by the hand to a table of people in parkas and combat boots.

I wouldn't have guessed they were all formerly Orthodox Jews, if it weren't for the subtle giveaways: an ashtray right near a plastic bag of Beigel's heimishe babka. A rolled-up sleeve revealing a tattoo that read, in Hebrew script, *gam zeh ya'avor*—this too shall pass. One girl texted furiously, puffed on a joint, and said, "Fuck if I know what that *chazzer* wants," mixing her Yiddish and English obscenities with ease.

"*Fin vi bist di?*" they asked. *Where are you from?* There was a sharp edge to the question, and in their looks. I was being tested.

"*Ich bin fin Ger—ober s'iz shoyn a lange tzayt tzirik.*" I dug up my best Yiddish to establish my bona fides: *I'm from the Gur sect—but that was a long time ago.*

I could tell I passed as acceptable, in the easy manner they adopted, and in the cigarette passed my way. When someone leaned over with a lighter, I knew I was truly one of them.

When Elle and I met next, we dove into each other headfirst, bodies pressed together on a hotel bed, breath mingling, tongues sweeping inside each other like it was the only possible thing we could be doing, like it was the only thing we would ever want to do. We didn't need to waste time with the formalities of a traditional "date." We had two thousand years of shared history. We knew what it was like to be each other, we knew what it meant to be where we had each been.

We didn't so much fall into a relationship as share a full spirit immersion, fast, deep, and complete. By Chanukah time we had met each other's children. We didn't even have to talk about the way we whipped our hands back to the sides of our own bodies when we heard the faintest sound of a child's footsteps in the hallway. Our children couldn't know, because their fathers couldn't know, and we didn't want to burden them with knowing things that they would have to keep secret.

Our children played video games and basketball together, as if they, too, had known each other forever. They spent Shabbos with us, and it seemed like no big deal that the moms shared a room, just like the kids did.

"Do you want to keep your kids in the dark forever?" I asked her eventually, hoping that she, too, had a plan toward freedom.

"It's just another six or seven years," she said, about her own middle schoolers. "I don't want to start anything."

I thought about the thousands of dollars I had already spent on attorneys and on therapy. I knew that Elle, who stocked the floor of conference centers, just didn't have access to that kind of money. I wanted to talk to her about legal aid, and gently ask if she'd like a referral, but I knew that was how Chavie Weisberger lost her children. Elle had a point. For many, the cost was just too high, in so many ways.

A few weeks later, Elle's ex-girlfriend reappeared. In true lesbian fashion, I met the ex, Shaina, and I liked her as a person. Shaina was the kind of mom that I was, and that Elle was, sacrificing everything for her children. For her, that meant still living in her parents' house on Thirteenth Avenue. She had her kids young, like me. Unlike me, she didn't get the chance to pursue a college education. She had too many tattoos to get a job within the community, where college degrees were not necessary, and so she settled for minimum wage jobs on the outside, not nearly enough to pay for both rent and childcare.

"I told them they got me into this situation and now they have to support me," she said of her parents, as she spit a wad of gum into a nearby trash can, rolling up a sleeve to reveal gray roses all the way up her arm.

I had been learning, in the backyard of Ditmas Park bars on Sunday afternoons, that very few ex-Hasidic parents leave their former communities with all four of these: custody of their children, financial independence, mental health, and the ability to be "out"—as gay *or* non-religious. At least one was always sacrificed.

Pinchas, who kept his beard after leaving and looked like a hipster with his beanies and fingerless leather gloves, was in an engineering program and lived on his own. He left a daughter behind, back in Williamsburg, with an ex-wife who allowed him one hour of visitation on Sundays. After those visits, he came to the bar and downed two beers in a row before he could speak.

Breindy, a petite girl who wore platform sneakers and cursed like a trucker, lived in a two-bedroom apartment with her children. "Oy stupid meds," she said, when she declined a second vodka-soda, and then turned to me and said, "You know those drugs, can I have three drinks on this?" She scrolled through her phone for photos of her pill bottles: escitalopram and clonazepam for anxiety and depression, and Ambien for sleep. Her ex-husband left strangulation marks on her neck, and so she got the kids and even managed to put them in a local public school. Three out of four.

I was trying to hit the jackpot. I felt greedy for wanting it all. I took a hit of the joint passed my way, wondering if I deserved anything at all. I dug a Timberland boot into the soil, leaned against Elle, and tried not to think about the way in which my own hair follicles could be tested for one puff of marijuana, and make me lose everything. But life just felt too stressful to give it *all* up, and so I took another hit, inhaled slowly, held it in my lungs.

Where Dreams Are Made True

"**S**ara!"

I was at a Manhattan middle school office, reviewing my notes and checking my stash of new business cards, when I looked up to see Mrs. Myers, a colleague from the past.

She waved me into her office. "Come in! Hello! It's been forever!"

While my Five Towns practice was full, I was trying to build a caseload for the new Manhattan office I had subleased. It was still empty for half of each designated Tuesday, and I hoped that networking would help.

"The city looks good on you!" I said, and sat down at a warm oak table across from her as we reminisced about her days on school faculties in the Five Towns.

I started to tell her about the work I was doing when she asked, gently, "Am I imagining it, or did you change something with your hair?"

It was a fair question. She and I had been mistaken for each other in the past, and we laughed about it. I had a natural scalp showing where my wig used to be, and I knew she could tell.

"I hope it doesn't affect this meeting. I got divorced recently, and I'm not covering my hair anymore."

She stood up, asked whether she could hug me, and just put her arms around me in a full, warm embrace. I could see tears in her eyes when she pulled away, after we sat back down. "You never need to worry about that. I know exactly what that's like. How are your kids? How are you?"

I was still in meeting mode, and so I told her we were okay, and we were looking at options for some school changes in our neighborhood.

She put a hand on my arm and said earnestly, "Your children would be so welcome here."

I thanked her, told her we were trying to stay local, but that her kindness was so very appreciated. She immediately invited me to come back and give a lecture to her students the following week.

When I returned to Manhattan Hebrew Academy for my lecture, I saw boys in kippahs and high-tops running through the lobby, talking excitedly about a basketball game. I could picture my Avigdor in a basketball jersey, his long athletic body midair. At his current yeshiva, there were no sports teams, no physical education program. I saw girls in casual hoodies sharing slices of pizza on the stairs outside the lunchroom. I was greeted by a teacher, who pressed the elevator button for me and proceeded to introduce everyone in the elevator by name, including the lunchroom server.

By the time I walked past the learning center and watched teachers high-five students in the hallways, I already knew: my children would feel so safe among them. I remembered the case of little Talia whose parents hired a private driver to bring her to the city, all the way from Long Island, so that her educational needs could be addressed. It came back to me, the information stored away in my mind, about the differentiated instruction and progressive learning style. By the end of my lecture, I asked for applications.

I texted Yossi:

Please look into the Manhattan Hebrew Academy.

I knew, however, that it was going to fuel our little kindling of a fight.

As it turned out, the source of my latest worry was, in fact, the light at the end of the tunnel. I had heard negative things about Footsteps, an organization that supports those who leave ultra-Orthodox backgrounds. *They are a bunch of angry losers*, people in the community said. When I finally dialed the number on their website, a cheery voice answered, "Welcome. Just tell me what you need." I stuttered a bit, tried to explain that I had left the Hasidics years ago, for the Orthodox, but that I was planning to truly challenge my Hasidic family and ex-husband for the first time. I hung up with a warm referral to Nina, a family law attorney who had been sympathetic to others in similar situations, and who had experience with rabbinical courts in some cases.

"Are you familiar with the concept of 'presumption in favor of the status quo'?" Nina asked during our first meeting.

I was embarrassed to say that I was not, but Nina put a comforting hand on my arm. "It's very simple. Judges will often rule in favor of keeping things just the way they are. By moving to Manhattan and getting the children into school here before any legal proceedings begin, there's a good chance a judge will see it best to keep it that way."

Before I could fully process it, Nina continued.

"You said you're living a double life. What do you mean by that?"

I told her about being gay, and terrified to be open about it. I described a more lax attitude to religious observance. "I wear pants when the kids are with their father, but I change into a skirt right before I pick them up."

"Don't take off the pants," Nina said before I could finish my thought. "You're smart, you're being cautious, but listen carefully: whatever you establish in advance, as long as the kids are doing well, the judge will see it favorably."

There was something so startlingly simple about her advice that I felt even more terrified. "If I do that, what if it doesn't work? I could lose everything!"

"How so?"

I told Nina about the divorce agreement I signed a decade earlier, promising to keep to all aspects of Orthodox observance.

"Let me see," Nina said.

I handed her the document that had been holding me in place for the last decade.

> *It is agreed by both parties that the children will be raised according to Halacha as stated in the Shulchan Oruch and the Mishna Berura. If it is determined by Rabbi Turkel of Lakewood, NJ, and Rabbi Levi of Jerusalem, Israel, that one party is not raising the children according to Halacha, custody will be transferred to the other biological parent.*

She looked up. "Was this entered in court as part of your legal divorce?"

It took me a moment to grasp what she meant, until I thought back to the day in Ocean County court, months after our religious divorce was completed. Yossi and I had both just stood there while the judge signed and stamped our papers, two pages of standard text purchased from the $399 divorce store, and then walked out without talking to each other. I smoked a cigarette on the side of the freeway and then drove to work. At the time, it meant nothing. To our religious minds, the only *real* divorce was the one issued by the rabbinical court.

"I don't think so," I said slowly, and handed her the document from Ocean County court.

Nina looked it over, then scoffed, picked up the document from the religious court, and waved it with a dismissive flourish. "Sara, this is not a legally binding document. Your legal divorce, issued in a New Jersey court, gives you full custody."

I noticed a tremor in my hand as I heard myself chuckle nervously, unsure about her wild ideas, about a legal system I could not fathom.

"Do you know what this *does* do?" she asked but didn't wait for my reply. "It's to establish a status quo. It's very clever of them, and it's quite common. This is how they get you to stick to a religious lifestyle, creating the religious status quo that *they* want. But you can act to establish a status quo to counter this, then petition a New York judge to grant you full custody with the facts as they are."

Her gaze was focused as she looked at me in silence, waited to see if I fully grasped what she was saying. She looked calm and assured, and I let a sliver of her demeanor crack the armor I had built up around my insides over ten long years.

"Are you saying that because I was *that* religious, I got myself this crazy ass loophole?"

"Yep," Nina said, nodding, still holding both documents. "Exactly that. Most people have their religious agreements at least entered into the record and stamped by a judge to make it legally binding. Yours is just a document some rabbi wrote and is completely irrelevant in a court of law."

Nina walked me to the door of her office. "Move to Manhattan if you can. Get those kids into the school you want. Live openly. And don't stress."

She squeezed my shoulder, and I wanted to hug her and cry. Instead, I walked out the door in a sort of daze. I was halfway home before I noticed the dryness in my throat, the sweat cooling under my arms, the sun bouncing off my windshield. I ran scenarios through my mind, all the possible ways that our plan could fail. I fought the flood of racing thoughts as I drove home. *I can still pull back. I can just go home and keep everything as is.* Then I thought, *The kids deserve better. I have to break this cycle.*

Slowly, my lungs took in big gulps of air, and I tried to let the new reality sink in: *I had someone on my side with a solid solution.*

For the rest of my drive home, I blared "Rockabye," the lyrics of another single mother that had become my anthem. She promised her child a better life, one that would be nothing at all like her own.

I put my skirt on over my jeans, but I kept the jeans on and let the ripped threads hang down my shins. One first step toward authenticity.

"Would you like to have cholent for Shabbos, or would you prefer French onion soup?" I asked the kids the following Friday morning. It was the first time in their entire lives that I asked, instead of cooking the same stew that my mother cooked, that her mother cooked, every week. They chose French onion soup, which we cooked overnight in the crockpot, and it was delicious.

When Shira said, "Can I have some milk?" just an hour after having chicken for dinner, I didn't encourage her to wait for five more hours, as the strict rules of my old brand of Orthodoxy ordained. Instead, I said, "It's up to you. I support you either way."

"Mom, you're really getting into this choices thing," Avigdor said. "What if I don't want to be Jewish?"

"I guess that's your choice, then." It sent some grief through my heart that my son had come to associate Jewishness with an oppressive system of rules. I did want him to choose for himself, but I also knew how hard it could be to lose everything familiar.

On weekends when I drove by Borough Park on my way to Park Slope for a date or to meet with friends, I felt the dark hollow in my chest. I wanted to drive by my mother's house and just sneak in and grab a bowl of chicken soup. I wanted to look into the window of my sister's kitchen and just see which of her children had grown taller, how many new strollers there were cluttering the hallway. I wanted to talk to God and know who it was that I was talking to. I missed everyone and everything so hard.

That 10 percent of fear that I described to Kyle hit me as I scheduled interviews for the kids at Manhattan Hebrew Academy, despite Yossi's express disapproval.

The kids spent the morning meeting with faculty and sitting in on classes. Afterward, they spoke excitedly about the new possibilities.

"They have junior varsity teams!" Avigdor said. "Like, official ones, where they play other schools and stuff."

Shira said, "So, I made, like, two friends, and I have their Snapchat and they love my coat."

I caught whiffs of their hope as it floated in the tiny space of our car on the drive home. Still, I was gripped by fear: What if something went wrong? Disappointing the kids after showing them hope would be even more brutal.

In March, I got an email from the academy, as promised. "We would be delighted to welcome Shira to join our seventh-grade class in the fall of 2018." I refreshed my emails. Again. Once more. I waited and refreshed again. There was no email mentioning Avigdor. Just the one.

I called the school and left a message for Mrs. Myers, and then stood out on my front porch, out of earshot of the children, pacing.

"Sara," she said gently when she called me back, "he's just too behind." She explained that their educational testing revealed that Avigdor, who was set to enter eighth grade in the fall, was on a second-grade reading level.

"What do you mean by that?" I asked, numb, as I stared at the peeling white floorboards. "He's been getting perfect *As*," I stammered.

But I knew the answer. Perfect *As* at his current school were not a measure of much, given its heavy focus on Judaic studies, with secular studies as an afterthought.

"I can get him tutors and bring him up to speed," I said quickly. "I will do whatever it takes, you know me, I really will."

"I'm sorry," Mrs. Myers said, "I really am."

Avigdor had been locked behind the door of his bedroom in recent weeks, no longer wanting to make sushi or hop into the car for impromptu acai bowl trips. It was just too much. Too many hours each day studying divorce rules, of being put down by his rebbes, of being made to feel not good enough.

"I cannot bring one of my children into a bright new world of opportunity, while leaving the other behind," I told Mrs. Myers.

I shuddered to think about how I would break the news to Avigdor, how crushing his disappointment would be.

As March turned to April, I realized that I would have to take concrete steps if I was really planning to move to the city. With Avigdor's acceptance in doubt, the whole plan felt even more precarious.

However, Nina advised that once I lived in Manhattan, the law would be on my side. A judge would be hard-pressed to send my children on a one-hour commute to their old schools each day. Plus, we could argue my case in Manhattan courts, where the judges were likely to be more liberal and less beholden to the Hasidic bloc vote.

I also had the children's ages on my side. At almost twelve and thirteen, their voices would matter. I had time on my side: the closer it was to the start of next school year, the more likely I could file for an emergency decision.

I was operating on so many levels simultaneously. Some days, it felt like playing five video games at the same time. I could never pause. Never stop. I needed to take big risks, and just play as hard as I could.

On other days, I felt like I was putting all my chips down on a hand of blackjack and hoping for the best. I'd never been that good at blackjack. Even if I got Avigdor into Manhattan Hebrew Academy, Yossi would likely not allow him to attend.

I signed a one-year lease on an apartment in Upper Manhattan, on a block of brownstones and residential doorman buildings. It was smaller than we were used to, but at five blocks away from the academy and minutes from my city office, it was perfect. I dropped off a cashier's check for first and last month's rent with my realtor, very aware that there was a chance I would have to default on my new lease and move back to the beach house.

As soon as the lease was signed, I let Yossi know that we were moving to the city. I gave him our new address and explained that we would be closer to his parents' home in Monsey, where he lived. I told him about my new building's resident lounge and invited him to visit weekly to learn with Avigdor. He turned the discussion to our plans for Avigdor's bar mitzvah, which was set for June.

"I got an extra tray of potato kugel for before the meal," he said. "It should be very nice."

For a moment, it seemed like he might have heard me. Like he might have started to accept that we were moving.

Then Yossi sent me a text message saying that the principal of an ultra-orthodox boys' yeshiva on the Upper West Side, Rabbi Menashe, was trying to contact me. "The principal is trying to reach you about the application."

I had Rabbi Menashe's phone number from some of our previous collaboration on cases. He had always seemed like a kind man, the type of person who worried about his students after-hours.

"I wasn't sure if that was you on the application!" he said. "How are you?"

I told him that I was not sure why Yossi had applied to his school for Avigdor, and that I was not aware that he was doing that. I heard the same confusion in Rabbi Menashe's voice.

"Yes," he said slowly, "I am sure your son is wonderful, but we don't usually recommend boys switching into our school in eighth grade."

I sent polite and pleading emails to Manhattan Hebrew Academy. "Just wanted to update you that we are so looking forward to moving to the Upper West Side next month."

It was mid-May, three weeks before we planned to move, when Mrs. Myers called me with a little lift in her voice.

"There's good news and bad news," she said. "We can accept Avigdor. But he would have to repeat seventh grade here with us."

I listened to her explanation, and it made sense. I thanked her, and I stayed up late googling the research in education and psychology. I learned that children who repeated a grade were often at an advantage when it came to college applications. I learned that they were often more mature than their classmates, which could pose challenges, especially if they looked older. I thought about Avigdor and his narrow shoulders, his hairless chin, his soft blue eyes. Some of his classmates were already shaving nascent mustache hair. Luckily, he still passed as a younger child.

After a year of teaching my children to make their own choices, I knew this had to be his.

I took him for a walk on the Atlantic Beach boardwalk later that week, and I laid it all out for him.

"The school likes you a lot," I said. "They see how sweet you are, and how well-mannered you are."

All true points that had him anxiously tapping his feet against the boardwalk. "Just tell me," he said. "I know when you're all serious."

I told him about needing to repeat seventh grade. I summarized the data I had gathered: He might have a better chance at getting into a good college. He might feel a bit distant from his younger classmates.

We walked and talked it all through, watching the dark waves rush onto the sand. He asked thoughtful questions about the Manhattan school schedule, and where we would live if he made the choice to stay at his current school, and what did I think. I told him I would understand either decision, and I just wanted him to be happy.

"I want to do it," he said finally. "Even though it will be hard to repeat a grade, I think I have a better chance of being happy."

I held him tight, my little boy who no longer liked hugs, but I couldn't help it. I was inspired by his mature choice, and for once, I felt confident that I got something right.

The next couple of days were frustrating. I got an email from the principal of a school in the middle of New Jersey, a religious all-girls' school that was an hour away from my new Manhattan apartment. The principal wanted to invite my Shira in for an interview.

Yossi texted me:

We will pay for a car service to school every day.

I didn't know who the "we" was, but I did know that my suspicions were confirmed. He was not acting alone.

Then a letter came in the mail.

I called Nina immediately. "I don't even know how to explain this."

I paced the floor of our small hotel room in Long Beach, where we were staying for a few days, until school was over. Our cottage had been emptied; keys returned. Our boxes were already in the new city apartment.

I read the letter to her over the phone. Under the seal of a Lakewood rabbinic court, it read:

You are hereby summoned to appear before the Rabbinical Court on Tuesday, June 26, 2018, at 2:30 p.m. Claim: Issues relating to children schooling and/or custody.

The document stated that if I did not appear, "the respondent may be in contempt of this Rabbinical Court, and will be liable to the sanctions set forth by Jewish Law."

I knew the penalty for defying a rabbinical court: excommunication.

The *Jewish Press*, and so many other publications, have sections for those who have refused to appear in rabbinical courts. They list the names of those offenders, and all Torah-observant Jews are urged to avoid having any contact with them.

I could not be excommunicated. My practice was in an Orthodox Jewish area, with Orthodox colleagues, and with a mostly Orthodox clientele. If I were outed as defying a rabbinical court, my practice would crash and burn. I couldn't afford that.

"They're going to end up with their father," I hyperventilated to Nina. "I'm going to be homeless. This is how they win. What do I do?"

Somehow, the rabbis had gotten me into full-on panic mode again, and Nina heard it through the phone.

"Breathe," she said. Nina sounded calm and collected, without even a hint of my own anxiety. She said she would be in contact with the rabbinical court on my behalf, and I didn't need to do a thing.

I was skeptical. "I don't know if the *beis din* will talk to a woman."

"Even better," she said, "we don't need them feeling comfortable with me. The more uncomfortable they are, the less they will want me showing up in person."

I heard myself let out a short chuckle, in spite of my mounting panic. There was nothing as reassuring as a professional who had a tense situation under control. Still, I had my doubts.

"I'll call you back shortly, and we'll draw up an emergency petition for Manhattan courts."

In my mind, I saw the stern faces of the rabbis in their long beards and pious overcoats and dusty fedoras, and I felt reduced to complete helplessness.

"I can't." I barely mustered a whisper. "I'm not allowed. I signed something saying I will never go to court."

I heard Nina sigh deeply, as if she had suddenly grasped why I was so immobilized by fear. She sounded slightly exasperated when she said,

"Sara, those documents have no legal force. But I understand your anxiety. Let's set up an appointment, and we'll work out a plan."

In June of 2018, one year after Eli and I split, our lives finally began to shift. Just over a week after Avigdor's bar mitzvah, the kids and I packed into the car for our final commute. School was over, and we were able to officially move into our city apartment. For seven days at least, until the kids went to summer camp.

The trunk of my compact Audi was stuffed with suitcases, backpacks, and random bags of clothing. We stopped at the Atlantic Beach kosher Dunkin' Donuts for the last time, to get some hash browns and egg wraps for dinner.

As soon as I parked in the beachfront lot, my phone rang, and the caller ID read, "Schwartz In-Laws," a call I had not received in a very long time.

I heard my mother-in-law's voice, and for a moment I thought it was a mistake. Then she started talking and her high-pitched voice turned sharp, sharper, until I felt the air seeping out of my lungs. I stepped out of the car, my legs trembling, and I leaned against a nearby railing.

"You have one chance to stop this," she said. "Just send the kids to the schools we chose, and it will all be over. We will get them a driver to and from school every day."

I listened for a moment before I said, "They are already accepted to a school near me, a good school—"

"We took you in even though you had a crazy family, and we always accepted you. But look at you now. You are destroying the children! *Destroying* them! You had to put them through another divorce, and now you are ripping them away from everything they know! We cannot stand by and watch you do this. It is one thing if you are crazy. We will not let you do this to the kids. We will do whatever it takes to get them out of your control."

I stared at the asphalt beneath me, and it shimmered in my gaze. I held on to the railing, hoped I wouldn't lose control of my shaky legs.

The kids gestured impatiently from inside the car, and I held up a finger, mouthed "one minute," as I gulped the hot ocean air.

"You have one chance, Malka. I can't promise you what will happen after that."

I hit the red button on my screen before I could really think about it. Call over.

"Just a work thing," I told the kids, who were already opening the car doors, already running up the ramp to place their orders.

I sat in the hot pink booth with them, held a cup of burnt coffee, and listened to their stories about the last day of school without hearing anything at all.

In our new city apartment, we unpacked our boxes and ate on the floor of our living room. We visited Crate & Barrel and picked out a table and couch. I took the children on some visits to new restaurants and new basketball hoops and to our building's indoor gym. Then we pulled their old duffel bags out and packed the same types of skirts and yarmulkes we had packed every year. We stocked sets of plastic drawers with deodorant and labeled bottles of shampoo and the requisite bug spray that I knew would come home entirely full. I drove them to bus stops where their former classmates and old camp friends waited, and helped them get safely onto their respective busses. Shira to her all-girls' camp, and Avigdor to his boys' yeshiva camp.

"Mom." Avigdor's voice was low, almost indiscernible, when he left me a message one week after camp started. "It's an emergency. Please call me. Something bad happened."

I dialed his camp, waited while they paged him to the office, ran every worst-case scenario through my mind. None of it prepared me for what he said next.

"Totty came to camp today. With Asher. They took me to their car and talked to me for a long time. I don't remember everything. They said I should go to a school in Monsey. That the Manhattan school is terrible for me. I told them it's my choice, Mom, but they weren't listening. I felt so trapped."

He sounded like he was crying. He told me how Yossi's brother Asher, a headstrong man, tried to convince him to go to some school he had never heard of.

"Zeeskeit, I'm so sorry. I'm going to contact your camp right now."

I was already pulling up the director's phone number, already planning a stern conversation and veiled legal threats, when Avigdor said, "Mom, don't call the head rabbi. He's part of it. He called me into his office yesterday and gave me a whole speech. The same thing that Totty said, just much calmer."

I wanted to drive up to camp to bring him home instantly. "I can be there two hours from now. Do you want to come home?"

"I'm having fun here, I just want this to stop," he said, and I could hear the breaking in his voice. As much as I wanted to bring him home, safe, away from all the rabbis who ran his camp, I didn't want to punish him for something that was not his fault. I promised to take care of it.

I contacted the camp and asked how they allowed unscheduled visitors on campus, without my approval. I sent a copy of my legal custody agreement.

I called Nina and told her what happened. We talked it through and decided that she would send a sternly worded email to Yossi.

Days later, I walked into my building after a long day of work, and my doorman called out, "Dr. Sara! I have a package for you." He handed me a manila envelope. "This was hand delivered earlier today."

I opened it in the elevator and saw very official-looking documents from a New Jersey legal firm: *Order to show cause.* An emergency motion filed with the Ocean County family court in New Jersey. Yossi was listed as the plaintiff, and there were pages and pages of descriptions of how I violated our divorce agreement.

I sent it to Nina, and instead of voicing alarm, she chuckled. "It's a crackpot move. They don't stand a chance."

"Nina," I said as I gripped the concrete edge of my dining room table, "they can take my children. It's happened before."

I knew that as irrational as it seemed, the irrational happened many times. I thought of the case of Gitty Grunwald, whose two-year-old was grabbed from day care, and who then lost custody over a failed hair follicle test. I thought of my sister Shani, whose children were grabbed, and who never regained custody, until the pain and heartache broke her already fragile mind and drove her to death. I thought of Chavie Weisberger, who lost custody by order of a New York State Supreme Court judge, because she was too lax in her religious observance.

"Listen," Nina said. "Here's one takeaway from this: *they* brought it into court. So, whatever promises you made about not taking this to court are now null and void. They've effectively rendered the *beis din* powerless."

It was a small relief. Nina had already formulated her strategy for appearing before the *beis din*. However, at least, I would not have to dig out my old wig and drive to Lakewood to face the rabbis.

I was so nervous about meeting with Yossi that I ran into a CVS on my way to the meeting, just to get some Advil for the headache I felt coming on. When I left the store, I saw my car on the back of a tow truck, being pulled down a city block. Dammit. I parked in the wrong zone. *I don't have time for this*, I thought, and called an Uber without even pausing. I would get the car later. The car was the least of my problems.

I arrived at Nina's conference room in my blazer and heels, my careful notes and file of documents in front of me. I had not talked to Yossi, face-to-face, in ten years. Not since our divorce.

He walked in behind a clean-shaven man in a pink button-down shirt. The man had a leather kippah clipped to his head, and he introduced himself as Kenneth, Yossi's attorney. Yossi sat down near him, his own balding head pointed down at the table, his beard longer than I remembered, his black velvet kippah faded.

Nina began, "This couple has managed to stay out of court and to interact amicably for years, and we hope to draw on that strength here."

She pulled out my children's individualized education plans and started to explain why I chose the Manhattan school for them.

"All due respect," Kenneth with the pink shirt said. "Mr. Schwartz will never allow this. The children are already accepted to another school that he finds acceptable."

He slid a sheet across the table, an acceptance letter signed by a rabbi of a yeshiva in Monsey, near where Yossi's parents lived. In the letter, the rabbi, who never met my son, claimed that his school could address Avigdor's educational needs.

I studied the letter. "Did the rabbi see Avigdor's educational evaluation?"

"No, no, the school is very good," Yossi mumbled, eyes cast downward, as if addressing the table. "I am telling you. They have a lot of learning specialists there. I talked to them a few times."

Nina put a hand on mine and took over. She explained that both of my children had already been interviewed and evaluated by the Manhattan school, and that their educational plans were already in place. Nina and Yossi's attorney sparred for a few more rounds, but we did not arrive at a resolution.

In late August, Nina told me that the Ocean County hearing date, scheduled for the next day, had been changed to attorneys only, and would take place by phone.

I clutched my phone the next morning, kept it in my hand as I poured bowls of cereal and wiped up the milk I had spilled all over my new counters.

Finally, Nina called.

"I need to know everything," I said, expecting the worst.

"Their order to show cause was denied," Nina said simply, like it was to be fully expected. "The judge didn't understand what Yossi was worried about. She didn't think moving to the city and switching schools harms the children in any way at all."

Nina spoke as if that were the natural order of the world, as if judges were expected to be sensible, unmoved by ultra-Orthodox powerbrokers and their almighty bloc vote and cozy ties to political elites.

"Oh," she added. "And jurisdiction is transferred to New York. So the next date is in Manhattan court, which is great."

But I could see nothing great about any of it.

"The children are to start school in five days. What am I supposed to do now? What if sending the children to school makes me look bad? What if they hold it against me in court?"

"Sara," Nina said, "*not* sending them to school would look bad." She paused to think, then said, "Send them to school on the first day as you've planned. This will be in your favor, Sara. Trust me."

But that *trust* was hard to muster after ten years of being terrified to make the slightest move in defiance of the rabbinical court.

I knew that Nina was right, though, except it didn't *feel* right. None of it did.

On the morning of September 17, I met Nina outside Manhattan's family courthouse. Her hair was sleek, her suit even sleeker, and she had heels on.

"You look great!" I said, grateful she was not having one of her messy-bun, rumpled-shirt days.

"So do you, just try to relax your face," she said.

We headed up to our assigned waiting area, rows of benches outside the courtroom. I looked around for Yossi. He was not there. Nina tried to contact his attorney but got no response. My heart pounded, I sweated through my makeup, and my blazer was stuck to my armpits. I imagined Yossi would arrive with a team, but what if they were already inside, paying off the judge? I knew it sounded delusional, but so much about the process had been insane, and I could no longer see the difference between baseless paranoia and legitimate concern. Everything bad seemed to have happened in some case, somewhere, and I was half-certain my kids and I were the next victims of another irrational development.

What felt like hours passed. I checked the large hanging clock: 9:20 a.m. Twenty minutes after our scheduled slot. Nina and I reviewed our documents. We had copies of every email and text message Yossi sent to me over the past year. We had copies of the motion filed in New Jersey, our response to the motion, and the judge's ruling. We had notes of the mediation meeting we attempted.

I was prepped within an inch of my life. I had the dates of each of those interactions nearly memorized, with a small notepad containing the timeline, in case I needed to refer to it on the stand. I had extra copies of the Manhattan Academy brochures.

I prayed, in my head, *God, if you exist, please please let me keep my children.* I hadn't had time to think about God much, but you could never be too prepared.

Finally, our case was called. "Schwartz vs. Schwartz!" a man yelled into the bench area.

Nina and I jumped up, headed to the courtroom door. At the last second, we saw a tall young man in a kippah rise behind us. Nina and I looked at each other, confused. Neither of us had seen him before.

Nina went up to him and spoke with him for a few seconds, then came back, her eyebrows raised.

"You're never gonna believe this."

We slid behind our table and stood to face the judge.

"All rise!"

We watched a thin woman in a judge's robe take a seat and wave to us. "Sit," she called. "In the matter of Schwartz vs. Schwartz, I have reviewed your petition to file this custody agreement in the county of Manhattan, the State of New York. Attorney for the plaintiff?"

Nina introduced herself and introduced me.

"Attorney for the defendant?"

The young man stood up, adjusted his kippah, flipped through some papers and asked, "My name?"

"Your name please. And where is your client?" The judge waved a hand in the air, gestured for him to hurry up.

Nina spoke with authority. "Your Honor, this gentleman is not an attorney in the state of New York or in any state. He is not licensed to address this court."

I turned my head slowly and watched.

"Is this true?" the judge asked, leaning forward.

"I, um, I am an assistant for the firm, um, the attorney. Mr. Yossi, he is on his way."

The judge looked at him for a moment, as if uncomprehending, then said, "Okay, but unfortunately, sir, you may not speak during these proceedings. You may watch and report back to your boss if you'd like."

The judge looked back to Nina. "Proceed."

Nina explained that I had a custody agreement from the state of New Jersey. We wanted to enter the custody agreement in New York because I had recently moved, and I switched the children's schools and needed an updated document.

The judge nodded. "Approved."

I saw a gavel hit the judge's podium. I heard it thunk, wood on wood, final.

"That was it," Nina said. "It's over."

That was it.

That was it.

It was over.

I heard her words and knew their meaning, but I was in a daze.

"You won, Sara."

"But—" I didn't know how to explain that it did not make sense. "We weren't even in there ten minutes."

She smiled and gave me a tight hug. "It's over, Sara."

I walked out of the courthouse and onto a downtown Manhattan street. I kept walking, past street vendors who sweated over giant pretzels in the September sun, past potholes that blew pollution into the air, past blocks of buildings.

I thought about the thirteen years of living in fear, since the moment my Avigdor was born. Thirteen years of modifying my wants, my needs, my dreams, to ensure they did not cost me custody of my children. I had hurt myself and so many other people along the way. I coerced my body into being a vessel for men, for too many men. I gave up the chance to mother my out-of-wedlock baby. I accepted the gift of Eli's heart, and then I broke it into pieces. I put my children through two divorces.

Thirteen years of stumbling through the world with a tightrope beneath me, never fully inhaling, never letting go.

After all that, he didn't even show up to fight me. The calculating part of my own brain wondered if he had planned that, all along. To intimidate me so hard, through so many rabbinic emissaries, that I would not even consider fighting him. Maybe he just miscalculated, forgot to consider my strength. Or maybe, I hoped, maybe a small part of him understood that I was trying to give our children tools for living ambitious lives. Maybe, at the end of the day, he wanted to step aside and allow them a chance at freedom.

I dialed Jay, the warmhearted, short-haired, gorgeous woman that I had begun to see over the summer, and kept walking as she asked, breathless, "What happened? I can't take it anymore, just tell me!"

"I mean, he didn't show up and the judge passed my motion, and my lawyer said I won," I said, walking past the Javits Center on the West Side Highway.

"YOU WON!!!" I heard her whisper *she won!* "Sorry, the whole office was praying for you. I just had to tell them."

Her voice reminded me that I had a body, and that my body was exhausted. I looked down at my feet, red and puffy in my heeled sandals. I realized that I was thirsty, parched. I went to the nearby deli to get an exorbitant, New York City–priced bottle of water. It was delicious.

I won.

We won.

I looked around as the sunlight bounced off the windows of so many tall buildings, sending prismatic arcs over my head.

The future, for the first time, had no limits.

Epilogue

In the months and years since Shani died, I would often feel a deep sense of guilt. At first, because I felt I could've saved her from her illness, and later, increasingly, for not helping more when her children were taken from her. Shani had severe bipolar disorder, but she was, at the same time, a proud and deeply devoted mother, who had never, not once, given her children anything but love and care. She never took having children for granted, and she worried about them and the impact her illness had on them.

Bipolar disorder is a terrible illness, and a disproportionate number of its sufferers attempt suicide. Nonetheless, stressors and other contributing factors play a role, and those can be alleviated with proper care and attention. I do *not* believe that Shani's suicide was her destiny. We will never know exactly what went through her mind in her final moments, but the taking of her children was the proximate cause of her final descent into depression, from which she would never escape.

I never did discover who made the decision to take her kids from her, who arranged it, who executed it. In the years that followed, as I came to understand the family court processes better, I realized the insidious manipulation allowed by the courts and upheld by the "family law industrial complex"—the armies of judges, attorneys, law guardians, therapists, fo-

282

rensic psychologists, and private investigators—who have strong vested interests in the adversarial process in which children's "best interests" are determined. For all who go through it, the process is grotesquely intimidating, expensive, and often decided capriciously by judges during pre-trial hearings, under the guise of temporary orders that then establish the very "status quo" judges tend to favor.

In my case, the rabbinical courts used this system to frighten me into submission. In Shani's case, she stood no chance without competent guidance, and she had few resources with which to acquire it. For both of us, the burden of proof was put on us, to prove we deserved our parenthood. That fact alone is an injustice.

I have a semicolon tattoo on my wrist, a symbol of suicide awareness, and I think about Shani every day. I talk to her in my head all the time, still. I tell her about my next plans to see her children. I tell her about things she would think are funny. I reassure her after I see her children. I beg her, sometimes, to look after me or them.

Before Shani's son's bar mitzvah last year, there were some difficulties in the arrangements, and I remember walking through Columbus Circle, pleading with her, *Please make sure this goes smoothly for him. Please, Shani. I will do everything I can.* I almost felt her there. Now, whenever I pass that spot, I nod to her or play a song in my AirPods for her—"Both Sides Now" by Joni Mitchell. I still blink back tears often, and sometimes I break down, mostly in the shower and mostly around the time of her death. It's been ten years, at the time of this writing. The pain is a little less intense now. But the moment I am reminded of it, it's back and very present. I loved her so much, and I miss her so dearly.

Shani taught me joy. She taught me that sometimes, you just have to laugh, even if a lot of negative things are happening—you either find the humor in that, or you go outside and spread your arms out and just laugh because you are alive.

Shani taught me what true sister love is. She never judged me. She never felt the need to control my decisions. She just loved me.

I wish I had been able to love her harder, to love her in ways that would have protected her from her own mind.

During my own legal battle, I begged her for help. I bargained with her. I said, *If you help me now, I promise you I will see your kids as much as I can and take care of them.* I remember sitting on my bed, head between my knees, sobbing and having this talk with her.

That bargaining was perhaps rendered ineffective, given how deeply I love my niece and nephew. My children and I went to visit Micki at Brown University last fall, where she is currently a junior. "I am gonna try to get it right," she said, when my children told her that since entering high school, they were going by their chosen names. She introduced my son, who now goes by Victor, to her friends on the pre-med track so he could ask questions about pursuing a career in medicine. My daughter, now Jordan, told Micki excitedly about our tour of RISD across the road, about how she felt like art school might be her calling.

Micki gestured to a familiar-looking bicycle. Long, '80s-style banana seat, worn handlebars. "My mom's," she said, tossing a curl behind her shoulder, bouncing down the hallway to show us the next thing. I stayed behind for a few seconds. Just enough to tell Shani, *Look at our kids! We did it! I love you.* I snapped a photo of the bike, of the sister I could see in its shadow.

I could almost see my children on a grassy campus one day, living inside the kind of dorms that I had only glimpsed from the outside, back when they were born. I could dare to imagine that they will have a chance to love, to live, to dream, and to become whoever they choose to be.

With Micki away at school, her brother Adam takes the train from Riverdale to the city to go thrifting with my kids. Their father, Felix, and I plan family picnics in the summer. We text. We share news. We send random selfies to each other. We are a true family.

I believe that Shani is in a heavenly place. I like to imagine her in a garden that segues to a sandy coast, with her long tie-dye skirt flowing behind her in the breeze. If there are other people in her heaven, she is picking wildflowers for an old man and taking a young child by the hand and running to the edge of the shore with them, where waves lap over their bare feet. She is wearing a flower crown and there is light in her eyes again, a twinkle. She is looking down at me and saying, "Hey, it's all going to work out. I am so proud of you."

The Greatest
Self-Disclosure of All

To my dear clients, past and present,

I thought about you through every stage of preparing this manuscript. I want to acknowledge that if this book does not match your impression of me, you are not imagining it. You and I have built a connection based on mutual trust, and so I am going to share some of my process here, with you.

I attended social work school in 2005, at which time Freud was considered the godfather of psychotherapy. Despite rumors of his cocaine snorting and pipe smoking, his lofty standards were passed on to me with great reverence. *Never bring yourself into the therapy room*, I was taught. My reactions were to be carefully measured inside my mind before appearing in my facial expressions. My personal life was to be kept entirely private. My job was to serve as a mirror for my clients, a reflective surface for their own self-exploration.

I worked to follow the guidance of Freud and my wise professors and saved my own feelings (or countertransference) for supervision sessions. There were times, like when my body revealed babies growing inside me, or when I removed my wedding ring from my finger, that my personal life was unconcealable. I planned careful conversations and executed them with my emotions at a safe distance, outside my office.

Then I began to attend postgraduate training in trauma-focused therapy. I was relieved to read the works of groundbreaking theorists like van der Kolk and Porges, who talked about another kind of mirroring—the kind that involved me being a human being in session. I learned that laughing, tearing up, and leaning in during sessions were powerful tools for healing a traumatized nervous system.

Still, when I began to write this book, I felt guilty. I worried about betraying the sacred space I had created in session, one where I only existed in service to your vulnerable, crucial, brave work.

Yet the words were bursting through my fingertips. The need to tell my story was visceral. I felt it in my breath, in my veins, as I struggled to restrain myself from writing the whole truth. I wrote stilted sentences, censored my searing grief and confusion and trauma, as I worried about a reality in which you felt obliged to hold space for my story. Less altruistically, I worried that my truths would impact my career, that no one would ever trust me with themselves again. I was half-sure that my unfiltered narrative would cause me to lose my job, my home, and possibly even my children.

Still, I wrote. I learned to visualize vacuum-sealed chambers for my words, to write as if no one would ever read my work.

In 2022, during an online, pandemic-era conference, Jet Setting Jasmine happened. I logged on to her lecture about sexuality from my bedroom, in my Zoom uniform of sweatpants and professional blazer. At first, I thought I had hit the wrong link. Jasmine was radiant in the center of my screen, ebony skin and long locks and *an exposed breast with a newborn suckling on it*. Several moments after my brain unfroze itself, I garnered that the tattooed, muscular man at her side was the father of her baby. Jasmine was a sex worker. And a psychotherapist. She kept two separate websites up. "My sex work clients know that I will not do therapy with them, and my therapy clients know not to ask for sex work. The boundaries are clear. But no part of it is a secret."

I watched Jasmine's partner cradle their baby and I thought about Freud. Specifically, about the ways in which he differed from the modern goddess on my screen. He was a white man. Most of his early successors were white men—Beck, Erikson, Piaget, etc. I wondered if they had wives at home, women who wore the evidence of their lovemaking, of their growing families, on their own bodies, miles away from their husband's offices. I thought about the privilege inherent in their lives, in their ability to keep two separate physical spaces for their existences. I thought about the clean lines of eras past, when people could close their office doors and then drive home without worrying that their sins or secrets were google-able.

What if I am keeping an oath I never took, I began to consider. Maybe, just maybe, the entire psychotherapy arena had been colonized by white men from decades ago, men who did not deserve to determine the extent of my own freedom. Maybe in our modern world, their expectations were moot anyway. Maybe if I owned my story, just one-tenth of the way Jasmine owned her bare skin, her dual professions, maybe that would inspire authenticity in others.

I listened to Melissa Etheridge as I jogged through Central Park in the early city daylight,

She sang about persisting through her own darkness and running in order to bring awareness to the suffering of women, of mothers and sisters and wives.

I replaced *run* with *write*. I thought about my fifteen-year-old self, about how many missteps, how many crashes and fractures she could have avoided had she been given access to a memoir like the one I was writing. I thought about my clients who lived in closets of their own, in terror that someday they would be exposed as queer, or as having doubts about religion, or as survivors of sexual trauma. So many people living in fear. I wrote for me, for them, for the hope of a world where we could all be free.

My dear client, know that I thought about you as I reviewed every single word of this manuscript. I hoped and prayed that my words would not cause you to doubt any of the growth you have achieved during our time together. The work you have done is yours alone, a result of your courage and your strength. Thank you for allowing me to be a part of it. Thank you for showing me that it is possible to forge ahead, even through the most wrenching of circumstances.

Please tune into your body as you read this book, and please honor any urge to put it down. Freud may not approve, but I will say this anyway: I hold deep love for you, always.

With my warmest respect,

Sara

Acknowledgments

I was afraid to write this book. The fear was visceral, borne of excruciating awareness of the consequences of revealing myself in public. For decades, my silence meant safety. I kept still, maintained a façade of heteronormativity and religiosity, and that façade bought me entry into a community filled with an imperfect but still essential love.

Back when I was silent, I read the stories of others who had broken free of similar façades. I kept their books near my bed, behind the covers of my permitted Jewish magazines, sometimes under my mattress. Their stories gave me words for that which I could not express, and their strength helped me find the steel core within myself. Thank you, Martha Beck, Elissa Wall, Glennon Doyle, Shulem Deen, Leah Lax, Cameron Esposito, Chanel Miller, Abby Stein, Melissa Febos, and Lamya H, for writing about queerness, trauma, and religiosity in ways that allowed me to clarify my own narrative. Thank you to anyone who has ever dug past the fear and told the truth about their life—you have carved a path out of stone, and I am so privileged to follow in your courage.

Thank you, Shulem Deen, for responding to my request for help in writing a nuanced memoir like yours, and for coaching me through every step of this process. Thank you for being generous with the lessons you gleaned from your life, for helping me see the blind spots and then guiding me in telling a more honest version of my story. Thank you, Sarah Perry, for being the most gentle, sensitive, and encouraging writing coach. Yours were the safe hands I knew were there, outstretched and waiting to hold the jagged segments of my story as I labored to eject them from my psyche. Thank you for getting it, and for being there. Thank you, Sarah Herrington, for seeing something in my first attempt at a Modern Love essay, and for teaching me how to refine and polish my work.

Thank you, Dan Jones, Miya Lee, Anna Martin, and the rest of the *New York Times* Modern Love team for bringing my words out into the world in essay and podcast form. I could not have wished for a better, classier way to publicly come out of the closet.

Thank you, Harvey Klinger, of the Harvey Klinger Literary Agency, for believing in my manuscript, for gently stoking the flames of my work, and for your fierce efforts on my behalf. This story is out in the world because you believed it should be, and I am forever grateful.

Thank you, Julia Cheiffetz for giving me the opportunity to see my story in print. I am so honored to be published alongside groundbreaking works at One Signal/Atria. Thank you, Nick Ciani, for your spectacular editorial guidance on this book, and for coming up with the perfect title. You took my life story and turned it into art. I am so very grateful for your talent and your expertise on this. Thank you to Hannah Frankel and the editorial team at Simon & Schuster, for answering my endless random questions and nurturing this book to completion. I hold deep gratitude for you all in my heart.

To the prolific members of our Tuesday Group, thank you for being my writing community, for granting me your warmth and wisdom and encouragement. Look out for these names on bylines: Cooper Minister, Jena Dropela, Jess DeCourcy-Hinds, Marshall Tarley, and Elizabeth Steiner.

To Justin Loeber, Jessica Sagstetter, Allie Cobb, and the team at Mouth PR, thank you for seeing me as a star and helping me find my own light.

Thank you for deeply understanding what this book is about, for amplifying my messages, and advocating for my voice to be heard. You are publicists in shining armor, and I am honored to be represented by you.

To Sydney Seifert, Juan Peralta, and the team at Soul Wellness NYC, I am so grateful for your support as we work together to treat those who have been silenced by systems and circumstances. I love you all. To Mordechai Levovitz, Rachael Fried, and the team at Jewish Queer Youth, thank you for allowing me to make meaning of my experiences by being a part of the pure joy that is JQY. You are my heroes.

Thank you, Chani Getter, for lifting me up, for believing that I could write this book, for the endless ways in which you have given me strength, spaciousness, grace, and wisdom.

There were angels who appeared along my path and gifted me with their wholehearted support. Jess Monterde, Albert Vilar, Leora Rosenberg, Tess Bjiere, Noa Green, Natasha Remillard, Aedin Frei, Goldie Junik, Cassie Cohen, Jennifer Nast, Meaghan Phelps, Angela DeRosette, Natashia El-Badewi, Darcey Merritt, Sarah McMahon, Medina B., Cassandra Davidson, Temima F, Ariella Azaraf, Shimmy Feintuch, and Shia Bochner, your presence in my life has been transformative. Frances Lyons, you always know when I need a shoulder to lean on and you gently offer yours, without needing to be asked. Thank you.

To my brother-in-law, Felix, thank you for reading early versions of this manuscript and encouraging me to stay true to the story, despite the complex emotions that engendered. Thank you for showing up, for being my family, for doing this life with me. To Micki and Adam, my beloved niece and nephew, thank you for allowing me to include you in this book, for being the most awesome, intelligent, brave humans, for granting me the absolute honor of being in your lives. I love you all to the ends of the earth and beyond.

To Victor, my firstborn, you have taken every obstacle and turned it into a stepping stone. It has been my greatest privilege to be the person who gets to raise you, to watch you reach for your goals with your unique blend of persistence and humor. Thank you for handling all our life changes with understanding and kindness, and for being so passionate about getting this book out there for those who need it most.

To Jordan, my favorite middle child, remember when I compared you to Ruth Bader Ginsburg's daughter, Jane, because you were inspiring me to write in ways that would truly impact others? And you said, "You realize, Mom, that means you think you're RBG herself," and then we both laughed so hard we nearly fell over. Thank you for always making me crack up at the ridiculousness of life, for styling me, and for allowing me into the beauty that is your life.

To Silas, my sweet love child, thank you for showing us all that there is bubbling joy in this world, mountains of it, right before our eyes. You are a miracle, and we are so grateful for you. To Jay, Silas's other mom, thank you for reminding me that I needed to tell my story, and for helping me believe people would be interested in reading it.

My children, this book would not be here without each of you. You have given me reasons to strive, to write, to laugh, and to forge ahead. There are not enough words in this language to express how much I love you, forever and ever.

About the Author

Sara Glass, PhD, LCSW, is a therapist, writer, and speaker who helps members of the queer community and individuals who have survived trauma to live bold, honest, and proud lives. She lives in Manhattan, New York. Find out more at DrSaraGlass.com.